God is not silent. However, often we are too busy to hear his voice. *How to Hear God* is a biblically based, historically illustrated look at the various ways in which God speaks. In reading and reflecting on its message, I have become a better listener. I highly recommend it for anyone who wants a more intimate relationship with God.

> **Gary D. Chapman,** PhD,
> author of *The 5 Love Languages*

A lot of people say God has told them something, but then you hear what it is, and it sounds more like a message from the devil. Other folks who don't even believe in God seem to have a word of truth for today. Well, here is a book by someone you can trust. Pete Greig has been a friend for years, and he is one of the wisest people I know when it comes to prayer. This book draws from the well of wisdom that has nourished the faithful for centuries. It is filled with voices of saints who have been not only people of prayer but people who get up off their knees and put feet on those prayers. This incredible book is a call to prayer and a call to action . . . which is exactly what our world needs right now.

> **Shane Claiborne,** author, activist,
> and cofounder of Red Letter Christians

Pete never fails to make my soul tremble with the good news of God's presence and guidance and invitation to pray. This book is sweet and salty—a perfect spiritual snack of deep spiritual truths with real-life wisdom and brevity. It's made me thirsty for living water, which is exactly the intent. I pray you will get this book, read it, and then get ten more to give to your friends. It will change lives.

> **Danielle Strickland,** speaker,
> author, and advocate

Trying to hear God can seem like a mysterious quest, and we can feel a bit lost and discouraged. At those times, we need some help, and Pete has given us some great guidance. Rooted in Scripture and filled with the experiences of many who have gone before us, this book shows that God really does speak to us and gives us some clear paths to hear him when he does.

> **Dr. Henry Cloud,** psychologist and
> *New York Times* bestselling author

I love the subtitle of this book: a simple guide for normal people. That's what Pete Greig is always good at—taking a deeply profound and mysterious subject like prayer and inviting us into it in such a beautifully ordinary way. His teaching here is a wonderful mix of the everyday and the eternal—and therefore such a powerful and helpful read. So good!

Matt Redman, worship leader and songwriter

Hearing the voice of God is essential to all our lives—and Pete Greig is an ideal guide. As the founder of 24-7 Prayer, Pete is a legend in the world of prayer. He also writes beautifully. I am so excited he has written this book.

Nicky Gumbel, author, pastor,
and pioneer of Alpha

Everything Pete Greig writes lights a fire in me. This book gripped me and awakened something in me. I found myself praying differently and listening to God differently, with more expectation and the willingness to step out in faith and risk feeling foolish. Pete takes what could be a daunting or confusing subject and disarms our defenses and dismantles our excuses with hilarious stories, down-to-earth examples, and simple practices. Every page will inspire your imagination, inviting you to believe that hearing from God truly is for everyone.

Glenn Packiam, associate senior pastor of
New Life Church and author of *The Resilient Pastor*

The most common question I am asked as a pastor is "How do I hear God?" I'm so thankful that my friend Pete Grieg has tackled this important topic. All of us have been designed to hear and discern the whispers of God, and when we do, our lives are forever richer.

Brady Boyd, author and pastor of New Life Church

Pete Greig has given us both a practical and profound book on how to connect more deeply with God. I believe it will enrich the lives of many people. I highly commend it to you.

Jon Tyson, lead pastor of Church
of the City New York

When generals speak, soldiers listen! While Pete won't like me saying this about him (humility will cause him to recoil), every generation has generals of the faith that command the church's attention. Not necessarily because they shout and orate with passion and skill but because the fruit of their lives and ministries demands that we listen. Pete is such a leader, and the truth contained in his book answers one of the most common questions: How do you hear God? Pete has the answer.

Glyn Barrett, senior pastor of Audacious Church, UK,
and national leader of Assemblies of God in Great Britain

Pete Greig has given us another masterpiece. Wise and winsome, profound yet playful, *How to Hear God* is the book we need. From the wild charismatics to the monkish contemplatives, there is a feast here for all. A hundred years from now, this book will remain a crucial resource on the journey of faith.

Daniel Grothe, associate senior pastor of
New Life Church and author of *The Power of Place*

In a world of noise and distraction, the people of God have an urgent need to learn to hear and be attentive to the voice of God. In this brilliant book, Pete unpacks the different ways we can grow in listening to God. If, like us, you long to better hear God speak in your everyday living, this is the book for you!

Tim and Rachel Hughes, lead pastors of
Gas Street Church, Birmingham

We have spent over twenty years teaching young people how to hear the voice of God. We wish we would have had this book the whole time—it would have made our jobs much easier! This is the most inspiring, empowering, and exhaustive book we have read on hearing God's voice. This book doesn't just fill your head with information but also will cause your heart to burn with inspiration. You could give this book to a brand-new believer, and they would be immediately empowered to hear God's voice. Or you could give it to a believer who has walked with God for many years, and they would be inspired and challenged to hear him in an even deeper way. The body of Christ has needed this book for very long time.

Jonathan and Melissa Helser, recording artists

Among the many church leaders I have known, Pete Greig stands out for his humility, openness to learning, and love for the whole of the body of Christ. I wholeheartedly join him in affirming that there is no greater adventure than intimate, ongoing conversation with God. Whoever you are, this is a wonder to which you are personally invited. Join Pete in this exploration of what it means to seek God's voice with all that you are—in Scripture, in tradition, in solitude, and in the precious communion of saints who stand with you throughout the whole of the earth.

Heidi G. Baker, PhD, cofounder and executive
chairman of the board of Iris Global

Don't we all want to hear from God? How much easier our lives would be if we could hear his voice and follow his direction. I love Pete's writing because it is easy to understand. The simple way he handles difficult subjects in *How to Hear God* makes this book compelling. If you really want to grow on this journey of hearing God, here is the book that will help you grow immensely.

Agu Irukwu, senior pastor of Jesus House London

How to Hear God

How to Hear God

A Simple Guide for
Normal People

Pete Greig

ZONDERVAN
REFLECTIVE

ZONDERVAN REFLECTIVE

How to Hear God
Copyright © 2022 by Pete Greig

First published in the United Kingdom with Hodder & Stoughton.

Requests for information should be addressed to:
Zondervan, *3900 Sparks Dr. SE, Grand Rapids, Michigan 49546*

Zondervan titles may be purchased in bulk for educational, business, fundraising, or sales promotional use. For information, please email SpecialMarkets@Zondervan.com.

ISBN 978-0-310-11462-8 (audio)

Library of Congress Cataloging-in-Publication Data

Names: Greig, Pete, author.
Title: How to hear God : a simple guide for normal people / Pete Greig.
Description: Grand Rapids : Zondervan, 2022. | Includes index.
Identifiers: LCCN 2021058970 (print) | LCCN 2021058971 (ebook) | ISBN 9780310114604 (paperback) | ISBN 9780310114611 (ebook)
Subjects: LCSH: God (Christianity)—Knowableness. | Desire for God.
Classification: LCC BT103 .G739 2022 (print) | LCC BT103 (ebook) | DDC 231.7—dc23
/eng/20220124
LC record available at https://lccn.loc.gov/2021058970
LC ebook record available at https://lccn.loc.gov/2021058971

Unless otherwise marked, Scripture quotations are taken from The Holy Bible, New International Version®, NIV®. Copyright © 1973, 1978, 1984, 2011 by Biblica, Inc.® Used by permission of Zondervan. All rights reserved worldwide. www.Zondervan.com. The "NIV" and "New International Version" are trademarks registered in the United States Patent and Trademark Office by Biblica, Inc.® • Scripture quotations marked AMP are taken from the Amplified*Bible. Copyright © 1954, 1958, 1962, 1964, 1965, 1987, 2015 by The Lockman Foundation. Used by permission. (www.Lockman.org). • Scripture quotations marked ASV are taken from the American Standard Version. Public domain. • Scripture quotations marked BSB are taken from The Holy Bible, Berean Study Bible, BSB. Copyright © 2016, 2018 by Bible Hub. Used by permission. All rights reserved worldwide. • Scripture quotations marked ESV are taken from the ESV® Bible (The Holy Bible, English Standard Version®). Copyright © 2001 by Crossway, a publishing ministry of Good News Publishers. Used by permission. All rights reserved. • Scripture quotations marked GW are taken from *God's Word*®. Copyright © 1995 God's Word to the Nations. Used by permission of Baker Publishing Group. All rights reserved. • Scripture quotations marked JBP are from The New Testament in Modern English by J. B. Phillips. Copyright © 1960, 1972 J. B. Phillips. Administered by the Archbishops' Council of the Church of England. Used by permission. • Scripture quotations marked KJV are taken from the King James Version. Public domain. • Scripture quotations marked MSG are taken from *THE MESSAGE*. Copyright © 1993, 2002, 2018 by Eugene H. Peterson. Used by permission of NavPress. All rights reserved. Represented by Tyndale House Publishers, Inc. • Scripture quotations marked NKJV are taken from the New King James Version®. Copyright © 1982 by Thomas Nelson. Used by permission. All rights reserved. • Scripture quotations marked NLT are taken from the Holy Bible, New Living Translation. © 1996, 2004, 2015 by Tyndale House Foundation. Used by permission of Tyndale House Publishers, Inc., Carol Stream, Illinois 60188. All rights reserved.

Published in association with The Bindery Agency, www.TheBinderyAgency.com.

Printed in the United States of America

23 24 25 26 27 28 29 30 31 32 33 /TRM/ 16 15 14 13 12 11 10 9 8 7 6 5 4 3 2

In memory of:

Floyd McClung (August 3, 1945–May 29, 2021)
Joel Edwards (October 15, 1951–June 30, 2021)
true fathers and sons.

Contents

Foreword

If there is a God . . .

If that God is not an abstract concept, a vague force, or an infinite sea of energy but a living community of trinitarian Love . . .

If this God-who-is-a-relationship, motivated by self-giving love, moved out of himself and became human . . . to draw as many as possible to share in the Trinity's inner life of Love . . .

If he incarnated as Jesus, a rabbi, a teacher from Nazareth . . .

If he called disciples after him, students, apprentices, sitting at his feet, listening to his teachings, and learning to say and do all that he said and did . . .

And if, upon this Jesus' return to the Father, he gave his Spirit to be with all Christians everywhere for all time . . .

Then surely learning to hear his voice is at the center of all that matters in life.

Many years ago a mentor said to me, "Learning to hear God's voice is the most important task of a disciple of Jesus." More recently, another mentor said, "The primary posture of a disciple of Jesus is sitting at his feet and listening." Same truth.

And yet: How? I don't wake up to an email from God every morning. Do you? Nor do I get a text message from heaven when I need to make an important decision, nor hear an audible voice from the sky when I'm feeling confused.

Enter my friend, Pete Grieg. I'm taking a bit of liberty calling him my friend; he is, but I view him more as a guide, a spiritual Sherpa for the heights of the kingdom, a living icon of the kind of Christian I want to grow and mature into in years to come.

And Pete has simply written the best book I have ever read on the most important thing you will ever do: learning how to hear God.

Pete calls this book "a simple guide for normal people." It is, but "simple" is not the same thing as simplistic. This book is disarmingly wise, deep, insightful. With his extraordinary grasp of the church down through history and across the globe, Pete transcends the Christian tribalism of our day—charismatic/noncharismatic/Reformed/Weslyan/Anglican/Anabaptist/convservative/progressive/etc, etc. He is rooting us in something far more ancient, unchanging, timeless. What the early Christians called the Way. This ancient form of Christianity (predating the term *Christianity* itself) is the antidote to much of the modern church's pain. The cure for our ills.

The future is ancient.

The timeless is timely.

And hearing God's voice is the key to everything.

John Mark Comer

How to Read This Book in Five Minutes

The Emmaus Road

> *Two of them were going to a village called Emmaus.*
> —Luke 24:13

This is a simple guide to one of the most astounding yet confusing things you will ever learn to do. The Bible says that you were created to enjoy a real, conversational relationship with God. Hearing his voice is therefore the most natural thing in the world. (You probably do it already more than you realize.) But whenever God's word is confused, abused, or ignored, it can become one of the most perplexing and painful things too. Throughout this book we explore one of the loveliest stories in the Bible. Christ's encounter with the couple on the road to Emmaus is a master class for anyone seeking to learn to hear his voice, not just because it models so many of the ways in which God speaks, but because the couple so consistently and reassuringly get it wrong.

Chapter 1: Hearing God's Word in Jesus

> *While they were talking and discussing together, Jesus himself drew near.*
> —Luke 24:15 ESV

Jesus is what God sounds like. He's literally the "living Word of God." Hearing his voice is not so much a skill we must master, therefore, as a master we must meet. All the other ways in which God communicates—through the Bible, prophecy, dreams, visions, and so on—come through Jesus and point back to him too. In fact, you are probably reading this now because the covert Christ is drawing near, just as he did on the Emmaus road, inviting you to embark upon a slow journey of deep discovery that will change your life.

Chapter 2: Hearing God's Word in the Bible

Beginning with Moses and all the Prophets, he explained to
them what was said in all the Scriptures concerning himself.
—Luke 24:27

When it comes to hearing God, the Bible is the language of his heart. Nothing he says in any other way in any other context will ever override, undermine, or contradict what he has said in the Scriptures. That's why Jesus doesn't just show up on the road to Emmaus and say, "Hi, it's me!" Instead, he takes considerable time to deliver a lengthy biblical exposition in which he reinterprets God's Word radically, in the light of his own life, death, and resurrection. This approach, the *christological hermeneutic*, can help you with the tricky business of hearing God's voice through the Bible and of making sense of its meaning in your life today.

Chapter 3: Hearing God's Word in Prayer: *Lectio Divina*

Were not our hearts burning within us while he . . .
opened the Scriptures to us?
—Luke 24:32

In this chapter we turn from *reading* the Bible to *praying* the Bible, using an ancient approach to spiritual listening known as *lectio divina*. By harnessing the power of imagination and meditation, *lectio divina* can leave "our hearts burning within us" as fresh revelation begins to flicker from familiar texts. The four traditional steps of *lectio divina* are simplified here into the acronym P.R.A.Y.: Pause, Read (*lectio*), Reflect (*meditatio*), Ask (*oratio*), and Yield (*contemplatio*).

Chapter 4: Hearing God's Word in Prophecy

Were not our hearts burning within us while
he talked with us on the road?
—Luke 24:32

The New Testament uses two Greek terms to describe the word of God: *logos* and *rhēma*. *Logos* refers to the expressions we've studied so far: God's living word in Jesus (chapter 1) and God's written word in the Bible (chapters 2 and 3). But the other term, *rhēma*, describes God's *spoken* word, living and active today, in prophecy. As the apostle Paul says, "The one who prophesies speaks to people for their strengthening, encouraging and comfort" (1 Cor. 14:3). In this chapter I set out some keys to help you grow in this important spiritual gift and some simple principles for handling it appropriately.

Chapter 5: Hearing God's Whisper

Jesus himself came up and walked along with them;
but they were kept from recognizing him.
—Luke 24:15–16

As we turn from *God's word* (his voice external) to *God's whisper* (his voice internal), we come to the heart of the problem that many millions of Christians have with hearing God; namely, their presumptions about what God sounds like and their expectations about how they think he should speak. His voice is relatively easy to hear when it comes to us loud and clear through an encounter with Jesus (chapter 1), through the Bible (chapters 2 and 3), or through supernatural prophetic utterance (chapter 4). But it's easy to miss when it comes, as it mostly does, in a voice hushed to "a gentle whisper" (1 Kings 19:12).

Chapter 6: Hearing God's Whisper in Dreams and the Unconscious

> *They recognized him, and he disappeared from their sight.*
> —Luke 24:31

One of the main ways God communicates in the Bible—and in which he continues to speak today—is through the subconscious realm of intuition. In this chapter I offer guidelines for those seeking to hear God in dreams and underline the importance of honoring the conscience, which is an essential yet fallible mouthpiece for the Holy Spirit. I also explore the Ignatian prayer of Examen, which can be such a powerful tool for connecting with our own inner worlds.

Chapter 7: Hearing God's Whisper in Community, Creation, and Culture

> *When he was at the table with them . . . their eyes were opened.*
> —Luke 24:30–31

The Emmaus road story is inescapably an account of God speaking through the actualities of community, creation, and culture. When Jesus was born, God's people already had his word in the Bible (the Hebrew books at least), but it clearly wasn't enough. They also had his word through prophets and prophecies, but this wasn't enough either. They knew God's whisper in the still, small voice of Elijah and in their consciences, dreams, and visions. In fact, they had almost every expression of God's word we've studied so far in this book, but none of it was enough. Eventually, God's word had to become flesh—not in a book but in a body, not just mystically in heaven but materially "among us" (John 1:14). There is no aspect of God's creation through which he cannot and does not speak. This chapter is, therefore, about discerning the voice of God in the whole of life, not just in religious contexts but also in the actualities of community, creation, and culture.

Chapter 8: The Word, the Whisper, and the Way

Then the two told what had happened on the way.
—Luke 24:35

It took perhaps three hours for the couple from Emmaus to realize that they were hosting the living Word of God. But the moment their eyes and ears were opened, their overwhelming attitude was, "Yes!" Hearing became doing. They hurried out of the house immediately, didn't wait until morning, and walked the seven miles back to Jerusalem, where they found the disciples and "told what had happened" (Luke 24:35). This is the pattern: the more we say yes to Jesus, the more familiar and precious his voice becomes until ultimately, at the end of the road, at the end of the day, at the end of our lives, we look back as the sun sets and whisper in wonder and joy, "Were not our hearts burning within us while he talked?"

Jesus is what God sounds like. He's literally the "living Word of God." Hearing his voice is not so much a skill we must master, therefore, as a master we must meet. All the other ways in which God communicates—through the Bible, prophecy, dreams, visions, and so on—come through Jesus and point back to him too. In fact, you are probably reading this now because the covert Christ is drawing near, just as he did on the Emmaus road, inviting you to embark upon a slow journey of deep discovery that will change your life.

1

Hearing God's Word in Jesus

Jesus himself drew near.
—Luke 24:15 ESV

---

*The wide world is all about you: you can fence
yourselves in, but you cannot for ever fence it out.*
—J. R. R. Tolkien

And so the great adventure begins.

Nothing could ever be wilder or more wonderful than the human capacity to hear God's voice. And for that very reason, few things hold such potential to confuse and cause pain when used, abused, or ignored.

Perhaps that's why you've picked up this book. You're wanting to grow in your ability to discern God's voice, aware that this must be the key to everything else in the Christian life, without which all the talk about a real, conversational relationship with the Lord is just hot air. "For prayer is nothing else than being on terms of friendship with God," said Teresa of Ávila five centuries ago.[1] But, of course, it's not easy.

As I write this, certain self-proclaimed prophets are scrambling to cover their tracks after falsely predicting the outcome of a presidential election. Meanwhile, the same old uncivil war rages on between the conflicting pronouncements of people claiming to know God's opinion on everything from global pandemics and medical genetics to the geopolitics of the Middle East. And sadly, this is deeply, painfully personal. Who hasn't been hurt by the misappropriation of God's word from the lips of a controlling parent, or the proud pronouncements of a cocksure preacher, or a troubled soul like the total stranger who informed me one day at the end of church that God had commanded her to marry me?

And so it seems both natural and necessary to follow my previous book, *How to Pray*,[2] with one on *How to Hear God*. Here we have the other side of the conversation. The bit in which we stop talking *about* God, *at* God, or even *to* God and start talking *with* him.

* * *

> Hear, O Israel: the LORD our God, the LORD is one.
> Love the LORD your God with all your heart and
> with all your soul and with all your strength.
> —Deuteronomy 6:4–5

The most important prayer in all of Judaism begins with this one word: *hear*. Known as the Shema (literally meaning "listen," "hear," or "heed"), Deuteronomy 6:4–9 was regarded by the rabbis and by Jesus himself as the core of the Law, the most important of the commandments, and thus the highest priority for all humanity.[3] Before we can love God with all our hearts and souls and strength, we must learn to listen. This, then, is the prerequisite that unlocks the purpose of life itself.

Our forefathers cherished these verses so deeply that they wore them in the phylacteries on their heads and their hands. Again and again, from generation to generation, these words reminded them to listen to God. "Hear," they prayed twice daily, reciting the Shema as the centerpiece of their morning and evening services. "Hear," they told their children, training each one to pray these words in bed at night. "Hear," they gasped with their dying breath, repeating the Shema as the final words they would pray.

Learning to hear God's voice—his word and his whisper—is the single most important thing you will ever learn to do. I'm not exaggerating. Hearing God is not peripheral; it is integral to human history. Neither is it an optional extra for wild-eyed mystics and those who happen to be spiritually inclined. Hearing God is essential to the very purpose for which you and I were made. Without it everything falls apart. But when we learn to love God's Word—to listen and obey—everything aligns. As Jesus says, "People do not live by bread alone, but by every word that comes from the mouth of God" (Matt. 4:4 NLT).

* * *

I settled into my seat as the door sighed shut and the train pulled away from the station. Gradually we gathered speed until the familiar streets became a blur of buildings whirring past the window on our way into London. The carriage was crowded, but no one was talking. I let out a little introverted sigh of contentment and popped a pair of white buds into my ears. Scrolling down to a podcast by cognitive neuroscientist Doctor Caroline Leaf, I pressed play, looking forward to losing myself in new ideas. The clattering of the tracks steadily got louder, and I turned up the volume to hear. The lady opposite caught my eye, and for a ghastly moment, I thought she wanted to talk. Smiling helplessly, I pointed at my earbuds and mouthed, "Sorry." She shrugged too and returned to her paperback. I turned up the volume a little more.

Dr. Leaf was interviewing a woman who'd suffered such extreme trauma that it had triggered premature ovarian failure—early menopause. But she'd learned to moderate many of the symptoms of the menopause, she said, by carefully monitoring her stress levels. Dr. Leaf asked how one does this, and without missing a beat, the woman explained how to test the pH of one's own urine. A little nervously I glanced at the lady opposite. The train had reached full speed.

The rain was coming down hard, drumming like gravel against the window and running in horizontal rivulets across the dirty pane. The noise was considerable, and I turned up the volume as loud as it would go.

It was not until I began to gather my things to leave the train that the terrible truth emerged: all this time my earbuds had been disconnected from my phone. For almost twenty minutes I'd been broadcasting Dr. Caroline Leaf's reflections on moodiness, memory loss, and menopause, at maximum volume, to the entire carriage. The person *least* able to hear her guest's detailed instructions on the personal art of pee-sampling had unfortunately been me. Everyone seated nearby, with the exception of the agitated lady opposite, had pretended not to notice, too English to make a fuss.

This is a simple book for normal people about how to plug in and hear the voice of God more clearly amid the clatter and clamor of daily life. It is, in other words, a simple guide to one of the most astounding yet confusing things you will ever learn to do. *Astounding* because, well, what could be more amazing? With four words—"Let there be light"—(just two in Hebrew) God created more than one hundred billion galaxies (Gen. 1:3). "The LORD merely spoke, and the heavens were created. He breathed the word, and all the stars were born" (Ps. 33:6 NLT). What on earth might happen if he were to speak a few words to me?

But it's *confusing* too because God does not for the most part speak audibly, the way we speak, and this means that we can easily misunderstand, misinterpret, or miss out altogether on what he is saying. The problem is generally not that God isn't communicating, and neither is it normally that we lack the capacity to hear. Rather, like me on that train, it's that we easily get disconnected, distracted, and distanced from the intimate and immediate connection we were created to enjoy. It's a disconnection that comes, as the Anglican Service of Communion puts it, "through negligence, through weakness, and through our own deliberate fault."

But if this is starting to sound a bit onerous, please don't worry. As usual, Jesus keeps the whole thing refreshingly simple, relational, and earthy: "My sheep listen to my voice," he says. "I know them, and they follow me" (John 10:27). In other words, don't concern yourself with one hundred billion solar systems and the odd, embarrassing disconnection. If stupid, dumb sheep can learn to recognize their shepherd's voice, so can you!

This is for everyone. He certainly won't be checking your baptismal certificate or testing your ability to recite the creed on the Final Day. His friends will be known, he says in this verse, by just two things: their ability to recognize his voice and their readiness to follow.

And, of course, this is why, if you've been around Christians for any length of time, you'll have heard someone say, quite matter-of-factly, "Oh, God told me this," or, "The Lord said that," as if it's the most normal thing in the world (which, in a way, as we shall see, it is). But just try using that line with your general practitioner: "Doctor, I'm hearing the voice of Jesus." Or in a court of law: "God told me to do it, Your Honor." They'll medicate you or detain you before you can shout, "Hallelujah!"

And yet many of the most eminent people who have ever lived have freely admitted to hearing the voice of God, from George Washington Carver, sometimes called the African American father of modern agriculture,[4] to Florence Nightingale, the mother of modern nursing who wrote in her diary, shortly before her seventeenth birthday, "God spoke to me and called me to his service. What form this service was to take, the voice did not make clear."[5] From Ben Carson, the pioneering American neurosurgeon and former presidential candidate who felt called into medicine through a supernatural dream,[6] to Dag Hammarskjöld, the Swedish economist who won the Nobel Peace Prize and was described by John F. Kennedy as "the greatest statesman of our century."[7] From the genius French polymath Blaise Pascal[8] to the escaped slave and trailblazing abolitionist

Harriet Tubman.[9] From the Scottish Olympian Eric Liddell, who famously felt God's pleasure when he ran, to the blind English poet John Milton, who dictated to his daughter each morning whatever he had heard from God the night before.

Survey after survey confirms that most people in our supposedly secular Western societies still interact with God.[10] We don't approach chemotherapy thinking, "I suppose I ought to pray about this, but I just can't be bothered." We tend not to welcome newborn babies into the world with the words, "Behold, a biological fluke born into a meaningless universe." No one ever stared up at a murmuration of starlings at dusk, or out to sea under a stormy sunset, and whispered, "Wow, I'm awestruck by my own magnificence." Human beings are hardwired to worship. You have been meticulously made with an extraordinary ability to walk and talk with God.

In fact, the Bible says that your primary purpose—the reason for which you were born—is to enjoy a real, conversational relationship with an infinitely loving divinity, which is why you almost certainly hear him already, more than you realize. Your Father in heaven invites you to walk with him in a relaxed daily conversation as Adam and Eve did in the glades of Eden (Gen. 3:8). He wants to talk with you intimately as he did with Moses, "face to face, as one speaks to a friend" (Ex. 33:11). Occasionally he will communicate thrillingly through dreams, visions, and audible voices, as he did with the apostle Peter on the rooftop in Joppa (Acts 10:9–19). But mostly he will speak quietly in "a still small voice" as he did with Elijah on Mount Carmel (1 Kings 19:12 NKJV), sounding surprisingly ordinary as he did when the boy Samuel confused his voice for that of the old man in the room next door (1 Sam. 3). Again and again the Lord will join you on your journey through life, stirring your soul and speaking through the Scriptures, as he did with the couple on the road to Emmaus, whose story is explored throughout this book.

The Encounter on the Emmaus Road

Two of them were going to a village called Emmaus, about seven miles from Jerusalem. They were talking with each other about everything that had happened. As they talked and discussed these things with each other, Jesus himself came up and walked along with them; but they were kept from recognizing him.

—Luke 24:13–16

So begins one of the greatest short stories ever told. "Learn to live inside this story," says theologian Tom Wright, "and you will find it inexhaustible."[11] As literature it is poignant and profound. As a vehicle for teaching, it is loaded with insight into how God speaks (and how we may listen). And as a piece of storytelling, it is tender, humorous, and luminous with wonder. In fact, its construction is so neat that some scholars have questioned whether it happened at all. And so, because we're going to return to it throughout the coming chapters, let me take a moment to explain why I believe that the Emmaus road narrative should be taken literally as an actual, historical encounter.

First, we are told that Jesus appeared to his disciples on at least ten occasions after his resurrection and that one of these was to a large crowd of some five hundred people (1 Cor. 15:6). With so many eyewitness accounts from which to choose, it stands to reason that Luke would have selected the most powerful and poignant for inclusion in his gospel and, of course, that he would do his best, inspired by the Spirit, to tell it well. It's a jaded view of the world that questions the veracity of an event just because it happens to be intrinsically meaningful and beautifully told.

Second, Luke consistently demonstrates a rigorous commitment to narrative accuracy both in this gospel and in his book of Acts. Where his fellow gospel writer John plays with chronology, poetry, and trope (to great effect), Luke remains a determined chronicler of facts. Why would he fabricate such a significant encounter?

Third, there are a number of important details in this story that lend it a distinct ring of truth. For example, why would Luke name one of the travelers and not the other if he were making the story up? And why does Jesus disappear after breaking bread without any mention at all of wine? Surely, if this story has been constructed, in part as a prototype of Communion, Luke should certainly have remembered both elements! And there's another interesting little detail. Why would he have chosen the relatively insignificant suburb of Emmaus as their destination? Wouldn't it have been more interesting if they'd been on their way, for instance, to Jericho, where Joshua first took hold of the promised land, where Bartimaeus had recently been healed, and where the parable of the good Samaritan had been set? Or they could have been walking to Bethany, where Jesus had been anointed with perfume just a few days earlier and where Lazarus had been raised from the dead. Now *that* would preach! But no, Luke says that the couple were walking some seven miles home to an obscure town not mentioned anywhere else in the Bible, presumably because this was the simple fact of the matter.

Finally, the depiction of Jesus himself in this story bears a striking resemblance to other accounts of his postresurrection appearances. Just as Mary had mistaken him for a gardener earlier that morning, and as seven of his closest friends would fail to recognize him a few days later on the shores of Galilee, so too, here on the road to Emmaus, the walkers fail to recognize the Lord. His appearance seems to have changed. It's also the way he speaks. Again and again, the resurrected Jesus approaches his friends with playful questions. He greets Mary with, "Woman, why are you crying?" He greets the fishermen on the Sea of Galilee with, "Haven't you caught any fish?" He asks Peter over breakfast, "Do you love me?" And here, on the road to Emmaus, he greets the travelers with another playful question: "What are you discussing together as you walk along?" (Luke 24:17).

In the light of all these biographical, stylistic, and circumstantial consistencies, there is no inherent requirement to take the Emmaus road story merely as metaphor and sufficient contrary evidence to accept it as fact. This matters because a literal reading of the story makes an actual, personal encounter with the living Lord Jesus thrillingly possible, tangible, and available to us all.

*　*　*

So let's take a deep dive now into this story that has so much to teach us about hearing God.

It's late afternoon and the sun is sinking, lengthening the shadows. As we discuss the horrors of recent events in Jerusalem, there is a weariness in our steps, as if the world has ended. He catches up to us easily with a spring in his step, as if it has just begun. We lower our voices, expecting him to pass us by with the usual pleasantries, but instead he slows down and falls in with our pace, wanting, it seems, to talk.

> He asked them, "What are you discussing together as you walk along?"
>
> They stood still, their faces downcast. One of them, named Cleopas, asked him, "Are you the only one visiting Jerusalem who does not know the things that have happened there in these days?"
>
> "What things?" he asked.

Does he really not know? Do we dare to trust him? These are dangerous times.

> "About Jesus of Nazareth," they replied. "He was a prophet, powerful in word and deed before God and all the people. The chief priests and our rulers handed him over to be sentenced to death, and they crucified him; but we had hoped that he was the one who was going to redeem Israel. And what is more, it is the third day since all this took place. In addition, some of our women amazed us. They went to the tomb early this morning but didn't find his body. They came and told us that they had seen a vision of angels, who

said he was alive. Then some of our companions went to the tomb
and found it just as the women had said, but they did not see Jesus."

The stranger's face is hard to read. Clearly, he's caught up in the things
we're recounting, but somehow he doesn't seem particularly distressed, impressed, or surprised. At one point he even seems (I must
have it wrong) to stifle a laugh. Finally, he stops, looks up at the sky,
and emits a long, frustrated sigh.

He said to them, "How foolish you are, and how slow to believe all
that the prophets have spoken! Did not the Messiah have to suffer
these things and then enter his glory?" And beginning with Moses
and all the Prophets, he explained to them what was said in all the
Scriptures concerning himself.

All our lives we've heard these stories of Abraham and Moses, but the
way he tells them now ignites something indescribable in our hearts.
Insight after insight we've never heard before. It's a couple of hours to
Emmaus on foot (three when you're tired and talking as we are now),
but before we know it, we're home, the sun has set, and dusk is falling fast.

As they approached the village to which they were going, Jesus
continued on as if he were going farther. But they urged him
strongly, "Stay with us, for it is nearly evening; the day is almost
over." So he went in to stay with them.

Our guest's feet are washed first, of course, and then, when it is done,
he looks directly at the servant and expresses a gratitude disproportionate to the menial duty rendered. By now the smell of fresh bread
is filling the house, lamps are flickering, and our best wine is waiting.
Eagerly we retire to the table, but before I can bless the food in the
usual way, our guest takes charge.

When he was at the table with them, he took bread, gave thanks, broke it and began to give it to them. Then their eyes were opened and they recognized him, and he disappeared from their sight. They asked each other, "Were not our hearts burning within us while he talked with us on the road and opened the Scriptures to us?"

The fire ignited in our hearts earlier on the road now consumes us entirely. With our own eyes we have seen him! In our own home we have hosted him! Suddenly we are more awake, more amazed, more alive than we have ever been before. Hurriedly we wrap our cloaks around us, all tiredness gone, and step out into the night.

They got up and returned at once to Jerusalem. There they found the Eleven and those with them, assembled together and saying, "It is true! The Lord has risen and has appeared to Simon." Then the two told what had happened on the way, and how Jesus was recognized by them when he broke the bread. (Luke 24:17–35)

The Word, the Word, and the Words

The encounter on the Emmaus road is not only, as Tom Wright says, "a wonderful, unique, spellbinding tale" but also "a model for a great deal of what being a Christian, from that day to this, is all about."[12] Here we find the covert Christ joining us on our journey through life. And here we are reminded that we must proactively invite him into our questions, our relationships, and our homes. Here our hearts catch fire and the Scriptures come alive. Here he walks and talks with us, patiently answering our questions, realigning our thinking, and teaching us to pray. Here at the table we share the bread and the wine, remembering his death and recognizing the reality of his resurrection right before our eyes. And here we are propelled out into the darkness as witnesses to the wonders we've seen.

And, of course, the Emmaus road story is also, preeminently, a model of prayer. Somehow these few verses distill more insight into how God speaks, and how we are to hear him speak, than any other passage, anywhere else in the Gospels. In fewer than twenty verses, the Lord communicates in at least five different ways: *conversationally* "as they talked and discussed these things with each other"; *exegetically* when he explained "all the Scriptures concerning himself"; *sacramentally* when he "took bread, gave thanks, broke it and began to give it to them"; *prophetically* when "their eyes were opened"; and *inwardly* when he spoke directly to their hearts, which were "burning . . . while he talked."

This is not an exhaustive list of all the ways in which God speaks (no dreams here, no angelic visitations, no talking donkeys, and so on), but it certainly provides a broad enough basis for a thorough exploration of the theme throughout this book. It also resonates deeply with our own Christian experience. The simple fact of the matter is that for every person who encounters Christ dramatically on the Damascus road with blinding lights and a booming voice, hundreds more meet him slowly and quietly, incognito on the Emmaus road, through friendship, Scripture, and conversation.

I said that God speaks in five ways through these twenty verses, but the list is incomplete without its most important component. The ultimate way in which God communicates in this story is not through the Bible (as some evangelicals might have it), nor through the breaking of bread (as sacramentalists might say), nor is it through "hearts burning within" (as contemplatives might think), but rather it is through Jesus Christ himself. He is the preeminent and ultimate Word of God (John 1:1) who animates and defines every other word God may speak in our lives. On the road to Emmaus, Jesus emphatically does not send a Bible or an angelic messenger or even a sudden epiphany to the couple, but rather goes to great lengths to appear to them personally, taking at least an hour to explain "what was said in all the Scriptures concerning himself." On another occasion he makes it perfectly clear that it's possible to "study the Scriptures diligently because you think that in them you have eternal life," but then he adds, "These are the very Scriptures that testify about me, yet you refuse to come to me to have life" (John 5:39–40). Elsewhere, the writer of Hebrews makes a similar point: "In the past God spoke ... at many times and in various ways, but in these last days he has spoken to us *by his Son*" (Heb. 1:1–2, italics mine).

What this means is that hearing God begins and ends with meeting Jesus. We understand the Bible in the light of Christ and not the other way round (more on this in the next chapter). Every other way in which God communicates—and in which we may therefore hear him speak—comes through Jesus and points back to him too. Nothing can replace, and nothing matters more, than a personal encounter with Jesus. "It is Christ himself, not the Bible, who is the true word of God," wrote C. S. Lewis. "The Bible, read in the right spirit and with the guidance of good teachers, will bring us to him."[13]

Some people will inevitably worry that such a focus on Christ as the preeminent Word of God might detract from the authority of the Bible as God's Word. Nothing could be further from the truth! The Bible is the primary means by which we become familiar with both the purposes and the personality of its subject, Jesus Christ. And here in the Emmaus road story, we have a dynamic picture of the dance between God's Word in the Bible and his final Word in Jesus. Each one points to the other. Our subjective personal encounters with Jesus are counterbalanced by our more objective examination of his Word in the Bible. One without the other simply doesn't work. Hearing God begins with Jesus and leads us immediately to Scripture, which, in turn, points us back to Christ.

Any revelation that claims to be from God, therefore, but does not sound like Jesus, and fails to push us deeper into relationship with Jesus, is fundamentally not Christian, no matter how supernatural it seems, how profound it sounds, and how many Bible verses come wrapped around its delivery.

The Vision Is Jesus

Many years ago, at the start of the 24-7 prayer movement, I scribbled some words on the wall of the first prayer room that unexpectedly self-seeded all around the world (now we'd say they "went viral"). It was a long, rambling prayer-poem-rant type thing called "The Vision," which began like this:

> So this guy comes up to me and says, "What's the vision? What's the big idea?" I open my mouth and the words come out like this: "The vision? The vision is Jesus! Dangerously, obsessively, undeniably Jesus."

It's been a long time since I wrote those words. The world has changed a great deal, and so have I. My faith has for the most part mellowed with the seasons, hopefully like a half-decent wine. Many of the things that seemed so intensely important back then have simply evaporated with time. Meanwhile, my hope in humanity's ability to sort itself out through politics, economics, and science has diminished drastically, and my trust in charismatic leaders to show us the way out of our predicament is almost completely gone. But the gentle allure of Jesus—the luminous beauty of his character and the startling defiance of his way—remains my vision, my glorious obsession, perhaps more now than ever before. Jesus really is the hope of the world.

I'm naturally nervous of prophecy and of the kind of people who claim to have a hotline to heaven, but because I'm into Jesus, I do deeply desire to hear whatever he has to say, no matter how he chooses to say it. I find myself invited to speak around the world about prayer, and this often leaves me feeling a fraud because I'm not especially interested in the subject. But because I'm into Jesus, we talk, and yes, I guess our conversations are going a little deeper these days. Hearing his voice remains tricky. I'm learning—becoming more discerning—but I still sometimes get it wrong. I'm also nervous because psychiatric wards are full of people hearing voices they attribute to God. And so, for that matter, is the Christian conference circuit. We need to think. We need to be biblical. But most of all we need to stay focused on Jesus.

The religious knowledge of the couple on the Emmaus road would have been extensive, but when they met the risen Jesus, everything—including their understanding of the Bible—had to change. Personally, I'm not particularly interested in becoming more devout or more informed or even better at hearing God. I aspire to discern his voice only insofar as it brings me closer to Jesus. My passion is still, in the words of Paul, "to know Christ" (Phil. 3:10). In spite of many failures, my focus remains, in the words of Hebrews, "Jesus the author and perfecter of our faith" (Heb. 12:2 ASV).

> **Pause & Pray**
>
> I pause here simply to focus my thoughts on Jesus, "the author and perfecter of [my] faith," asking him to draw near to me now by his Spirit, just as he drew near to the couple on the Emmaus road. Sitting still and breathing slowly, I become aware of his presence. And thinking about these two words—author and perfecter—I ask myself how my story is still being written and in what ways my faith still needs to be perfected.

Going *Ghar*

The wonderful truth is that Jesus Christ still appears and speaks to people today the way he did on the Emmaus road. I'll never forget the testimony of a Kurdish woman called Asrin, who first shared her story with me one evening over dinner and has given me permission to recount it here. Asrin grew up in northern Iran, where six of her cousins were killed by the ruling Ayatollah's forces (with whom the Kurdish Iranians are at war). Her earliest memories, therefore, are of playing in the cemetery where her mother would go to mourn.

Then, at the age of sixteen, Asrin was arrested, accused of crimes she had not committed and forced to sign a declaration of guilt.

"I had done nothing wrong, and still they held me guilty," she said, and I detected a flicker of fire in her eyes. "These people had killed my cousins, and now they were accusing me of crimes I had not committed. So I decided I might as well go and do the things they had forced me to confess. I would travel to the mountains of Iraq and join the Kurdish militia."

Up to this point, Asrin had always dutifully attended the mosque to pray, but, she said, Allah had never responded. As communists, the Kurdish militia denied God's existence, and Asrin began to wonder if they were right.

"Either God was going to speak to me," she said, with a flash of that same fire, "or I would have nothing to do with him. I gave God an ultimatum," she said with a grin. "I told him he had seven nights to speak to me, or I would go *ghar*—that's a Persian word for being permanently upset with someone."

On the seventh night, just before bed, Asrin reminded God of his looming deadline: "Either you appear to me tonight," she said, "or that's it. I will live the rest of my life as if you don't exist." That night she had a dream. She dreamed she was in a vast reception room full of many people, feeling very alone until she recognized a man in front of her, leaning against a wall. It was *Hazrat Isa,* Jesus the holy, highly honored in the Qur'an as a prophet (but not as the Son of God). "He was standing so close I could feel his breath," she said. "All around him there was brilliant light."

Nervously, Asrin addressed Jesus. She told him she was here to talk to God. "He looked straight back at me and said the strangest thing: '*Talk!*'"

"No," she protested. "You don't understand. I need to talk to *God.*"

Again, Jesus looked at her and said, "*Talk!*"

Then, very slowly, he repeated the most astounding phrase: "I am God," he said. "'I am God. I am God.'"

Asrin's face seemed to be shining with the memory. "As I heard this," she whispered, "all doubt drained away from my tired heart. We talked and talked and talked. I just poured out my heart to him—to God in Jesus—and for the first time in my life, I experienced God speaking back into my life."

When Asrin awoke from her dream, she hurried to share the news with the local mullah, but he told her angrily that Jesus could not be God. Next she told her family, but they just laughed at her. And then one day, as she was sitting in a park far from home, a total stranger gave Asrin a New Testament in the Persian language.[14] It was the first Bible she'd ever seen. The stranger also invited her to church, where she was amazed to hear the preacher say that God is love. Reading her new Bible in the park afterward, Asrin finally found the words that made sense of her dream. Jesus said, "I am the way and the truth and the life. No one comes to the Father except through me" (John 14:6). No wonder he'd invited her to *Talk!*"

Right then and there, sitting in that park, Asrin acknowledged Jesus Christ as the Son of God. And as she did so, she experienced an unfamiliar sense of hope flooding into her body, displacing the many years of despair.

Asrin shared this story with me quietly and calmly, but I just kept shaking my head in amazement and forgetting to eat. A couple of times I wanted to scream, "Hallelujah!" At the end I wanted her to tell it all again, this time to the whole restaurant, until I remembered that most of our fellow diners were also Persian Christians—members of the fastest-growing church in the world—many with their own equally amazing tales to tell.

"So what did you do," I asked, "after you became a follower of Jesus?"

"Oh," she laughed. "I never joined the Kurdish militia. I didn't want to kill people anymore. I wanted to bring life. So I trained to plant churches instead."

"Of course," I said encouragingly, pretending that this is *precisely* the sort of thing I expect women to be doing in Iran. "And, um, how's it all going?"

"Well, I've planted five churches so far," she replied casually. At this point I decided that I was not going to be the person to tell Asrin that some Christians in the supposedly emancipated West don't think women can do things like this.

"Isn't that a bit . . . dangerous?" I asked instead, already feeling like a complete coward.

Asrin fixed me with a steady gaze. "Pastor Pete," she said, "I was willing to die fighting to kill for the Kurdish militia. Don't you think it's much better to die fighting for Jesus Christ?"

When I meet people like Asrin, I want to become a Christian all over again. That beautiful verse from Colossians loops in my mind: "Christ in you, the hope of glory" (Col. 1:27). Like the couple on the road to Emmaus, Asrin had never expected to meet Jesus, and yet when she did, he spoke in such a way that the Bible came to life, her heart burned within her, and the entire trajectory of her life was transformed. How did he speak? First through a dream, then through a preacher, and finally through the Bible. And the result of these different types of revelation was a wonderful, ongoing conversation with the Lord that continues to this day.

*　*　*

Growing up, I never really learned to hear God's voice in the kind of conversational way experienced by the couple on the road to Emmaus and by Asrin in Iran. I learned to listen for God's voice in sermons and in Bible verses that seemed relevant enough to my situation to be appropriated as such. I suppose I also expected God to speak when I needed particular guidance for big decisions and never really doubted that he could speak supernaturally to missionaries and people who seemed more deserving than I am. But I never really learned to hear the Lord for myself, not as a natural part of a living relationship. Looking back now, I think I had unwittingly developed three fundamental problems with the very notion of God speaking to me either supernaturally or in any consistently conversational way: *psychological*, *theological*, and *experiential*.

Psychologically, I felt unworthy of any kind of special attention from God, and my experiences backed this up. When I prayed for a miracle, it never seemed to work; when I read my Bible, it often seemed irrelevant; and when I needed God to speak dramatically, there was never an audible voice or an angelic visitation or a supernatural dream. Asrin's story would have left me secretly thinking, "That could never happen to me." I didn't feel spiritual or special enough to hear God in the ways people do in the Bible, or in places like Iran.

Theologically, I had absorbed some of the prejudices of dispensationalism, although I would never have known what that term meant. This is the idea that we should no longer expect God to speak and act miraculously today in the ways he once did in the Bible because that sort of thing died the day the ink dried on the New Testament. These days, the argument goes, we have God's Word in the Bible, which is far more reliable than all that other whacko stuff. One of the many problems with this view is that it disregards the fact that people can, and do, misunderstand and misapply the Bible just as much as any other means of divine communication. It also ignores that the Bible itself teaches that God speaks outside the Bible![15] Dispensationalism only really makes sense in the absence of miracles, which leads me to the third problem I had with hearing from God . . .

Experientially, I was unfamiliar with the voice of God. Apart from the Bible, I only really expected him to communicate through my conscience (which seemed basically to be God saying no a lot) and through something we referred to as "having peace." The idea here was that when you made a good decision, you would be flooded with a sense of well-being, but when you made a bad one, you would lose that peace altogether. For me this was never a good test. In fact, most of the best decisions I've ever made have been accompanied by feelings of blind terror. The night I proposed to Sammy, for example, I had no peace at all. I was absolutely petrified. The night before we married, I was worse. The day I started the internship that revolutionized my relationship with the Lord, I walked down the driveway literally doubled over with anxiety. My lack of peace was epic. I could go on, but you get the point. Peace is a pretty subjective means of making important decisions, especially if you're as uptight as I am.

This matters because we often confuse theology with psychology. The fact that God speaks is a matter of *theology*. It's about God's nature. But how we hear God speak is a matter not of theology but of *psychology*. It's about how our neural pathways have learned to receive and process data, which varies from person to person. One individual may indeed be flooded with feelings of peace when they propose to their girlfriend, while another may be utterly terrified. This probably says more about the way that person is wired than it does about the will of God for their lives.

Psychology and Theology

St. Joseph's School in the town of Walgett in the remote Australian outback was founded by the Sisters of St. Joseph in 1896. Its motto, proudly emblazoned everywhere from the school crest to the school uniform, is *I hear, I see, I act*. Students at St. Joseph's are left in no doubt that theirs is a broad education involving hearing, seeing, and doing. But perhaps seeking a little extra gravitas, and with a nod, no doubt, to the school's Catholic roots, a decision was made a few years ago to translate this excellent motto into Latin. Which is how a school in the Australian outback came to have the utterly brilliant epigram: *audio, video, disco*.[16]

Of course it's not just the pupils of Walgett who learn by hearing, seeing, and doing. Everyone processes information in all three of these ways, with a clear bias, particularly earlier in life, toward one or the other. We learn most effectively through either seeing (visual processing), hearing (auditory processing), or doing (kinesthetic processing). And these preferences affect us subconsciously all the time.

For instance, I was sitting in a restaurant with three other people preparing to order a meal. One of them said, "The steak looks good," pointing at a plate on the next table. Another said, "Yes, I've heard the steak's delicious here." And the third (my wife) said, "Can I have a taste of yours?" Clearly I was preparing to dine with *video, audio,* and *disco.*

Many people struggle to hear God because they have been taught to listen for his voice in ways that are difficult or even impossible for them to process. An academic study in America discovered a correlation between certain psychological attributes and the way spiritual phenomena are experienced. Certain personality types, it seems, simply find it harder to hear God's voice than others.[17] This is not helped by the fact that a disproportionate amount of the material on listening to God has been written by introverts (representing approximately 35 percent of the population), who understandably advocate their own preference for quietness, stillness, and solitude. Countless extroverts struggle to hear God in such introverted ways and conclude that they are simply inherently bad at prayer. How desperately they need to know that it's equally possible, and no less spiritual, to discern the voice of God in public spaces, with other people, and through processes of external interaction. Yes, the Bible says, "Be still, and know that I am God" (Ps. 46:10), but it also says, "Let us shout aloud to the Rock of our salvation' (Ps. 95:1)!

Toilet-Cleaning Blues

Because I grew up without a natural conversational relationship with the Lord, everything changed the year I left school in quite a surprising way. It was to be an unwanted crash course in hearing the voice of God.

My exam results had been bad, and I felt like a failure. My girl-friend had dumped me, which didn't help. My friends had all gone away to university, and I felt lonely. To make matters worse, I was working as a toilet cleaner in a local hospital. Slowly but surely the world was turning gray. I longed for God to say something, but my prayers just seemed to bounce off the ceiling. I attended church dutifully, but everyone seemed fake. In desperation I went away on a solitary retreat and read the entire book of Jeremiah, but none of it made any sense. I was seeking God with a mixture of determination, desperation, and desire, but either he wasn't there or didn't care. Eventually, I ran out of energy and gave up praying altogether. It all seemed such a sham.

C. S. Lewis famously observed that "God whispers to us in our pleasures, speaks in our consciences, but shouts in our pains. It is his megaphone to rouse a deaf world."[18] I look back now and see how true this has been in my own life. He certainly used my eighteen-year-old angst to rouse me from my deafness, just as he had used a deep desperation to get Asrin's attention in Iran and had used disappointment to open the hearts of the couple on the road to Emmaus.

Having given up my faith a few weeks earlier, I went to a concert where a stranger approached me apologetically, introduced himself as a Christian, and said that he had a message for me from God. I held my breath because I was trying to stop believing in God, and yet I was also still desperate to hear his voice. The man said that he'd been staring at the back of my head for most of the gig and kept seeing a random, recurring mental image of a flickering candle that suddenly went out, plunging the room into darkness. "Does this make any sense?" he asked and reluctantly I nodded.

"Well, the flame just kind of reignited," he continued. "I saw it burning brighter than before. Lighting up the whole room." And with that he wandered off.

I knew that God had finally spoken to me. He was there and he cared. The light in my life was going to return. But how and when? For several months I asked God this question, again and again, and he said precisely nothing. Outwardly, nothing changed. Inwardly, I still felt depressed. And then one day I was shuffling through some Christmas cards when a Bible verse printed on one of them unexpectedly knocked the breath out of me: "If you spend yourselves in behalf of the hungry . . . your light will rise in the darkness" (Isa. 58:10). Here at last was the answer to my question, as clear as day. My light would shine again when I began to care for the poor.

And so, straight after Christmas, I threw in the towel as a toilet cleaner (quite literally) and got a job working for a homeless charity. I also poured out my heart to an older, wiser Christian called Nicole. What, I asked, did she think I should do? When and how would that flame get reignited in my life? She listened patiently as I described quitting my faith, the flickering candle, and the verse on the Christmas card. When she heard me mention Isaiah 58, she lit up, jumped from her seat, ran out of the room, and then returned with a letter. It was from Jackie Pullinger, the famous missionary to Hong Kong, and it had the whole of Isaiah 58—the entire chapter—printed as its header. Nicole told me that this was a sign from God and fixed me with a penetrating stare. She said that I should get on the next flight to Asia.

And so that is where and how the fire of faith was finally reignited in my life. Slowly, over several months in Hong Kong, I was healed, changed, and commissioned to do the very things I've been doing ever since. The key? Naturally and supernaturally, I began learning to hear the voice of God for myself.

God had spoken to me in at least four ways: through a vision, a Bible verse, the wise counsel of another Christian, and a simple willingness on my part to obey. This isn't a bad checklist of the various ways in which God speaks, and it mirrors much of what we have seen in both the Emmaus road story and the testimony of Asrin. But it is also significant that these different moments of revelation, which have been deceptively distilled here into just a few paragraphs, were actually spread out over the better part of a year. There were weeks and even months between his speaking in one way and then another. At the time this felt like forever.

Listening Slowly

God is rarely in a hurry to speak. Testimonies of his intervention are often unhelpfully condensed into a sort of highlight reel, leaving us to read quite carefully between the lines in order to notice the tedious months or even years of asking and waiting in between the dramatic moments of epiphany. It's striking how long Jesus takes to reveal himself to the couple on the road to Emmaus and later in their home. Here he is, resurrected from the grave, physically present, exclusively engaged with this highly favored couple, and still he refuses to speak in a sound bite or to behave dramatically. And it was the same for Asrin. She had given the Lord seven nights, and he said nothing for six. Even then, Jesus having revealed himself powerfully to her in a dream, there was a gap of several months before she finally received a Bible, found out what it all meant, and was able to fully respond. "In the spiritual life God chooses to try our patience first of all by His slowness," wrote Frederick Faber almost two hundred years ago. "He is slow: we are swift and precipitate. It is because we are but for a time, and He has been for eternity. Thus grace, for the most part, acts slowly. He works little by little."[19]

In her book *Walking on Water*, Madeleine L'Engle quotes Mother Alice Kaholusana, a Hawaiian Christian:

> Before the missionaries came, my people used to sit outside their temples for a long time meditating and preparing themselves before entering. Then they would virtually creep to the altar to offer their petitions and afterwards would again sit a long time outside, this time to "breathe life" into their prayers. The Christians, when they came, just got up, uttered a few sentences, said AMEN and were done. For that reason my people called them *haoles*, 'without breath,' or those who failed to breathe life into their prayers.[20]

I admit that I am often breathlessly hurried in my dealings with God. I expect him to be at my beck and call on some kind of celestial speed dial. I bluster into his presence and make my demands without due reverence. I am terrible at tarrying on the other side of asking to slowly breathe life into the embers I have spread before the altar of the Lord.

But God is not in a hurry, and he is also—as we see in these stories—inclined to speak to those who show themselves truly hungry. We see glimpses of this in the couple on the Emmaus road, who weren't just shooting the breeze, passing the time in idle chatter, when Jesus appeared by their side. Rather, they were earnestly "talking with each other about everything that had happened." Similarly, Asrin had been seeking God with an audacious determination for seven days, even issuing the Almighty with an ultimatum before her breakthrough came.[21] As for me, I can't compare my teenage angst with the passion of either Asrin or the couple from Emmaus, but I had certainly been seeking God more seriously than ever before when he finally broke in.

If your hope in reading this book is simply to learn a few principles about hearing God, I hope it helps. But if your desire is for something more, if you are thirsty for a fresh encounter with Jesus and longing to become more familiar with his voice, or simply wanting to want him more, I would encourage you to pause and pray whenever something stirs your soul as you read. Resist the temptation to rush. Try to make this a process of personal interaction with God. Embark upon a season of seeking his face. Begin to do your own deals with him, as Asrin did. Earnestly process your questions with other people, as I did with Nicole before Hong Kong and as that couple did too on the Emmaus road. As you do these things, I believe that the Lord will respond to your requests in generous proportion to your desire. "You will seek me and find me," he says, "when you seek me with all your heart" (Jer. 29:13). God does not say here, "You will inevitably find me the moment you seek me." Rather, he promises to be found "when you seek me with all your heart." There is something about the posture of my praying and the wholeheartedness of my seeking—the determination, desperation, and desire—that moves the heart and attracts the attention of God. Eventually.

Ears to Hear

There's a favorite saying of Jesus—one he used more than almost any other—that acknowledges how difficult we often find it to hear his voice. On fifteen separate occasions he urged his listeners to have "ears to hear,"[22] presumably because it was perfectly possible to stand in the crowd staring at Jesus Christ himself, listening to his words but missing his meaning entirely. I recognize this tendency in myself. I often need God to show up and speak more than I show up and listen.

People in Jesus' day got similarly distracted. Many joined the admiring crowds, but few became his disciples and friends. And although some two billion people today call themselves Christians, surely if even a fraction of us truly had "ears to hear" what the Lord is saying, the world would soon be changed.

My aim in the rest of this book, therefore, is to help you find your ears! I'm not particularly interested in teaching truths about God's Word. (This might actually, ironically, reduce your ability to hear him speak. As Jesus says to the Pharisees, "You study the Scriptures diligently because you think that in them you have eternal life. These are the very Scriptures that testify about me, yet you refuse to come to me to have life" [John 5:39–40]). Instead, I want to help familiarize you with the voice of Jesus so that you will become more alive than you've ever been before to the "great and unsearchable things"[23] he wants to say to—and through—you. Perhaps we should simply pray.

> *Lord, I am here before you now, wholeheartedly.*
>   *Speak as I seek your face.*
>   *Give me ears to hear what you are saying and a greater willingness to wait.*
>   *Insofar as I am also here before you now half-heartedly, fuel the fire of my desire.*

Do whatever it takes to renew in me an all-consuming passion for your name.

Lord Jesus, open my eyes to perceive you.

Holy Spirit, soften my heart to receive you.

Father God, grant me faith to believe that when I pray in this way, you hear and draw near with words of infinite love. Amen.

Living Word: Sojourner Truth (1797–1883)—Encountering Jesus

I jes' walked round an' round in a dream. Jesus loved me! I knowed it, I felt it.

—Sojourner Truth

Nineteenth-century abolitionist and women's rights activist Sojourner Truth could not read the Bible for herself, and yet she encountered Christ and heard his voice in ways that changed not just her own life but also those of countless others ever since. To date she has given her name to a library, a NASA space rover, a US naval ship, and an asteroid. She has been featured on a US postage stamp and a Google Doodle, in a Broadway musical, and with a sculpture that stands in the US Capitol Building in Washington, DC. She is honored in the calendar of saints by the Episcopal Church and in the list of 100 Most Significant Americans of All Time by the Smithsonian Institution. There are plans to make her the first woman of color to be featured on a US banknote since Pocahontas in the 1860s. Not bad for an illiterate woman born into slavery in south-eastern New York in 1797 as one of ten (or perhaps twelve) children.

As a child, Isabella (as she was originally known) was bought and sold several times. At the age of thirteen she became the "property" of a cruel rapist called John Dumont. After seventeen years she escaped and found sanctuary with a godly Quaker couple who paid for her freedom.

Isabella could neither read nor write, so the Bible was a closed book unless someone read it aloud. But then one day she received a vision: "God revealed himself to her, with all the suddenness of a flash of lightning."[24] Terrified, she began repenting of her sins until "a friend appeared . . . beaming with the beauty of holiness and radiant with love." Recalling this epiphany while dictating her autobiography, Sojourner smiled: "I jes' walked round an' round in a dream. Jesus loved me! I knowed it, I felt it."[25]

This was her Emmaus road encounter, and it was to become the defining moment of her life. There were a few false starts in her fledgling faith, not helped, I suspect, by her inability to read the Bible for herself. But she asked God for a new name to reflect her new life, and he answered, appearing to her once again to name her Sojourner "because I was to travel up an' down the land, showin' the people their sins, an' bein' a sign unto them," and Truth "because I was to declare the truth to the people."[26]

And so it was that Sojourner Truth began traveling around, attending prayer meetings, and speaking out against slavery and (even more controversially) in favor of the emancipation of women. She was often threatened, sometimes attacked, and on one occasion beaten so badly she had to walk with a cane for the rest of her life. But she never backed down. "The Lord has made me a sign unto this nation," she said, "an' I go round a'testifyin' an' showin' on 'em their sins agin my people."[27]

Her most famous speech, Ain't I a Woman?, was delivered at the Women's Rights Convention in 1851:

> Look at me! Look at my arm. I have plowed, I have planted, and I have gathered into barns. And no man could head me. And ain't I a woman? I could work as much and eat as much as man–when I could get it–and bear the lash as well! And ain't I a woman? I have borne children and seen most of them sold into slavery, and when I cried out with a mother's grief, none but Jesus heard me. And ain't I a woman?[28]

Quite rightly, the world today applauds Sojourner's defiant and determined stand for freedom, but some would prefer to forget her motivation. The defining moments in her trailblazing life were encounters with the Lord Jesus Christ. First, he spoke to assure her of his love—and by this she found a fierce confidence. Next, he spoke to give her a new name—and by this she found her call. Ultimately, he spoke not just to her but also through her as "a sign unto this nation . . . showin' on 'em their sins."

Listening Exercise:
Hearing God's Word in Jesus

To truly encounter Jesus is to be knocked sideways, astonished, overwhelmed. Mild interest means you have not yet met him.
—Simon Ponsonby

In this chapter we've seen that hearing God is relational rather than technical. At the heart of the Emmaus road story is an encounter with Jesus Christ: "Jesus himself drew near" (Luke 24:15 ESV). Elsewhere he says, "My sheep listen to my voice; I know them, and they follow me" (John 10:27). So let's take time now to do precisely that: to listen to his voice, to allow him to draw near, using one or more of the exercises described below.

Worship Exercises

> Let us fix our eyes on Jesus.
> —Hebrews 12:2 BSB

We become familiar with the voice of Jesus by spending time in his presence, and we do this primarily in worship. There is no better way to prime yourself to hear God's voice than to draw near to him regularly, giving your undivided attention to him in love. It surprises me how many faithful churchgoers don't make space for worship in their everyday lives. Why not create a series of worship playlists tailored to different moods and occasions? Personally, I find it refreshing to explore a wide range of musical genres in personal worship. It doesn't all have to be guitar led! There are such astoundingly beautiful hymns to Jesus freely available to each one of us, written by many of the greatest musicians of all time, from Handel's *Messiah* and Bach's *St. Matthew Passion* to Aretha Franklin's rendition of "Amazing Grace" and Chance the Rapper's mix of "How Great (is our God)."

While audio processors can easily get lost in worship music regardless of environment, those who process life more visually or kinesthetically may enjoy linking their listening to a participatory experience or a special place. Your chosen moment might be a particular journey alone in the car with the music playing loud, or a serene walk in the country with your earphones in, or a regular time of physical exercise accompanied by praise.

And, of course, worship is more than music. This morning I sat in silence for a while, simply staring at a beautiful view as I slowly became aware of God's presence. There are certain poems and pictures that move me to wonder. The Psalms are a timeless treasure trove of praise, used by Jesus himself. And you probably know someone who makes you fall in love with Jesus all over again. Why not see them in order to ply them with leading questions such as, "What's God been showing you recently?" or "What does the voice of Jesus sound like for you?"

Questions for Personal Reflection and Group Discussion

- Is there a time in my life when "Jesus himself drew near"? How did he speak? What did he say? Do the particular circumstances of that encounter reveal anything about my own predisposition when it comes to hearing God?

- In November 2017 a painting of Jesus entitled *Salvator Mundi* (*Savior of the World*), attributed to Leonardo da Vinci, became the most expensive painting ever sold. If I look at it now online, does anything seem familiar? Is there anything I "recognize" in his features? In what ways do I perceive and experience Jesus differently from the way Leonardo da Vinci experienced him?

- *(For groups)* Take time to share testimonies of how you became followers of Jesus. (This is invariably a wonderful, faith-building thing to do, and it doesn't matter at all if you've shared like this before.) At the end of each person's story, go round the group, each saying, "The thing that story shows me about Jesus is . . ."

For Further Reflection

Simon Ponsonby, *Amazed by Jesus* (Edinburgh: Muddy Pearl, 2021).

Philip Yancey, *The Jesus I Never Knew* (Grand Rapids: Zondervan, 1995).

Dane C. Ortlund, *Gentle and Lowly: The Heart of Christ for Sinners and Sufferers* (Wheaton: Crossway, 2020).

PART 1

GOD'S WORD:

VOX EXTERNA

Jean Louis Forain, *The Road to Emmaus*
Artokoloro / Alamy Stock Photo

And beginning with Moses and all the Prophets . . .
—Luke 24:27

When it comes to hearing God, the Bible is the language of his heart. Nothing he says in any other way or in any other context will ever override, undermine, or contradict what he has said in the Scriptures. That's why Jesus doesn't just show up on the road to Emmaus and say, "Hi, it's me!" Instead, he takes considerable time to deliver a lengthy biblical exposition in which he reinterprets God's Word radically, in the light of his own life, death, and resurrection. This approach, the *christological hermeneutic*, can help you with the tricky business of hearing God's voice through the Bible and of making sense of its meaning in your life today.

2

Hearing God's Word in the Bible

*And beginning with Moses and all the Prophets, he explained
to them what was said in all the Scriptures concerning himself.*

—Luke 24:27

---

*Christians read the Bible not as a document from history but as
a world into which they enter so that God may meet them there.*

—Rowan Williams

Our old GPS offered a range of voices, including a man who barked
commands like a soldier, a woman so breathy Sammy said she couldn't
be trusted, and an option for recording your own voice. Since Sammy
had vetoed the breathy woman and we were both quite scared of the
military man, I asked if she would like to be the voice that guided
me flawlessly around the scribbled streets of England. Directions are
not Sammy's strong point (she still muddles her left and right), and
it would be fair to say that we've had a few "fraught" moments in the
car over the years as a result. And so I added that, perhaps, if she did,
it could be quite healing for our relationship.

Sammy frowned and immediately came up with an even better
idea. And so that night I found myself sitting on the sofa between our
two little boys, with them taking turns to read the sixty or seventy
predetermined phrases, ranging from "turn left" to "you are approaching a ferry." In subsequent years my heart would often melt as these
two squeaky voices steered me through Britain's notoriously confusing road system. On the rare occasion I did in fact approach a ferry,

their voices on my GPS broke into Rod Stewart's "I Am Sailing." And whenever I pulled up outside our house late at night and all the lights were off, a little voice, fast asleep inside, would invariably catch me off guard: "Welcome home, Daddy. You have reached your destination."

Our boys are now young men with deep, gravelly voices and a pretty decent ability to read a map, but I can't bring myself to discard that old GPS. Its technology may be hopelessly out of date, but the voices it contains are becoming more precious with every passing year.

One day we were driving through the center of Edinburgh, Scotland's ancient capital, on our way to the train station. The roads were busy and the one-way systems confusing, but somehow the little voices on our GPS were successfully guiding us to our destination. We were just about to make our final turn into the station when Danny's prerecorded voice chirped up, right on time, "Turn right here!"

Feigning amazement, I looked at him in the rearview mirror. "How do you know where the station is?"

Danny stared at me, wide eyed and open mouthed, clearly quite impressed by his own navigational abilities, and then said something that has passed into the folklore of our family: "I don't know how I know; I just know!"

How We Know What We Know

In that statement, Danny encapsulated one of the greatest philosophical conundrums of all time: How do we know what we know? It's a branch of philosophy known as epistemology, concerned with the nature of knowledge. If you've ever engaged a conspiracy theorist online, you will have become embroiled in an epistemological debate. Quite quickly you realize that the issue (flat earth, antivax, the Bilderberg Group, whatever) is not the issue. The actual discussion is really about the nature of knowledge. Whom do you trust? How do you know what you know?

Some people say they know what they know because of science and rationality, but no one is purely rational, and empirical analysis has its own inherent limitations and distortions. Or perhaps I know what I know on the basis of whatever feels right in any given situation. But if there's one thing I learned as a teenager with a broken heart, it was that my emotions are not a reliable basis for anything. My feelings change all the time, mostly at the mercy of the weather, espresso, and Nina Simone.

Some people say they know what they know because it's what they've always known. They simply accept whatever worldview they happen to have inherited from their own particular culture and tradition. This might work very well indeed if you are a rural medieval basket weaver in a long line of basket weavers who have lived in the same village for centuries. But it doesn't work so well in the global village where you find yourself confronted with completely different views of reality at the click of a button or for the price of a discount flight. Whose truth is the true truth?

For every Christian who has ever lived, the Bible is ultimately how we know what we know. Our epistemology is anchored in this vast and ancient record of God's revelation regarding the nature and purpose of reality. Like that GPS leading me through the chaotic streets of Edinburgh, the Bible is a constant source of guidance, wisdom, and direction through life's many twists and turns. "Whether you turn to the right or to the left," said the prophet Isaiah to Israel, "your ears will hear a voice behind you, saying, 'This is the way; walk in it'" (30:21). And just like that GPS, the voice of Scripture, which can certainly seem formal at first, quickly becomes familiar and even familial. It speaks intimately to our hearts and somehow becomes more precious with every passing year. "Welcome home," says the voice again and again. "You have reached your destination."

When it comes to hearing God, the Bible is the very language of his heart. Nothing he says in any other way or in any other context will ever override, undermine, or contradict what he has already said in the Scriptures. I suppose this is why Jesus doesn't just show up on the road to Emmaus and say, "Hi, it's me!" You might think that would suffice. Instead, he takes considerable time to conduct an exhaustive biblical exposition that carefully contextualizes his own life, death, and resurrection within the canon of its orthodoxy. What an incredible Bible study that must have been! How amazing to have listened as Jesus personally unpacked "what was said in all the Scriptures concerning himself." No wonder the couple said to each other a little later, "Were not our hearts burning within us while he . . . opened the Scriptures to us?"

Christ's commitment to biblical exposition on the road to Emmaus reveals three important truths that we will explore over the next two chapters.

First, it shows that the resurrected Jesus continues to look to the Bible for *authority*. A brand-new world may have been inaugurated by his death and resurrection, but the Bible is still the means by which Jesus *knows what he knows*.[1] Perhaps this seems strange to us today. Notions of absolute truth and ultimate authority are fiercely attacked, and the Bible itself is no longer accorded unconditional respect in Western societies. Even within some wings of the church, the authority of the Bible is being undermined. No wonder so many people are losing their confidence in Scripture. And this is why we're going to take a little time over the next few pages simply to remind ourselves of the unparalleled authority of the Bible as the inspired Word of God, the epistemological foundation for life, and the primary means by which we may hear him speak today.

Second, on the road to Emmaus Jesus *interprets* the Scriptures in a radical new way, explaining "what was said in all the Scriptures *concerning himself*" (v. 27, italics mine). In other words, he took the lens of his own life, death, and resurrection and reviewed the entire Bible through its unique perspective. This Jesus-shaped approach to understanding the Bible is such an important key to hearing his voice that it's going to be our focus throughout the second half of this chapter.

Third, in this story we see that when the Bible is interpreted in this way—in the light of Jesus, inspired by the Holy Spirit—it has a remarkable power to speak directly and personally into our lives. Like the couple on the Emmaus road, we will sometimes find "our hearts burning within us" as the Lord reveals himself to us through the Bible. And so, in the chapter after this one, we are going to focus on one of the most powerful tools I know for hearing God speaking directly to our hearts through his Word: the *lectio divina*.

I'm excited about the biblical focus of these chapters because I believe that Jesus wants to do for you precisely what he did for that couple on the Emmaus road. His nature hasn't changed. Ask and he will draw alongside you as he drew alongside them and open the Scriptures for you as he did for them until your heart, like theirs, begins to burn. "Call to me and I will answer you," he says, "and tell you great and unsearchable things you do not know" (Jer. 33:3). Wonderful and surprising new discoveries await as you call on the Lord and learn to listen for his voice in Scripture.

The Ultimate Authority of the Bible

The Bible was effectively illegal in mainland China when I lived in Hong Kong, so I took the exciting opportunity to smuggle as many as possible across the border in a couple of suitcases, buried under dirty laundry. Having made it through customs, I deposited the precious contraband (minus underwear) in a series of lockers in a hotel in Guangzhou and mailed the locker keys to an address in northern China. Secrecy was paramount, I was told, because the recipient of these keys might well risk his life, and certainly his freedom, traveling from the other side of China to collect the illegal load.

Why on earth was he willing to take such risks for a book considered boring and irrelevant by many in the West? Because the fast-growing church in China was, and is, ravenously hungry for the nourishment of God's Word. And as a result of that hunger, things are changing quite dramatically. In fact, the biggest Bible-printing factory in the world today—the size of twelve soccer fields, with the capacity to print twenty million Bibles a year—is in China. These are shipped out to a network of sixty thousand churches through eighty distribution centers. And this vast enterprise still struggles to keep up with demand.[2]

Worldwide, the Bible is indisputably the most successful literary creation of all time. No other book even comes close. Every year, more than one hundred million copies are sold or given away. The *New York Times* omits the Bible from its list of bestsellers because it would almost always be on top.[3] And this is not just because it is old and profound—so is Plato's *Republic*—but because the Bible points to Jesus, resonates profoundly with every culture, and ultimately changes lives.

This precious anthology of sixty-six books written by at least forty authors in three languages over fourteen hundred years has always been a source of incomparable comfort, correction, and direction in my own life. Again and again, God has spoken truth and wisdom to me through its words.

Here I am, for instance, as a scared kid at a brutal boarding school sleeping in a dormitory with thirty other boys, hiding under the blankets after lights out, reading my pocket New Testament by the glow of a tiny flashlight and whispering, "I can do all things through Christ who strengthens me" (Phil. 4:13 NKJV).

And now I'm enjoying a McDonald's hot fudge sundae in Hong Kong, and my mother is on the phone: "It's Dad," she says, sounding frail. "Heart attack." The words go through me like a knife. "They tried to resuscitate him; he'd been swimming in the sea. But your dear dad's gone to be with Jesus. I'm so sorry." I stumble to my room feeling utterly alone and very far from home. Kneeling by my bed in that tiny tin hut, dwarfed by a forest of neon skyscrapers, I turn to one of my dad's favorite psalms, and the tears begin to flow: "Even though I walk through the darkest valley, I will fear no evil, for you are with me" (Ps. 23:4).

Several years later, I'm worrying about a piece of graffiti on the wall of the first 24-7 Prayer room: "GIVE. GOD. NO. REST." Isn't it a bit . . . irreverent? Perhaps I should take it down. But then, embarrassingly, I discover that this "heresy" is actually a direct quote from Isaiah 62, which quickly becomes a rallying cry for the entire 24–7 movement:

> I have posted watchmen on your walls, Jerusalem;
>   they will never be silent day or night.
> You who call on the LORD,
>   give yourselves no rest,
> and give him no rest till he establishes Jerusalem
>   and makes her the praise of the earth. (Isa. 62:6–7)

And now I'm with our 24–7 team on the Mediterranean island of Ibiza, trying to shine a little light slap bang in the middle of Europe's biggest party scene. The island is suffering a major drought, and its small Christian community has asked us to pray for rain. This feels like a very big prayer indeed, and I don't have a lot of faith. But then, as I climb into my car at the end of our prayer time, two remarkable things coincide. First, some rain starts splatting on the windshield, and soon we're being drenched by the heaviest storm Ibiza has seen since 1976.[4] And second, just as I'm doubting that our prayers have anything to do with the rain, I receive a random text message. A guy called Vanya is sitting in a prayer room thousands of miles away in St. Petersburg, Russia, knowing nothing about our prayer request in Ibiza but sensing the Holy Spirit giving him a particular Bible reference for us: 1 Kings 18. I looked it up and let out a little gasp of surprise. An entire chapter of the Bible about praying for rain, concluding with a mighty downpour ending years of drought: "Meanwhile, the sky grew black with clouds, the wind rose, a heavy rain started falling" (v. 45).

And now it's the dog-end of winter, and Sammy is chronically ill with uncontrollable epilepsy and a massive brain tumor. We're more scared than we've ever been before, but the Bible is speaking hope and peace to us in ways nothing else, and no one else, can. The first time she goes into the MRI, Sammy vomits all over the expensive machinery. The second time, she memorizes Psalm 91 and meditates on each line. As a result, she somehow experiences something of the presence of God in that desolate tube: "Whoever dwells in the shelter of the Most High will rest in the shadow of the Almighty. I will say of the LORD, 'He is my refuge and my fortress, my God, in whom I trust'" (vv. 1–2).

It would be easy to go on, but I'm sure you have your own stories of God speaking into your life through the Bible. What a priceless gift he has given us! How easily we take its riches for granted. How often we leave it unopened or trade its treasure for lesser things. "Oh, give me that book!" cried John Wesley. "At any price give me the book of God! . . . Let me be *homo unius libri* [a man of a single book]."[5] And, of course, his prayer was answered emphatically. John Wesley went on to ride some 250,000 miles carrying his Bible, preaching 40,000 sermons from its pages, unleashing its power to change nations. And the moment that fire was first ignited in Wesley's heart was remarkably similar to the one that caused the hearts of the couple on the road to Emmaus to burn within. On May 24, 1738, at a Moravian Bible study in Aldersgate, London, during a reading from Martin Luther's *Preface to the Epistle to the Romans*, Wesley famously found his heart "strangely warmed." This, then, was the spark that ignited the wildfires of the Great Methodist Awakening.

Encounter Culture

We talk a great deal today about "encountering" the Lord. Books, conferences, and organizations use this term a lot. We design worship events and ministry times explicitly to create space for encounters with God. And the Emmaus road story is perhaps the ultimate example of just the kind of life-changing encounter to which we aspire. And yet it is marked less by the feelings and phenomena we tend to associate with such moments than it is by a lengthy Bible study. Let me say that again. This archetypal encounter with the resurrected Lord is signaled not by a dramatic *experience*, nor by an overpowering *emotion*, but rather "merely" by an extensive *exposition* of Scripture.

We live in an age when people increasingly measure truth experientially. What began in the 1960s counterculture as, "If it feels good, do it," is now, "If it feels true, believe it." A subjective approach to ethics has reached its inevitable conclusion today with an experiential approach to epistemology. And this shift has profoundly affected the way we evaluate the truth of God. Back in the postwar years, Billy Graham's voice could ring out around the world with a single, simple refrain: "The Bible says . . ." And this proved enough for millions of hungry souls. "If it's in the Bible," they reasoned, "it must be true." As the twentieth century unfolded, Christians had to work a lot harder to justify their beliefs. And so we witnessed the rising popularity of apologists like C. S. Lewis, Francis Schaeffer, and Josh McDowell, whose classic *Evidence That Demands a Verdict* sold more than a million copies.

With the erosion of many of the old absolutes and this rise of experientialism, even Christians began to expect doctrinal truth to come seasoned with powerful feelings, and the charismatic movement was happy to oblige. A new generation of millennial preachers learned to inspire and emote, while the old guard dryly informed and equipped. Around the same time, an industry grew up to monetize worship music so that today, when someone refers to "a good time of worship," we know perfectly well that they're referring to an emotional time of singing. And, of course, it is now normal to respond to a sermon by receiving personal prayer ministry, hoping—let's be honest—for an experience: a prophetic word or a physical sensation such as tears, tingling, or tumbling to the floor. Anything to verify that something actually happened through the time of prayer.

I am not against all of this. In fact, I think it's wonderful that our heads and our hearts have been reconnected. Experiences are important. Emotion matters in faith as in life. Two thousand years ago on the Emmaus road, the couple measured the power of Christ's words experientially, by the sensation of their hearts burning within. So none of this is new or unhealthy.

But however wonderful an experience may be (and no experience could ever be more wonderful than personally encountering the risen Lord), the Bible remains the primary arbiter of truth for Christians—whether we feel it or not—and the main way in which we hear God speak. This must surely be one of the reasons why Jesus is so discreet on the road to Emmaus. He knows that an extraordinary *experience* and a personal *encounter* are insufficient unless accompanied by a biblical *explanation*.

I've enjoyed recounting exciting stories of God speaking supernaturally in this book, and I make no apologies for seeking to inspire you to expect such encounters in your own life too. But by far the most important and consistent way in which God speaks is perhaps the least dramatic. Learning to hear him through the Bible may well seem far less exciting than dreams, visions, and angelic visitations. But just as Jesus took time to unpack the Bible on the Emmaus road, and as John Wesley's life was transformed by a Bible commentary, so God wants to set your heart on fire with a fresh passion for the Scriptures. As it says in the longest psalm, which is itself a hymn to the glory of God's law, "How sweet are your words to my taste, sweeter than honey to my mouth!" (Ps. 119:103).

Pause & Pray

Boring? Confusing? Disappointing? Do I have feelings about the Bible I try to hide? Seeking to be utterly honest, I talk with the Lord now about my relationship with his written Word. I ask him to speak to me through the Bible, to open my eyes to see it in new ways and to make my heart burn within.

Letting the Lion Out of the Cage

Open the door and let the lion out; he will take care of himself. . . .
He no sooner goes forth in his strength than his assailants
flee. The way to meet infidelity is to spread the Bible. The
answer to every objection against the Bible is the Bible.
—Charles Spurgeon

From the catacombs of Rome to the arms of the *Cristo Redentor* out-stretched over Rio de Janeiro, from Michelangelo's *Creation of Adam* to Aretha Franklin's "Oh Happy Day," from the Celtic monasteries that saved European civilization after the decline of the Roman Empire to the American Bill of Rights, Western society is forged, founded, and framed by the Bible. The historian Tom Holland, in his bestselling book *Dominion: The Making of the Western Mind,* argues that modern science could only have arisen from a biblical understanding of the world as a created entity, subject to universal laws (and not from the predominant Eastern view of the world as a cosmic illusion). The medievalist Brian Tierney, of Cornell University, traces our idea of universal human rights back to the notion of humanity made in God's image as described in the book of Genesis and as expounded by Christian canon lawyers in the twelfth century.[6] Meanwhile, classicist Kyle Harper has demonstrated that the idea of sex needing to be consensual was a startling new concept that came into the world through Christianity.[7] According to contemporary rabbi Ari Lamm, the Bible is "the only common language we've ever known for remembering our past and bettering our future. It is," he adds, referring to America, "our moral founding document no less than the Constitution is our foundational political document."[8]

There was a day in 1381 when a preacher named John Ball delivered such an incendiary open-air sermon to a crowd gathered on London's Blackheath Common that it ignited an uprising against the injustices of English society. His voice rang out, using the biblical book of Genesis to challenge the very infrastructure of the nation at that time, and he did so with a question in rhyme:

When Adam delved and Eve span,
Who was then the gentleman?[9]

It was a good question, and a defiant one. In God's original plan, where, Ball wanted to know, were the feudal overlords? Hadn't Adam and Eve been ordinary working people who ploughed and span just like the members of the crowd gathered that day on Blackheath Common? This was rabble-rousing stuff in a feudal society, divided by a vast disparity in wealth and power, built upon a form of bonded slavery and ultimately justified by divine right, especially at a time when the church carefully controlled access to the Bible, reserving it solely for priests schooled in Latin. "Therefore I exhort you," the preacher cried that day, "to consider that now the time is come, appointed to us by God, in which ye may (if ye will) cast off the yoke of bondage, and recover liberty."[10] With these words, the so-called Peasants' Revolt began.

John Ball paid the ultimate price for letting the lion of biblical truth loose in medieval England. He was hung, drawn, and quartered on July 15, 1381, in the presence of King Richard II. His head was then mounted on a spike on London Bridge as a warning to other dissenters. Meanwhile, in Oxford, his distinguished contemporary John Wycliffe continued his life's work of translating the Bible into English, seeking to put it into the hands of the people, arguing strongly for its primary authority and for the priesthood of all believers, some 133 years before Martin Luther's Bible-led Reformation in Germany. For this Wycliffe was later excommunicated as a heretic, his body exhumed and burned, and his ashes scattered without ceremony on the River Swift.

John Wycliffe and John Ball lost their lives, but they won the war. If you walk across the Central Lobby of London's Houses of

Parliament today, you will find a Bible verse set in its floor as a constant reminder at the heart of British government of its proper political priorities: "Unless the LORD builds the house, the builders labor in vain" (Ps. 127:1). Next door in Westminster Abbey, when Elizabeth II was crowned queen of the UK, Canada, Australia, New Zealand, South Africa, Pakistan, and Ceylon (now Sri Lanka) in 1953, she was presented with a Bible and these remarkable words, which echoed out around the abbey: "We present you with this book, the most valuable thing that this world affords. Here is wisdom, this is the royal law, these are the lively oracles of God."[11]

The Bestselling, Least-Read Book

But if the Bible really is "the most valuable thing that this world affords," the very foundation of Western culture and the primary medium by which God speaks today, why is it increasingly disrespected in public by the very societies it has built and neglected in private even by Christians? There has never, in any of our lifetimes, been a moment like this when the Bible was so easily accessible yet so little read. Six centuries after John Wycliffe paid such a price to put Scripture into the hands of ordinary people, the YouVersion app alone offers 2,062 versions of the Bible in 1,372 languages, all completely free of charge. Meanwhile, research shows that 78 percent of Americans own a physical copy of the Bible, but only 9 percent of them read it regularly.[12]

At the start of the COVID-19 pandemic in 2020, there were signs that this sad state of affairs might be about to change as Bible sales soared in most Western countries and many people suddenly had more time to read it. But between January and June of that year, our engagement with the Bible actually declined by 6 percent among men and 7 percent among women.[13] "We revere the Bible, but don't read it," observed famous pollster George Gallup Jr. dryly. "It is the bestselling, least-read book in America."[14]

Why is there such a gulf between what we say we believe about the Bible and what we do in practice? One of the problems seems to be that no one ever teaches us *how* to read it, with both our heads and our hearts. We pretend that the Bible is easy, obvious, and straightforward, when much of it is not. Some people spout pious phrases like, "If it's in the Bible it's good enough for me," but in doing so they fail to acknowledge how complex it can be. In rabbinic tradition, every word of Scripture is considered to have seventy faces and 600,000 meanings![15] The simple fact of the matter is that the Bible is very long (about 1,200 pages), very old (written between two and three thousand years ago), and very different in its cultural context from our own. As a result, it's not always easy to make sense of its meaning and apply its message to the complexities of life in the twenty-first century.

There are two particular skills that every single Christian needs to develop, therefore, in order to hear God in and through holy Scripture. First, we must learn to read the Bible *with our heads*, in order to understand what is actually, objectively, being said. And second, we must learn to read it *with our hearts*, in order to experience God's voice through its pages. By carefully studying the Bible, we come to understand what its writers were originally saying. And by prayerfully exploring it, we learn to discern what the Holy Spirit is saying to us now. It's important to do both. If I understand what the Bible means but never hear what it says to me personally, I have information without revelation. But conversely, if I disregard its original context and ignore the bits I don't like or don't understand, I will be in grave danger of abusing God's Word by confusing it with my own feelings, preferences, and prejudices.

Making Sense of the Bible

The greatest gift of God is often either rejected outright or treated as if it is of little worth. But if we really began to study the Bible, we would be impressed with the proper value of this gift. It seems ludicrous that we have to exhort people to study the Bible.
—William Wilberforce

There are two Greek terms you may find helpful when seeking to make sense of the Bible (but don't worry, it's not essential you remember these). The first is *exegesis* (from the Greek *exegeisthai*, meaning to "lead" or "guide out"). Exegesis is the art of explaining, interpreting, and applying Scripture. It's what a preacher does when he or she unpacks the meaning of a particular Bible passage. Exegesis asks what the author of each book was intending when they first wrote it, and indeed what God was intending when he first inspired it. Exegesis also recognizes that different parts of the Bible need to be understood in different ways according to their literary genre. For example, the Song of Songs is a terrific erotic poem and a profound metaphor about the relationship between God and humanity, but we should not expect it to be a helpful teaching manual on how to run a church. That is not why it was written.

Similarly, the book of Genesis teaches profound and timeless theology, but it was certainly not written by someone (or a group of people) with a modern scientific mindset. This means that we read Genesis wrongly, and may even miss its message altogether, if we expect it to be the equivalent of a science textbook. Certainly, none of the early church fathers interpreted the six days of creation in such a literalistic way.[16]

Understanding the context of different parts of the Bible can help us to make sense of many (not all) of the bits of the Bible we tend to find difficult today. For example, the apostle Paul is often dismissed as sexist by people who don't understand the cultural context in which he was writing. As members of Western liberal societies, we wince when we read his words, for example, about women wearing head coverings in worship. But in the Middle East it's completely different. I remember reading 1 Corinthians 11 in the United Arab Emirates, surrounded by women wearing either the hijab, which covers hair and neck but leaves the face fully visible, the niqab, which covers everything except eyes, or the burqa, which fully covers the entire face. In this context I was surprised to find that Paul's counsel to the women of Corinth seemed both sensitive and even quite progressive, certainly not repressive. He seems to have been urging members of the fledgling church in Corinth to avoid unnecessary cultural offense, not because the churches were horribly oppressive patriarchal environments but rather because these newly converted women were feeling so liberated by the gospel that they had abandoned even the most basic cultural norms of decorum. Far from being an example of chauvinism, these instructions may well underline the extraordinary emancipation of women in Christ.[17]

Another passage frequently cited as evidence of Paul's patriarchy is his "Instructions to Christian Households" in Ephesians 5 and 6 ("Wives, submit yourselves to your own husbands," etc.). What the critics tend to misunderstand, however, is the first-century Greco-Roman family unit in which husbands and wives were not expected to have any form of friendship, and in which masters had unlimited power to use and abuse their slaves, and where children were not viewed with the sentimentality we attach to them today. Addressed to such an austere domestic hierarchy, Paul's instructions are not oppressive but radical. For instance, when he asks each husband to love his wife "just as Christ loved the church" (Eph. 5:25) and "as their own bodies" (v. 28) and "as he loves himself" (v. 33), Paul is advocating a level of tenderness and self-sacrifice unknown in the surrounding culture at that time and, frankly, still rare today. Once again, he is not being repressive but liberating.[18]

Context changes everything. You probably know the story about the man who decided to let his Bible fall open randomly and then to take the first words he read as God's specific guidance. Closing his eyes, he allowed his finger to fall on a page: "[Judas] went away and hanged himself" (Matt. 27:5). Fortunately, this wasn't the direction the man was seeking, and so, needing clarification, he tried again. This time his finger fell on Luke 10:37: "Go and do likewise."

The problem with this approach is, first, God is not a fortune cookie and, second, God's Word in the Bible is the Bible itself—not just isolated words picked at random from within its text. The wider story of Judas hanging himself is one of guilt, shame, betrayal, and utter tragedy. It might well have spoken to that man's heart had he taken time to reflect on this context. Similarly, the instruction, "Go and do likewise," comes at the end of the parable of the good Samaritan about loving others sacrificially. This too might have addressed that man's situation had he come to the text carefully and prayerfully.

But, of course, God has every right to break the rules of sound exegesis and hermeneutics, and one of the greatest Christian leaders of all time was converted through this questionable potluck approach to Scripture (see the "Living Word" section at the end of this chapter). Clearly, however, it would be neither healthy nor sensible to make this technique our normal means of divine guidance!

Some people view exegesis with suspicion, worrying that it stops us taking the Bible at face value (which it does) and that it therefore undermines the authority of Scripture (which it does not) and detracts from our ability to engage with the Bible devotionally (which it can actually enhance). In fact, reading the Bible with our heads, so that we understand it intellectually, only strengthens our ability to receive the Bible as God's Word with our hearts. Let me give you an example.

A Tale of Two Rembrandts

Rembrandt painted the biblical story of Simeon blessing the baby Jesus in the temple courts twice: once when he was twenty-five years old, at the start of his career, and again at the age of sixty-three, in the year of his death. The first is entitled *Simeon's Song of Praise* and hangs in the Mauritshuis Museum in the Dutch city of The Hague. This painting is magnificent, brilliant, and full of civic pomp. It depicts Simeon as a grand, priestlike figure in the temple courts and Jesus as a baby clearly born to be king. There is a strong theatricality about the way the temple architecture swoops up like a backdrop in a stage set, while its key characters gather center stage, lavishly costumed and dramatically spotlighted. This is the work of an artist brimming with ambition, determined to prove his unbounded abilities to the world.

Rembrandt's second depiction of this same scene, painted thirty-eight years later, is entirely different. Entitled simply *Simeon in the Temple*, it hangs today in Stockholm's National Museum. The pomp of his earlier work has been reduced to an intimate study of an old man's face. Gone is the grandeur, the costumery, and the admiring crowd. The spotlight has been replaced with the warm glow of candles. The decisive lines of a steady hand belonging to an artist in his prime are now shaky, mottled, and soft. The baby looks sweet, vulnerable, and real. Simeon himself seems frail, tender, and tired. It might perhaps be a self-portrait. Here we see an old man, done with the theatrics of kingly courts, gazing past the face of the baby, his mouth ajar as if sighing or perhaps preparing to pray his *Nunc dimittis*. It's a scene haunted by life's transience and transcendence entwined.

Rembrandt,
Simeon's Song of Praise, 1631
Fine Art Images / Heritage Images /
Alamy Stock Photo

Rembrandt,
Simeon in the Temple, 1669
The Picture Art Collection /
Alamy Stock Photo

Clearly, both of these paintings are great works of art, but it's not immediately clear that they are painted by the same artist, let alone that they depict the same scene. Our ability to feel the power and receive the messages of paintings like these is only enhanced by an understanding of their relative historical and biographical contexts. In a similar way, if we approach the Bible without reference to its context, we may well fail to grasp the original journey of its authors, the way it all holds together, and the extraordinary power of its message speaking directly to our hearts today.

You don't have to become an expert in theology or learn the Bible's three original languages to benefit from a little personal research. I would encourage you, as someone serious about hearing God, to invest in a study Bible, a few commentaries,[19] and an introduction to hermeneutics, such as the classic *How to Read the Bible for All Its Worth* by Gordon Fee and Douglas Stewart.[20]

The other term you may find useful in seeking to make sense of the Bible is *hermeneutics* (from the Greek word *hermēneuō*, meaning to "translate or interpret"). Hermeneutics is the particular key you use to unlock the meaning of the text. I sometimes think of it as the pair of glasses you put on to read the Bible. There are a number of different hermeneutical keys you can use to unlock the meaning and power of Scripture in this kind of way. These include:

- A *covenantal hermeneutic*, which takes the various covenants established between God and his people and uses them as a map for navigating the rest of the Bible.
- A *dispensationalist hermeneutic*, which divides the Bible into different eras (or "dispensations") in the belief that God deals differently with humanity at different times in history.
- A *feminist hermeneutic*, which pays particular attention to its moments and messages of emancipation or oppression toward women.

- A *liberation hermeneutic*, which interprets the Bible primarily as a message of justice and freedom for captives. In this paradigm, the story of the exodus from slavery, reenacted by Jesus, becomes the lens through which everything else is viewed.

A Christological Hermeneutic

On the road to Emmaus, Jesus introduces another, brand-new hermeneutical model that sets the hearts of his listeners on fire. We are told that he "explained to them what was said in all the Scriptures *concerning himself*" (Luke 24:27, italics mine). Earlier, in John 5:39, he said of the Bible, "These are the very Scriptures that testify about me." Jesus reframed the Old Testament (his Bible) entirely in the light of his own life, death, and resurrection. It was a breathtakingly audacious thing to do—either an act of such barefaced narcissism that it would probably be diagnosed today as a form of psychiatric delusion, or a moment of epiphany with eternal consequences. Clearly, for the couple who heard him and for his billions of followers ever since, it is the latter: a moment of truth. I'm reminded of C. S. Lewis' famous trilemma: a man making any such claim must either be a liar, a lunatic, or indeed the Lord.

But Jesus isn't just teaching here about himself from the Bible; he's also teaching about the Bible itself, modeling the way in which we are now to read it in the light of his existence and through the lens, therefore, of the Gospels. This approach, known as the *christological hermeneutic*, is one of the most radical and exciting keys to biblical understanding I've ever found. *Radical* because it gets to the root of the Christian faith. If we truly believe that the life, death, and resurrection of Jesus changes everything, that must surely and especially include the way we read the Bible. And it's *exciting* too because a christological hermeneutic enables us to catch glimpses and hear whispers of our Lord on every page of the Bible.

The christological hermeneutic means that we read the Old Testament in the light of the New Testament, and the later New

Testament epistles in the light of the Gospels.[21] So, for example, the apparent brutality of God's instruction to Abraham to sacrifice his only son Isaac is reframed completely by the moment, centuries later, when God himself sacrifices his only begotten Son on the cross. Elsewhere, the difficult Old Testament passages in which God apparently commands or condones genocide clearly have to be reevaluated in light of Jesus revealing once and for all that the heart of the Father is neither nationalistic nor aggressive, but rather overflowing with love toward all people and nations.[22]

The christological hermeneutic can also be deeply challenging. For instance, it is relatively easy to derive a justification for violence and war from parts of the Old Testament, but much harder to do so when these passages are seen through the lens of the life and teaching of Jesus Christ. He commands us to love our enemies, refuses to take up arms, and rebukes and then even reverses Peter's violence against one of the men who came to arrest him.

A christological reading of the Bible may well unsettle hierarchical models of church governance based on the Old Testament temple and its Levitical priesthood. It will dismantle the arguments used by some people to justify nationalism and racism based purely on the Old Testament view of Israel.[23] It will also challenge attitudes that subjugate women in ways that he himself clearly and consistently redressed.

Perhaps I'm rattling a few too many cages here. But see for yourself! On the Emmaus road, Jesus reinterprets the Bible in the light of himself, and the writers of the New Testament follow his lead. Perhaps it would be strange if such a radical review of the text did not challenge our presumptions profoundly.

The ultimate challenge of a Jesus-centered hermeneutic is that it makes love the lens through which we must henceforth read, interpret, and apply all Scripture. "The whole Bible does nothing but tell of God's love," says Augustine of Hippo.[24] And Raniero Cantalamessa, preacher to the papal household, puts it beautifully like this:

If the written word of the Bible could be changed into a spoken word and become one single voice, this voice, more powerful than the roaring of the sea would cry out: "the Father loves you!" (John 16:27). Everything that God does and says in the Bible is love, even God's anger is nothing but love. God "is" love![25]

No wonder the hearts of the couple on the road to Emmaus burned within them! Jesus makes the Bible God's love letter to our souls.

Having underlined the importance of understanding the Bible with our heads using hermeneutics, it's now time to think about hearing God's word through its pages more personally in our hearts.

Living Word: Augustine of Hippo (354–430)— Hearing God in the Bible

Augustine of Hippo was one of the greatest theologians and Bible teachers of all time, but the defining moment in his life came when God spoke to him personally and powerfully through a very simple song sung by a child exhorting him to pick up the Bible and read.

> Suddenly a voice reaches my ears from a nearby house. It
> is the voice of a boy or a girl (I don't know which) and
> in a kind of singsong the words are constantly repeated:
> "Take it and read it. Take it and read it."[26]

Augustine was born in the ancient North African city of Thagaste, in modern-day Algeria. There he lived until the age of seventeen when he traveled to Carthage to study rhetoric. In that great metropolis he immersed himself enthusiastically in "a hissing cauldron of lust."[27] As T. S. Eliot put it in his poem *The Waste Land,*

> To Carthage then I came

> Burning burning burning burning[28]

Augustine completed his studies and fathered a son before moving to Milan, where he worked as a professor and met Ambrose, the renowned bishop of that city. Having experimented with various philosophies and cults in a perpetual quest for truth, Augustine found himself deeply attracted to the gospel as preached by Ambrose. Confronted by the call of Christ, he famously prayed, "Give me chastity and self-control, but not yet."[29]

Augustine's inner battle finally became unbearable on a summer's day in 386. He was sitting in a garden in Milan in great distress, literally banging his head and tearing at his hair, when suddenly, "a huge storm rose up within me bringing with it a huge downpour of tears."[30] And it was at that precise moment a child's singsong voice came drifting across the garden. "Take it and read it, Take it and read it." Taking this as a word from God, Augustine opened his Bible and read the very first words he saw: "Not in carousing and drunkenness, not in sexual immorality and debauchery, not in dissension and jealousy. Rather, clothe yourselves with the Lord Jesus Christ, and do not think about how to gratify the desires of the flesh" (Rom. 13:13–14).[31]

Through these two sentences, God spoke so powerfully into the condition of Augustine's heart that he immediately, finally, repented of his sins. "It was as though," he recalled later, "my heart was filled with a light of confidence and all the shadows of my doubt were swept away."[32]

Augustine (a natural leader) immediately persuaded several friends to retreat with him for six months to a villa at the foot of the Italian Alps so that they could study the Bible together in depth without distraction. And then, on Easter Sunday, 387, at the age of thirty-two, Augustine was baptized.

Turning his back on Milan's many temptations, Augustine returned to his hometown to establish a community centered on prayer and scriptural study. He heard one day about a man who was open to the gospel some sixty miles north in the city of Hippo, and diligently traveled there hoping to lead him to Christ. But by pursuing that one lost sheep, Augustine became the shepherd to countless more. Members of the church in Hippo were so impressed by Augustine's zeal that they dragged him before the bishop and demanded that he be ordained on the spot. In many ways, the rest is history.

Augustine's training in rhetoric, his great learning, and his newfound passion for the gospel combined to make him an indomitable evangelist: "Preach wherever you can," he said, "to whom you can, and as you can."[33] Having been converted through God's written Word, and having studied it with such hunger as a new believer, he now began to unpack its treasures in countless sermons that would shape Christian thought—and indeed Western civilization—to this day. He also used God's truth to defend the faith from various heresies. But, ultimately, it was not his intellect but his heart that preached the loudest message of all. One of his most famous prayers captures this passion exquisitely:

> Late have I loved Thee, O Beauty so ancient and
> so new; late have I loved Thee!
> For behold Thou were within me, and I outside;
> and I sought Thee outside and in my unloveliness
> fell upon those lovely things that Thou hast made.
> Thou were with me and I was not with Thee.
> I was kept from Thee by those things, yet had they
> not been in Thee,
> they would not have been at all.
> Thou didst call and cry to my and break open my
> deafness:
> and Thou didst send forth Thy beams and shine upon me
> and chase away my blindness:
> Thou didst breathe fragrance upon me,
> and I drew in my breath and do not pant for Thee:
> I tasted Thee, and now hunger and thirst for Thee:
> Thou didst touch me, and I have burned for Thy peace.[34]

Listening Exercise:
Hearing God's Word in the Bible

*By the reading of Scripture I am so renewed that all
nature seems renewed around me and with me. . . .
The whole world is charged with the glory of God
and I feel fire and music under my feet.*
—Thomas Merton

In this chapter we've seen that the Bible is the language of God's heart. Nothing he says in any other way or in any other context will ever override, undermine, or contradict what he has said in the Scriptures. When God's Word is allowed to inform our thinking and feed our souls frequently enough, our lives are totally transformed.

A survey of forty thousand people aged between eight and eighty discovered that reading the Bible has a profound effect on both our mental health and our spiritual growth, but only if it is done at least four times a week. Once or twice a week provides a negligible benefit, and three times results in only a slight improvement. But among those who study the Bible at least four times a week, there is a dramatic inflection point, a sharp uplift in their mental and spiritual well-being. In fact, these regular Bible readers are 30 percent less likely to feel lonely, 32 percent less prone to anger issues, 60 percent less likely to report feelings of spiritual stagnation, and 228 percent more likely to be active in sharing their faith.[35]

Reading the Gospels

> The good news about Jesus the
> Messiah, the Son of God.
> —Mark 1:1

If we want to learn to discern the voice of Jesus so that his words become deeply familiar to our souls, we must get to know what he is actually like. And, of course, we can do this most effectively by absorbing the four multifaceted accounts of his life and teaching presented so beautifully in the Gospels. It's true that "all Scripture is God-breathed and is useful for teaching, rebuking, correcting and training in righteousness" (2 Tim. 3:16), but it is the Gospels that provide the center of gravity, the focal point for the whole of the rest of the Bible, and they should certainly preoccupy us the most. If you're wondering where to start with personal Bible study, I would always recommend one of the Gospels.

If we are to bridge the gap between what we say we believe about the Bible and what we actually practice in terms of biblical engagement, we need to think about psychology as well as theology. Here are a few simple, practical suggestions of how three different psychological preferences might approach Scripture meaningfully and enjoyably.

Auditory processors: Instead of just reading the words on the page, you may find it helpful to *listen* to the Bible, either by reading it aloud to yourself or with one of the excellent audio versions available online. For me this has been a wonderful discovery in recent years. I love listening to the Bible, sometimes allowing the words simply to wash over me. Remember that this is how the Bible was originally experienced by most people! As recently as the seventeenth century, Bishop Francis de Sales clearly assumed this when he urged his congregation to "Be devout to the word of God: whether you listen to it in familiar conversations with your friends, or at sermons, hear it always with attention and reverence."[36]

Visual processors: You may well find it helpful to deface your Bible! Write in its margins. Highlight the text in different colors. Make the pages a feast for the eye. Similarly, you could try doodling a meditation by writing out a verse, perhaps in your journal, and then drawing images, underlining, going on bunny trails. You might also take a trip to an art gallery to find a depiction of a scene from the Bible. Sit quietly in front of it, journal in hand, ready to record your reflections.

Of course, there are also great pictorial depictions of Scripture in films, from Mel Gibson's *The Passion of the Christ* to DreamWorks' *The Prince of Egypt*, and Dallas Jenkins' *The Chosen* series.

Active processors: You may well engage powerfully with the Bible by putting its words into practice. This is, of course, a necessary approach to Scripture for everyone, and there are many ways of enacting God's Word. Most obviously, you might obey one of its clear commands in a practical way. For example, having read the words of Jesus in Luke 3:11—"Anyone who has two shirts should share with the one who has none, and anyone who has food should do the same"—resist the temptation to spiritualize it, or merely to think, "I really shouldn't have so many clothes." Instead, you might get up, go to your pantry, and fill a box for the food bank. Then go to your closet and fill a bag for the charity shop (including at least one favorite item!). You will experience great joy—the smile of Jesus—as you do this, and it will be the best Bible study you could possibly do on this verse!

You will find more practical ideas on how to hear God in Scripture at the end of the next chapter too.

Questions for Personal Reflection and Group Discussion Having Read a Particular Scripture

- What is the cultural context and original intention of the writer? (A study Bible will help here.)
- What does it mean to read and interpret this passage in the light of Jesus?
- What question do these verses make me want to ask the Lord?
- How are these verses relevant to my life today?
- What is God saying to me through these verses?

For Further Reflection

Nicky Gumbel, *The Bible in One Year* (London: Hodder & Stoughton, 2019), a commentary on the entire Bible from Nicky and Pippa Gumbel, pioneers of the Alpha course, available both as a book and as an app with audio.

A study Bible or a good set of commentaries, such as The Bible Speaks Today series from IVP.

Kenneth E. Bailey, *Jesus Through Middle Eastern Eyes: Cultural Studies in the Gospels* (London: SPCK, 2008).

In this chapter we turn from *reading* the Bible to *praying* the Bible, using an ancient approach to spiritual listening known as *lectio divina*. By harnessing the power of imagination and meditation, *lectio divina* can leave "our hearts burning within us" as fresh revelation begins to flicker from familiar texts. The four traditional steps of *lectio divina* are simplified here into the acronym P.R.A.Y.: Pause, Read (*lectio*), Reflect (*meditatio*), Ask (*oratio*), and Yield (*contemplatio*).

3

Hearing God's Word in Prayer: *Lectio Divina*

Were not our hearts burning within us while he . . .
opened the Scriptures to us?

—Luke 24:32

Scripture is, in some sense, the music of God, which we hear;
in another sense, it is the instrument of God, which we play.

—Origen of Alexandria (185–254)

I was already deeply regretting inviting my friend Rob to church. The fact that he'd made it out of bed before lunchtime on a Sunday was, frankly, a big deal. Rob suffered from a dependency on various drugs, but mostly skunk, a potent form of herbal cannabis that made him anxious and triggered enormous mood swings. I'd been praying all week that the Lord would speak powerfully into his broken life. As a result, I saw the whole service through his eyes, and it wasn't pretty. The person leading proceedings was trying to be funny, the venue was chilly, and the worship leader was asking men and women to sing different parts, which Rob found hilarious, joining in heartily with the women in his highest, warbliest, most Mrs. Doubtfire voice. I began to wonder if he was stoned.

But, actually, all of this was okay because the thing I was awaiting, the thing on which I'd been focusing my prayers, was the talk. Surely, if God was going to break in and say something to Rob, it would be during the talk. "Please, Lord," I prayed in my head as a man with his hair in a side part and a prominent Adam's apple approached the podium, "let this be good."

After a nervous sip of water (which made his Adam's apple bob up and down), the preacher announced his theme. My heart sank. I'd been hoping and praying he'd say something like, "Today we're going to focus on freedom from addiction." Or at least, "Today I'm going to explain the gospel and give you an opportunity to give your life to Jesus Christ." Something, anything that might make Rob mutter that classic line from almost every testimony I ever heard: "Wow, I felt like he was speaking just to me."

But instead, the preacher announced that he had a message regarding Cain and Abel, the sons of Adam and Eve, from Genesis 4. Inwardly I groaned. "How on earth," I wondered, "is this going to relate to the long-haired, vegetarian, McDonald's employee sitting next to me? A man who just swapped his van for some weed and does not believe in Jesus, let alone the historical existence of Adam and Eve?"

The preacher set the scene, describing how Cain, the farmer, offered the Lord some of his vegetables, while Abel, the cow herder, popped a couple of steaks on the altar. God preferred Abel's meat, which threw Cain into a fit of such jealous rage that he killed his younger brother. Hearing this familiar story through the ears of a non-Christian made it sound awfully peculiar. I mean, why do we get out of bed on a Sunday morning to think about this stuff? My toes were sort of curled in my shoes, my buttocks clenched like cannonballs. "Remember to breathe," I told myself. The preacher was explaining how God banished Cain to "the land of Nod" (honestly, look it up), where he built a city and fathered many children (which obviously begs the question, "With whom?").

It had been quite a morning. In the space of an hour, we'd had fratricide, the ire of a meat-loving God, and rumors of incest in the land of Nod. All before Sunday lunch. I resigned myself to an awkward conversation with Rob later and zero chance that he would ever attend church again.

"So, um, what did you think?" I asked nervously at the end of the service.

"It was incredible, man!"

"It was?" I replied, trying to conceal my surprise. "Which particular part?"

"The speech," he said.

"That's incredible," I replied.

"Incredible," he said again, slowly shaking his head like a man trying to process its cosmic significance. "Pete, it was like the dude with the big Adam's apple was speaking *just to me*."

"It *was*?" I said again, this time completely failing to hide my amazement.

"Weren't you listening, Pete?"

"Um, yes, trust me, I was listening."

"So you *know*! It was just for me."

"Absolutely," I said. "I mean it was all amazing, but, just out of interest, which bit in particular was it that, um, hit you so powerfully?"

"Dude, he just kept saying it: 'caned' and 'able.' Over and over again. I guess you're either caned or able, right? And, well, look, Cane's the bad guy. Able's the good un. So, yeah, I get caned. I get caned a whole *lot*. I guess that makes me the bad guy here. I'm the great hairy dude wandering around in the land of Nod, in a daze having sex. So, yeah, I need to stop getting caned, man. I need to be able instead. Honestly," he kept shaking his head in amazement, "it all pans out, just like the guy with the Adam's apple said."

"Wow," I replied. "I mean really, wow. That is really, truly *remarkable*." And it really, truly was.

Rob might not have been listening carefully with his head that morning, but he was certainly listening with a wide-open and beautiful heart. As a result, I suspect he heard from God more powerfully than anyone else in the room. And this was to prove life-changing. Gradually, Rob stopped getting caned and got more able. Eventually he would even become a follower of Jesus.

Rob's story reminds me that how we listen is sometimes (always?) more important than what is said. Maybe that's why Jesus was forever asking people if they had ears to hear what he was saying. And I suspect it's also why the very first word of the great Benedictine Rule, which has guided monastic communities for 1,500 years, is this one little word: *listen*. Fifteen centuries of successful community built on the power of mere listening.

In the previous chapter, I underlined the importance of properly understanding the Bible, but we all know that head knowledge does not necessarily transfer to the heart. This was true for the scribes and Pharisees in Jesus' day, whose encyclopedic knowledge of God's word in the Scriptures blinded them to his ultimate word in Jesus standing right there under their noses. "We all possess knowledge," observed the apostle Paul, who was himself a brilliant intellect and a former Pharisee. "But knowledge puffs up while love builds up. Those who think they know something do not yet know as they ought to know. But whoever loves God is known by God" (1 Cor. 8:1–3). The heart is more important than the mind.

I emerged from undergraduate studies in theology and sociology with a head full of knowledge about the Bible—and a diminished capacity to hear God speak through its pages. My times of Bible study were just that—times of dry, dutiful study. In learning about God's Word in general, I seemed to have lost my ability to hear his word to me personally. The medieval Franciscan Bonaventure said that we all have three sets of eyes: the eyes of the *body*, through which we see physically; the eyes of the *mind*, through which we reason; and the eyes of the *heart*, through which we gain spiritual insight. I knew that I needed to rediscover the art of reading the Bible with the eyes of my heart, not just with the eyes of reason, so that God could speak to me in whatever way he saw fit, even if it was going to be through the world's worst exegesis of Cain and Abel!

Pause & Pray

Placing my hand over my heart, I repeat Psalm 119:18 three times.
"Open my eyes that I may see wonderful things in your law."

Pictures and Windows

Jews have two approaches to the Torah. The first is analytical and seeks to discover the one objective, true meaning of the text. This is reading with our heads. But the second is more subjective in that it seeks the deeper and more personal spiritual meaning. This is reading with our hearts.[1] The writer Evelyn Underhill says that we can approach the Bible as either a *picture* or a *window*.[2] Sometimes God's Word is there simply to be studied with admiration and fascination, like a great work of art. But if we only ever do this, we are committing idolatry—worshiping the Bible itself. God has given us the Bible to point us beyond the Bible. That's why it's essential (I can't say this strongly enough) that we learn how to approach the Bible as a window frame as well as a picture frame, not just looking *at* it but also *through* it to the world, and the Word, beyond.

So how do we actually, practically, do this? How do we move from studying Scripture objectively and hearing its message generally to receiving God's Word personally in our own lives? Well, the most powerful tool I have ever discovered, one that has revolutionized my own personal relationship with the Bible and has become the model for the devotional I help to write, record, and release each day, is the ancient tradition of *lectio divina*—the slow, prayerful reading of Scripture.

Lectio Divina

> *This practice will bring to the Church—I am convinced*
> *of it—a new spiritual springtime . . .* lectio divina
> *should therefore be increasingly encouraged.*
> —Pope Benedict XVI

I was setting the scene at the start of a retreat for our church leadership team at which we desperately needed to hear from the Lord. I suggested we start our time together by prayerfully exploring a bit of the Bible, listening for anything the Holy Spirit might want to say to us using the *lectio divina*. Noticing a few blank faces, I explained that this literally just means "holy" or "sacred reading" and that it's an ancient way of meditating on the Bible (and other inspired literature) by reading slowly and prayerfully, listening more with our hearts than with our heads. I explained that to do this we would simply go around the circle, taking turns to read a couple of verses each from a single chapter. Having done this, we would pause to share any word or phrase that had caught our attention. And then, instead of rushing on, we would linger and repeat the whole exercise again.

"Try to switch off the bit of your brain that wants to make sense of it all," I said. "Try to listen intuitively. Use your imagination." Those familiar with this model of prayer were nodding, knowing that, although it sounds simple, it can be a very powerful way indeed of listening to the Lord.

That morning, before heading out to the retreat, I'd been reading part of Revelation 15, which had struck me as a pretty good note on which to kick things off:

> Great and marvelous are your deeds,
>   Lord God Almighty.
> Just and true are your ways,
>   King of the nations.
> Who will not fear you, Lord? (Rev. 15:3–4)

And so I explained that I'd chosen these verses as a word of encouragement from God for us. It was, I added, a passage through which the Lord had been speaking to me personally that morning. I was overdoing it a bit, but everyone was beginning to look pretty interested, putting down their coffee cups and reaching for their Bibles.

I gave them the reference but unfortunately got the chapter number wrong. Instead of saying Revelation 15, I said Revelation 16. And so the first person cleared her throat and began to read in her most thoughtful voice, "The first angel went and poured out his bowl on the land, and ugly, festering sores broke out on the people who had the mark of the beast and worshiped its image" (Rev. 16:2).

Realizing my mistake, I clearly should have stopped and started again in the correct chapter. But instead, I thought, "Oh well, it's got to get better." And so we proceeded through the second, third, and fourth plagues, each one worse than the last, as the members of the group valiantly tried to read their allocated verses with something other than total despair. Sammy was staring at me quizzically. Did I really think that the seven plagues of the apocalypse were making a beeline for our beautiful little community? But I was determined. Isn't *all* Scripture supposed to be "useful for teaching, rebuking, correcting and training in righteousness (2 Tim. 3:16)?

But then, just when I thought it couldn't get any worse, the next reader continued in her best, most earnest voice, "The fifth angel poured out his bowl on the throne of the beast, and its kingdom was plunged into darkness. People gnawed their tongues in agony . . ."

She paused, glanced up, and I smiled back, nodding as enthusiastically as I could.

"Um, okay. 'People gnawed their tongues in agony,'" she repeated, "'and cursed the God of heaven because of their pains and their sores, but they refused to repent of what they had done'" (Rev. 16:10–11).

At this point my friend Scot, one of the elders of the church, emitted a sort of snorting noise, and I distinctly noticed his wife, Misty, kicking him. Someone other than Sammy was now looking at me, clearly wondering why I thought this was God's word to our fledgling church plant. But we soldiered on, one reader after the next, expecting things to take some kind of turn for the better. Surely, I thought, it's got to finish on a happier note. And then, when it lifts, we can just focus on that and pretend the rest of it didn't happen. But it turns out that the final verse of Revelation 16 goes like this: "From the sky huge hailstones, each weighing about a hundred pounds, fell on people. And they cursed God on account of the plague of hail, because the plague was so terrible" (v. 21).

Yes, the chapter actually does end with giant hailstones, the cursing of God, and the word *terrible*.

Apocalyptic writing of this type was common for the people of the ancient world.[3] The symbols that seem so confusing to us were much easier to decipher for its original readers. They would have known, for example, that the beast from the sea described in chapter 17 was not a despotic twenty-first-century antichrist but rather the cruel emperor Domitian, who had recently instituted an idolatrous cult in Ephesus, requiring its citizens to worship members of his own family. The book of Revelation was written in part to reassure struggling first-century Christians that justice would ultimately be done and that their powerful enemy would eventually be vanquished. It was not written to terrify a tiny team of twenty-first-century church planters during a time of devotional prayer!

In spite of this excruciating experience of *lectio divina*, I continue to believe in the life-changing power of reading the Bible slowly, attentively, and imaginatively, whether alone or with others, seeking *conversation with* God (rather than *information about* God) from the text, approaching the Scriptures not just as a picture to be studied but as a wide-open window to the world.

Ancient Roots

The monastic practice of *lectio divina* was first formally established in the sixth century by Benedict of Nursia, the great synthesizer of monasticism, although its origins are much older, rooted in the Bible itself, as we shall see.[4] Benedict's Rule required members of his communities to spend up to three hours every day prayerfully reading sacred texts or listening to them being read. This was a startling commitment of both time and energy and utterly countercultural in a world where books were rare and so was the ability to read them (increasingly so because of the cataclysmic decline of the Roman Empire at that time). The fact that Benedictine monks spent as much as one in every six waking hours practicing the *lectio divina* reveals first a radical commitment to learning—no hint of anti-intellectualism here. Second, it reflects Benedict's confidence in the power of inspired literature to speak powerfully into the lives of its readers. And third, it demonstrates how highly he valued this practice in particular as a tool for transforming the minds, hearts, and lives of its practitioners. Benedict knew that if society were to be rebuilt, Christian communities would have to become centers of intellectual and spiritual formation and that *lectio divina* was essential to both.

The *lectio divina* was eventually systematized into a distinct four-step process by a Carthusian monk called Guigo II in the twelfth century using a Latin word to describe each stage:

1. *Lectio*—"read" the text.
2. *Meditatio*—"meditate" on the text.
3. *Oratio*—"pray" the text.
4. *Contemplatio*—"contemplate" the Lord.

Before I unpack what these steps mean, please note that it took six hundred years for *lectio divina* to be systematized in this way, so you shouldn't feel constrained to take Guigo's process too rigidly. Personally, I find his four steps helpful as a teacher but poor as a companion in prayer. For example, I will often start by praying (step #3: *oratio*) before I have finished meditating on the Scripture (step #2: *meditatio*). If a thought comes into my head that I want to express to the Lord, I do so, regardless of Guigo's process! As for step #4 (*contemplatio*), I don't always do it. This is either because I'm just too mentally distracted for contemplative prayer or because I find myself so caught up in talking with the Lord that we never move beyond words into the silence of a more contemplative interaction (more on this later). *Lectio divina* is meant to be a delightful relational exchange, never a rigid religious straitjacket.

In my previous book *How to Pray*, I recommended a very simple framework for prayer using the acronym P.R.A.Y. One of the lovely surprises we've had since that book came out, and particularly since launching the Lectio 365 devotional,[5] is how well this framework also works with the *lectio divina* (incorporating Guigo's four steps without all the Latin!). The framework is this:

P.R.A.Y.	Guigo II	Action
Pause	-	Quietly prepare your heart
Read & Reflect	*lectio* and *meditatio*	Slowly read, rejoice, reflect, and repeat
Ask	*oratio*	Turn your reflections into prayer
Yield	*contemplatio*	Enjoy the presence of God

In the rest of this chapter, I'm going to walk you through these four steps, unpacking some of the thinking behind each one.

Step #1: Pause

Jesus himself drew near.
—Luke 24:15 ESV

Draw near to God and He will draw near to you.
—James 4:8 NKJV

On the Emmaus road, Jesus first "drew near" (Luke 24:15 ESV), next he initiated conversation (v. 17), and only then, a little later, did he begin to unpack "what was said in all the Scriptures concerning himself" (v. 27). In other words, he took a little time before diving into the Bible, and so should we. Since the aim of *lectio divina* is meditation, conversation, and contemplation through Bible reading, it's a good idea to stop before you start. Pause for a moment to settle your heart before reading the text. Consciously slow down and draw near to God as he draws near to you.

More than 1,500 years ago, in the Babylonian Talmud, Rabbi Shmuel ben Nachmani said, "We do not see things as they are. We see things as we are."[6] He was right. If we hurry into the holy without preparing our hearts, we will see things not as they are but as we are. We will come to the Scriptures frenetically and functionally, projecting our own subconscious preconditions on the text, carrying with us whatever emotional and psychological baggage we happen to have accumulated that day.

Of course, it's impossible to silence our head noise entirely. No one can come to the Bible with complete objectivity. This is just one of the reasons why we all need the mitigating fellowship of other Christians—living and dead—in seeking to hear God's voice (see chapter 4). But although we can't remove our preconceptions entirely, it's certainly possible to reduce our distractions, deletions, and distortions significantly through the simple act of stilling ourselves before opening God's Word.

As it says in Psalm 46:10, "Be still, and know that I am God." This is a psalm that begins with "trouble" (v. 1), continues with "mountains fall[ing] into the heart of the sea" (v. 2), and climaxes with "nations . . . in uproar" (v. 6). It's an invitation to stillness *in spite* of our circumstances, not *because* of them. "Meet me," says the Lord, "in the eye of the storm." Stillness, especially in a culture as frenzied as ours, amounts to nothing less than a counterintuitive act of defiant trust in the sovereignty of God. The deceptively simple act of pausing, even just for a few minutes each day, can be a form of peace-making with our own battle-weary souls. Those rare people who learn to do this—who carry a quality of stillness with them through life—are attractive and authoritative because they are modeling something, whether they know it or not, of God's own nonanxious presence in the world.

So how do we do this? How do we actually, practically, still our souls? It's a good idea to begin by sitting quietly (or walking slowly) and simply taking a few deep breaths. As you do this, pay attention to any tension you are carrying in your body, and consciously relax in those areas. You may also find it helpful to repeat a short prayer phrase, such as the Franciscan, "My God and my all," or the Eastern Orthodox Jesus Prayer, "Lord Jesus Christ, Son of God, have mercy on me." I often whisper, "Thank you, Jesus," in time with my breathing.

Before opening the Bible, some people also pray in tongues to prime their spirits to be edified by the Holy Spirit (1 Cor. 14:4). Others find it helpful to memorize a set prayer of approach, such as Psalm 119:18 (KJV): "Open thou mine eyes, that I may behold wondrous things out of thy law." The prayer with which we begin Lectio 365 each day is this:

As I enter prayer now, I pause to be still; to breathe slowly;
to recenter my scattered senses upon the presence of God.

In pausing to recenter ourselves on the presence of God, we are making space for the Holy Spirit to fill our lives again. He is the one, according to Jesus, who will "teach you all things" and "remind you of everything I have said to you" (John 14:26). He "will testify about me" (John 15:26), will "guide you into all the truth," and will even "tell you what is yet to come" (John 16:13). There's little point in *lectio divina* without the Holy Spirit's help.

Slowing down, breathing deeply, relaxing physically, and inviting the Holy Spirit to come. Don't be deceived by the simplicity of such things. These are God-given practices, highly effective and historically proven to help move our minds from what Michael Polanyi called "subsidiary awareness" to "focal awareness": "If a pianist shifts his attention from the piece he is playing (focal awareness) to the observation of what he's doing with his fingers while playing (subsidiary awareness), he gets confused and may have to stop."[7] In other words, subsidiary and focal awareness are mutually exclusive. If I come to the Bible carrying distractions, it's futile to expect the act of reading the Bible in and of itself to magically make my head noise go away. Instead, by stopping to be still in the ways described above, *prior* to opening my Bible, I can prime my heart to hear from God in a focused way with far fewer distractions.

RESPECTING THE TEXT

Pausing before reading the Bible is not just a way of preparing myself to receive from God; it's also a simple act of common courtesy toward the Bible. Reverence may not be a familiar posture for citizens of a secularized and cynical age more used to writing reviews than removing our shoes, but it is intrinsic to *lectio divina*, which is explicitly the art of prayerfully reading sacred texts.

Muslims approaching the Qur'an are expected to dress appropriately, to wash thoroughly (*wudhu*), and to say a prayer. They must never place their holy book on the floor or under another book. When a Muslim witnesses a Christian treating the Bible casually, they have good reason to conclude that we don't really respect or revere it as God's Word. Perhaps they are partly right.

But approaching the Bible with appropriate reverence doesn't need to be complicated. I'm certainly not advocating ritual washing or special clothing before opening its pages! The book of Hebrews leaves us in no doubt that "we can now—without hesitation—walk right up to God, into 'the Holy Place'" because "Jesus has cleared the way" (10:19 MSG).

Step #2: Read and Reflect (Lectio and Meditatio)

If you read [the Bible] quickly it will benefit you little. You
will be like a bee that merely skims the surface of a flower.
Plunge deeply within to remove its deepest nectar.
—Madame Guyon

If you have paused to prepare your heart, the moment has come to begin reading the Bible (*lectio*). If you're wondering where to start, I would recommend working systematically through one of the gospels—perhaps John—and limiting yourself to fairly short passages of no more than twenty verses each time. This will constrain you to go slow and deep, remembering that you will be cycling back to read the passage at least one more time. The aim here is quality rather than quantity, learning to "let the word of Christ dwell in you richly" (Col. 3:16 ESV). Or, as it says in one translation, letting the word of Christ "have its home within you [dwelling in your heart and mind—permeating every aspect of your being]" (AMP).

FIRST READING: *LECTIO*

The aim of your first reading is to gain an overview of the passage before returning a second time to go deeper. To do this, you may want to use some of the tools set out in the previous chapter to help you understand the basic context and meaning of the text. It's okay that you are reading more with your head than your heart at this stage, but resist the temptation to overthink or to start researching ideas that pique your interest. There's a time and a place for Bible study, but this is not it! If certain words or phrases capture your attention, make a mental note to look out for them on your next reading. View this first read-through as setting the table in preparation for a meal to come.

Sammy was washing the dishes after supper one night when she dropped her engagement ring into the soapy water. Letting out a yelp, she began fumbling around furiously in the bowl. Failing to locate the missing item, she had a look of total concentration came over her face. This time she began searching the bowl systematically, carefully running her fingers under each submerged plate, slowly feeling around every item, until at last, triumphantly, she lifted the lost item out of the water, covered in bubbles.

Imagine how peculiar it would have been if Sammy had not reacted in this way. If she had just casually dibbled one hand in the water, withdrawn it without the ring, and shrugged, saying, "Oh well." Or, stranger still, if she had immediately emptied the bowl on the off chance of spotting her jewelry before it disappeared down the drain. Only two conclusions would be possible: either she didn't really believe that the ring was in the water in the first place, or the ring was of no real worth to her.

Jesus tells three parables about similar situations: a woman sweeping her house until she finds her lost coin (Luke 15), a man stumbling upon treasure buried in a field (Matt. 13:44), and a merchant looking for a pearl (Matt. 13:45). In these stories he teaches us to seek with all our hearts for the riches of the kingdom, just as Sammy searched for her ring. Give up anything, he says, to gain that one thing of ultimate worth.

I'm ashamed to admit how often I've dipped into Scripture casually, unwilling to search, to linger, to hunt for the pearl of great price hidden within its text. And this is, I suspect, because (should I admit it to you?) I don't always expect to find anything precious in there.

What would happen, I wonder, if I were to approach the Scriptures the way Sammy immersed her hands in that bowl: fully focused and determined not to leave until she found what was hers? What buried treasure might be awaiting my discovery if I would always open my Bible convinced that something infinitely precious is in there just for me and that, if I search long enough and carefully enough, I will surely find it eventually? "When you meditate," said Archbishop François Fénelon, "imagine that Jesus Christ in person is about to talk to you about the most important thing in the world. Give him your complete attention."[8]

I believe that this is precisely how Benedict of Nursia and the monks for whom he wrote his Rule felt whenever they opened a sacred text in order to practice *lectio divina*, because all books at that time (most especially the Bible) were intrinsically precious, considered inherently authoritative and worthy of respect.

It wasn't until the sixteenth century, almost a thousand years after Benedict, that Aldus Manutius began printing the first mass-produced, small-format, inexpensive books. Before that, prior to Gutenberg's invention of the printing press in 1450, it had taken months and even years to transcribe a single text onto parchment. The exquisitely illuminated Lindisfarne Gospels, transcribed by a monk called Eadfrith a hundred years or so after Benedict, and the equally sublime *Book of Kells* testify to the reverence with which transcription took place, especially with regard to the Bible. And making books wasn't just costly in terms of time. Ink and parchment were expensive items. It is estimated that a single book was worth thousands of dollars in today's currency. Monasteries therefore counted themselves blessed to own even a few books, and they certainly thought very carefully indeed before deciding to make one (which could take years) or to buy one (which could cost a small fortune) or to read one (which could hardly be done without reverence and awe).

I'm told that if you imagine the amount of information available to a Benedictine monk in the sixth century as a single unit, it took perhaps a thousand years for that knowledge base to double. After the invention of the printing press, it's estimated that the amount of information ordinary people could access began to double every hundred years, and then every fifty. By the end of the twentieth century, it was doubling every seven months, *and this was before the internet really took off.*[9] Today I can fit three thousand books on a single Kindle device, and there are thirty-three million titles available to me right now on Amazon, most for less than the price of an hour's work at minimum wage. The sight of a book today rarely makes our hearts beat faster with excitement and expectation, let alone reverence and awe. We speed-read pulp fiction. Some people pride themselves on reading dozens of titles a year. Others barely bother reading at all. Exhausted and numb, drowning in data, we have lost the art of reading wisely and well. We no longer know how to interact reverently, humbly, and slowly with a worthwhile text—even the Bible.

And so, having read the text once, we now return to read it again, determining—like Sammy searching for her engagement ring—to keep searching until we find the treasure hidden within its depths.

SECOND READING: *MEDITATIO*

> *You should meditate not only in your heart but also externally . . .*
> *reading and re-reading . . . with diligent attention and reflection,*
> *so that you may see what the Holy Spirit means by them.*
> —Martin Luther

Because you "set the table" in your first reading, it's finally time to feast! On this second reading you will take a little longer and go a little deeper, seeking to apply "diligent attention and reflection" to the text. "You should meditate," said Luther, "so that you may see what the Holy Spirit means."[10]

Some people get unnecessarily worried about any mention of meditation because they associate it exclusively with non-Christian religions and New Age techniques, but Martin Luther is talking here about biblical meditation rooted deeply in the Jewish and Christian traditions. As such, it's not about emptying your mind but rather filling it with God's Word, focusing your thoughts intensely on his truth. This is a fundamentally biblical approach to the Bible! In fact, the very first sentence of the very first psalm pronounces a blessing on "the one . . . whose delight is in the law of the LORD, and who *meditates* on his law day and night" (italics mine). And then there's

Psalm 19, which might almost have been composed as a description of *lectio divina*: "May these words of my mouth [*oratio*] and this meditation of my heart [*meditatio*] be pleasing in your sight, LORD, my Rock" (v. 14). Elsewhere, the psalmist simply cries, "Oh, how I love your law! I meditate on it all day long" (Ps. 119:97). When the Israelites were about to enter the promised land, the Lord's instruction to Joshua was to *"meditate* on [the Book of the Law] day and night" (Josh. 1:8, italics mine). Not just to study or teach it but actually, personally, to meditate deeply on its meaning.

The original Hebrew root word for "meditation" used in all these passages is *hagah* (הָגָה), which literally means "to moan, growl, muse, ponder or utter." God's command to Joshua was, as it were, to "mutter" the Scriptures, to "muse" on their meaning night and day, to ruminate like a cow chewing the cud, to "ponder" them deeply in his heart. This is what Mary the mother of Jesus did when she "treasured up all these things and *pondered them* in her heart" (Luke 2:19, italics mine). It's what Jesus himself inferred when he quoted Moses to Satan in the wilderness, saying, "Man shall not live on bread alone, but on every word that comes from the mouth of God" (Matt. 4:4). We are not just to *read* God's Word; we are also to *feed* on it, receiving it as our "daily bread" (Luke 11:3).

"Don't swallow it in a big lump," Bernard of Clairvaux said of the Bible in the twelfth century.[11] Chew over each word. Savor its flavor and sample its depths.

The psalmist uses another food analogy: "How sweet are your words to my taste, sweeter than honey to my mouth!" (Ps. 119:103). It's as if he's rolling God's Word around in his mouth like a piece of chocolate, slowly enjoying its texture on his tongue, delighting in its sweetness. This is meditation! Too often I've hit on Scripture like a kid on a sugar rush, seeking instant gratification. Instead of savoring its sweetness slowly, I've merely scanned the text for an easy epiphany, a catchy quote for social media, or, God forgive me, a ticked box on a daily list of chores.

THREE KEYS TO MEDITATION

There are three particular keys that help me to slow down and savor the sweetness of Scripture, to meditate on its meaning and hear God's voice through the text: *embracing interruption, exercising intuition*, and *engaging imagination*.

1. Meditation Means *Embracing Interruption*

It is deeply engrained within us, primarily by our educational systems, to process data in a regimented way. When it comes to reading books, we are trained to start methodically at the beginning and progress as quickly and efficiently as possible to the end. But meditation is cyclical, not linear. It's a labyrinth in a world of ladders, more concerned with discoveries made than distance traveled. That's one of the reasons why we return to read the passage several times, excavating a little deeper with each cycle.

One of the great proponents of this way of reading the Bible was Bernard of Clairvaux, the reformer of medieval monasticism and pioneer of the Cistercian Order. Bernard preached no fewer than forty-three sermons just on the Song of Songs.[12] It's a book that opens with quite a bang: "Let him kiss me with the kisses of his mouth" (Song of Songs 1:2). Lesser preachers might be tempted to make a quick point and move swiftly on, but not Bernard. He preached an entire sermon on this one opening verse. And then another. And another. In fact, he preached no fewer than eight sermons on these ten words! Clearly, he knew how to let a text interrupt him, as he circled and recircled its meaning, continually excavating greater depths of intimacy and insight.

When it comes to biblical meditation, interruptions can become invitations from the Holy Spirit. I'm not talking here about external interruptions such as a phone call when you're trying to pray. In fact, for *lectio*, switch off your phone and try to find a quiet space without distractions. What I'm talking about is the kind of interruption that arises within you as you read the text. Pay attention to the unexpected trains of thought triggered by the things you are reading. And when you realize that this has happened, instead of automatically shutting those thoughts down and returning dutifully to the text, you may want to pursue them a little further to see where they lead. Some bunny trails take you down dark holes, but others lead out into the light.

The book of Hebrews says that by welcoming strangers, "some people have shown hospitality to angels without knowing it" (Heb. 13:2). I'm pretty sure I have occasionally hosted the very messengers of God in my life simply by opening the door to the interruption of an unexpected thought while reading the Bible. Sometimes this is as simple as a sudden prompting to stop and pray for a particular person, which later turns out to have been prescient in a way I could never have known at the time. At other times it has been a tangential thought triggered by the text, which goes on to open an entire new vista in my life. As it did for the couple on the road to Emmaus, whose conversation about God was interrupted and redirected by a stranger, the living Word will sometimes interrupt the written Word.

2. Meditation Means *Exercising Intuition*

> *Deep calls to deep*
> *in the roar of your waterfalls.*
> —Psalm 42:7

Meditation is partly an instinctive process that bypasses our natural tendency toward deductive reasoning. Reading intuitively is easy for some people but not at all for others. One of the simplest ways I know of tuning into intuition when reading a text is to pay attention to the words or phrases that stand out to me, even if I don't initially know why. It's easy to do this. I rarely fail to find such a word or phrase when I look for one, and I'm pretty sure this will be your experience too.[13] Don't try to make sense of your reaction or analyze why it's speaking to you. Just acknowledge it and ask the Lord to show you why it's captured your attention. You're not looking for an exegetical explanation; the original significance or context of the phrase is of secondary importance. You're seeking to understand the personal, highly subjective meaning this phrase might be carrying just for you. As with my friend Rob with Cain and Abel, the Holy Spirit may even speak to you through the text in ways that exceed its original meaning.

Even as I write this, I can imagine all the "heresy alarms" sounding like air-raid sirens in a thousand well-meaning minds. But an insight that exceeds the bounds of sound biblical interpretation does not need to lead to heresy, provided it reflects the word, character, and example of Jesus. Rob's misunderstanding of Cain and Abel is a good example of how even bad biblical interpretation can sometimes lead to a profoundly Christian revelation resulting in transformation.

Maybe it's helpful if I give you an example of this process at work in my own life. During my prayer time this morning, I read (or rather listened to) Romans 12. There's a great sweep to this classic chapter that begins with its famous call to "offer your bodies as a living sacrifice" (v. 1). A quick glance at my study Bible reminded me that the big theme of this letter, addressed to the gentile church in Rome, is the importance of relying solely on God's grace for salvation. So far so good.

But when I got to verse 9, something unexpected happened: "Love must be sincere. Hate what is evil; cling to what is good." That simple phrase, "hate what is evil," is the one that jumped out at me. It's surprising because this chapter is loaded with great, inspiring quotes, and "hate what is evil" is certainly not the one I would naturally have picked for meditation today or any other day. I've never seen it turned into an Instagram post or a Christian T-shirt. But I've learned to pay attention to these kinds of interruptions and intuitions, so I paused to wonder why.

I think it was the strength of Paul's language that stopped me in my tracks. I hadn't expected to be told to exercise hatred today. And I didn't like being told to classify some behaviors as "evil" either. (Not just "misguided," "unhelpful," or even "wrong," but "evil"!) This kind of thing doesn't sit well with my kind of Christianity. We're into grace. Paul's theme in Romans is meant to be grace. But if he'd been preaching like this at our church, I'd have asked him to dial it down a bit. And, of course, the minute these thoughts crossed my mind, I realized quite uncomfortably that perhaps we were drifting away from a biblical view of sin. Maybe our grace was, in Dietrich Bonhoeffer's language, a bit "cheap."

Do I really *hate* what is evil, I asked myself, or do I merely mildly disapprove? In what particular ways am I tolerating, excusing, or even entertaining things that are, in fact, evil? Within seconds, the Holy Spirit was answering this question, shining an embarrassing light on a bad attitude in my life that I had been justifying to myself. Until now. And that is how I came to be apologizing to God this morning at 7:15 a.m. as I unloaded the dishwasher!

As I did this, my mind circled back to consider the strength of Paul's language, and I found myself muttering, half to God and half to myself, "Boy, that guy wrote in primary colors." He was so strong. So passionate. So fiery. So absolute. I sighed and put a mug on the countertop: "Lord, my beard is going gray, and my life is going beige. Wake me up. Shake me up. Make me passionate like Paul. Set my heart on fire once more."

As I prayed this, I felt a little surge of energy that I've come to associate with the Holy Spirit touching my life.

Reflecting now on all of this, I realize that I'd been challenged and convicted, I'd repented and received a fresh touch from the Holy Spirit, all in a few minutes while cleaning the kitchen! In fact, I'd been so engrossed in these four unlikely words, "hate what is evil," that I had completely tuned out the rest of the passage with its magnificent exhortation to "be joyful in hope, patient in affliction, faithful in prayer" (a verse I'd much rather have unpacked with you here!).

So how did this happen? How did I "hear" God speaking to me

this morning? First, by making a little space for the Bible at the start of my day (*lectio*). Second, by allowing a particular phrase to interrupt my thoughts and using my intuition to reflect on its meaning in my life (*meditatio*). And third, by turning these reflections into prayerful conversation with the Lord (*oratio*).

> The word of God is alive and active. Sharper than any double-edged sword, it penetrates even to dividing soul and spirit, joints and marrow; it judges the thoughts and attitudes of the heart. Nothing in all creation is hidden from God's sight. Everything is uncovered and laid bare before the eyes of him to whom we must give account. (Heb. 4:12–13)

3. Meditation Means *Engaging Imagination*

> *I long to see the imagination released from its prison and*
> *given to its proper place among the sons of the new creation.*
> *What I am trying to describe here is the sacred gift of seeing, the*
> *ability to peer beyond the veil and gaze with astonished wonder*
> *upon the beauties and mysteries of things holy and eternal.*
> —A. W. Tozer

Having explored the role of *interruption* and *intuition* in biblical meditation, we turn our attention now to the necessity of *imagination*. Whenever we take words and evoke worlds, we are at our most godlike. No other animal can visualize things it has never seen and visit places it has never been to. With our imaginations we invent, innovate, create, play, pioneer, solve problems, fall in love, and weave ten thousand bedtime stories. And it is with our imaginations too that we destroy.

The Bible talks continually about the power of the human heart and the battleground of our thinking. Unlike contemporary culture, it never suggests for a single second that human imaginings are merely nebulous, essentially harmless, entirely disconnected from physical reality. Jesus could not be clearer. He equates a sexually rapacious imagination, for instance, with adultery (Matt. 5:28) and a violent imagination with the act of murder (Matt. 5:21–2; 1 John 3:15). "Out of the heart come evil thoughts," he says elsewhere. "These are what defile a person" (Matt. 15:19–20).

We understand the power of our imaginations—and use them to the full, without hesitation—whenever it comes to reading fiction or watching a film. From rom-coms to action thrillers, we know perfectly well how to immerse ourselves in a plot, identify with its protagonists, and lose ourselves in the story. But a strange thing happens whenever we approach the greatest library of stories ever told. The moment we open the Bible, we seem to switch off our imaginations completely. Perhaps this is because we are overfamiliar with the material, which has merely made us lazy. (Although this should surely be good reason for doing the exact opposite and applying fresh imagination to the old tales.)

But, for most of us, I suspect the problem goes a little deeper than one too many flannelgraphs at Sunday school. When it comes to the inner world of our thought life, we often struggle with shame, and we are also understandably cautious of taking flights of fancy with holy Scripture. Where, we wonder, might our thinking lead us if left unchecked? How on earth are we to know the difference between God's thoughts and our thoughts, things imagined and things imaginary?

These are important questions because our imaginations are indeed both powerful and impure, but the answer is not to switch them off (even if this were possible), but rather to use them wisely and enthusiastically for God's glory. We don't need to be afraid of doing so, provided we apply the usual tools of discernment. Surely, if God can speak through a burning bush to Moses, and to the prophet Balaam through a donkey, and to King Belshazzar through graffiti at a party, he must be willing and able to speak to me through the quirkiness of my own imagination.

Imagination is one of the most powerful faculties God has given us, particularly when it comes to hearing his voice with our hearts as well as our heads. As Mark Twain put it, "You can't depend upon your eyes when your imagination is out of focus."[14] And the fact that our minds are such a battleground merely underlines the tactical importance they hold. Richard Foster, who has spent much of his life researching such things, concludes, "The devotional masters of nearly all persuasions counsel us that we can descend with the mind into the heart most easily through the imagination."[15] Conversely, conservative Bible teacher A. W. Tozer warned starkly of the dangers of ignoring our imaginations when it comes to the Bible, saying, "The weakness of the Pharisee in days of old was his lack of imagination, or what amounted to the same thing, his refusal to let it enter the field of religion. He saw the text with its carefully guarded theological definition and he saw nothing beyond."[16] Perhaps we might say that he saw the Scriptures as a picture frame containing God's Word but not as a window frame opening his imagination to something more.

A true understanding of the Scriptures requires both divine revelation and human imagination because its object lies far beyond the bounds of ordinary human experience. The Bible cannot possibly be both comprehensible to us and comprehensive to God. This is why we need the Spirit who inspired its writing in the first place to help us interpret and apply its meaning today, engaging our imaginations as well as our intellects to grasp its true message.

Have you ever noticed that wide-eyed, faraway look on the face of children as they listen to stories? It's as if they're gazing across the threshold of another world, seeing, hearing, and feeling the actual things described and imagining other realities barely implied. Tragically, as adults we tend to lose this magical ability. But one of the easiest ways of reawakening it is to read the text using all five senses. Learn to ask yourself questions such as, "Where am I standing in this story and what can I see?" "What background sounds am I hearing?" "How am I feeling?" And even, "Am I tasting or smelling anything?"

* * *

There was an evening, not that long ago, when I came to the Lord
with a heavy heart. The sheer scale of pastoral need in our church at
the time felt overwhelming. I was exhausted. I was also under attack
for the stance I'd taken on a particular issue. Complete strangers were
accusing me of all kinds of crazy stuff. I know I should have developed
a thicker skin by now, but the truth of the matter is that I was deeply
hurt and unable to defend myself. Sammy seemed worried. "Pete, how
are you going to keep this up?" she asked. "You've got nothing left to
give. This isn't sustainable."

I escaped to my study, collapsed into my old leather armchair,
and opened my Bible. Rarely had I felt such a need for a word from
my Father in heaven. Before beginning to read, I paused, but it was
little more than a series of heavy sighs. As for my prayer of approach,
it sounded like blasphemy: "Oh God," I groaned. "Oh God, Oh God."
I opened my Bible, more out of duty than desire, and found the day's
set passage. Deuteronomy 33. Moses on his deathbed, blessing the
tribes of Israel. Not particularly promising. First, there was a prayer
for Reuben to "live and not die" (v. 6), which made me think that at
least things weren't quite that bad. Next there was something about
Levi's "Thummim and Urim" (v. 8). And then these words unexpectedly wrapped themselves around me like a hug:

> Let the beloved of the LORD rest secure in him,
>   for he shields him all day long,
>   and the one the LORD loves rests between his shoulders.
>   (v. 12)

Here was my interruption, and it took no intuition whatsoever to
work out why. It was a beautiful reassurance for a troubled soul
like mine. I loved that image of "the one the LORD loves [resting]

between his shoulders," and began to imagine myself into the scene. There's an old, faded photograph somewhere of me as a baby, maybe eighteen months old, in a carrier on my father's back. That's how I imagined myself now. Held tight on my dad's back, safe and secure between his shoulder blades. I liked the solidity of that position. Could smell his thick holiday sweater. Felt his strength and the warmth of his back. Knew simply that I was loved. It was the physical sensation of trust. Of being carried. Nothing needed. Nothing required. And I could hear him singing as he walked. Emanating such a very deep contentment. And there I was, in the middle of this moment, bound to his back, caught up in his contentment, drifting off to sleep.

"Thank you, Father," I whispered, leaning into the embrace of my old leather chair, feeling the strain lifting from my shoulders. "I love you, Lord."

It was by my lingering to imagine the scene in this highly subjective way, not worrying too much about its original context and meaning, that this ancient blessing had become my blessing too. Had I noted the words appreciatively but moved on right away, although it would certainly still have encouraged me, it would not, could not, have ministered to my soul in the same kind of way.

I had engaged my senses by asking what I could see, smell, hear, and feel, and I had also positioned myself within the story. In this instance it had been pretty straightforward, since there were only two characters and the other one was God! However, it's often possible to read and reread a single story from a range of viewpoints, imagining yourself as a different character each time. Alexander Whyte, a moderator of the Free Church of Scotland in the nineteenth century, strongly advocated this method: "At one time you are the publican: at another time you are the prodigal . . . at another time, you are Mary Magdalene: at another time, Peter in the porch . . . till your whole New Testament is all over autobiographic of you."[17]

Step #3: Ask (Oratio)

PAUSE   READ & REFLECT   ASK   YIELD

If you've "Paused" and "Read and Reflected" with interruption, intuition, and imagination, it's now time to turn your meditations into prayerful conversation with the Lord. In his book *The Circle Maker*, Mark Batterson gives some great advice on the way you pray and the way you read the Bible:

> Prayer was never meant to be a monologue; it was meant to be a dialogue. Think of Scripture as God's part of the script; prayer is our part. Scripture is God's way of initiating a conversation; prayer is our response. The paradigm shift happens when you realize that the Bible wasn't meant to be *read through*; the Bible was meant to be *prayed through*. And if you pray through it, you will never run out of things to talk about.[18]

Reading the Bible certainly gives us plenty of things to talk about with God, but it is the way we read the Bible that sets the tone. I suspect you can see this just from the personal examples I've already given. As we explore and enter into the text, it is the most natural thing in the world to turn our thoughts to God in prayer. In fact, it's such a natural overflow that—like me repenting over the dishwasher this morning and then rejoicing in that old leather chair—you will often find yourself praying almost without noticing it.

There are many types of prayer that can flow from reflection on Scripture. I've already mentioned repentance and rejoicing, but don't forget petition (asking for your own needs) and intercession (asking on behalf of others). I am inordinately grateful to the contemplative tradition, which has taught me so much, having nurtured and championed the *lectio divina* for centuries. However, I am also grateful for the evangelical and Pentecostal traditions, which have taught me much about the power of intercessory prayer. This is a type of prayer that many contemplatives barely practice (and this is something we try to redress each day in the Lectio 365 devotions). There is more to intercession than just holding others silently before the Lord, valuable as that can be. The Bible leaves us in no doubt about the power and necessity of specific, defiant, expectant, fervent, miracle-making, intercessory prayer (see, for example, Exodus 17:8–16; Acts 4:23–31).

Jesus asks us, as he asked Bartimaeus, for a particular, specific, verbal answer to the question, "What do you want me to do for you?" (Mark 10:51). Insights that we receive during *lectio divina* may lead into thanksgiving, adoration, repentance, and personal petition, but they may also lead us outward and upward, into intercession for others. Take, for example, the way God spoke to me this morning through that verse from Romans 12, "Hate what is evil." I responded personally with repentance but could easily have enlarged my prayers to ask for God's mercy on people known to me who are currently undoubtedly afflicted by evil. Similarly, when God comforted me that night through Deuteronomy 33:12, I might easily have gone on to intercede for those with an even greater need to know the Father carrying them "between his shoulders."

Step #4: Yield *(Contemplatio)*

Therefore, I urge you, brothers and sisters, in view of God's mercy, to offer your bodies as a living sacrifice, holy and pleasing to God—this is your true and proper worship.
—Romans 12:1

Seek in reading and you will find in meditation; knock in
prayer and it will be opened to you in contemplation.
—St. John of the Cross

In this chapter I have talked about the essential role that Benedict of Nursia played in the development of *lectio divina*, but not yet about a character almost equally influential in popularity: Ignatius of Loyola, founder of the Jesuits. Arising in sixteenth-century Europe, the Jesuits championed a practical spirituality that sought to find God in all things. They became the great popularizers of such ancient practices for spiritual formation as the examen, the Spiritual Exercises, and, of course, *lectio divina*. Armed with these powerful tools, Jesuits went out and truly changed the world. It was Jesuits, for instance, who located the source of the Blue Nile, discovered quinine, invented the humble trapdoor, founded the Brazilian city of São Paulo, championed Baroque architecture, wrote the first dictionaries of North America's native languages (enabling cross-cultural communication), gave their names to thirty-five craters on the moon, and provided education for leaders from Descartes and Voltaire to Bill Clinton and Denzel Washington.[19] The Jesuits embody the intrinsic link between spiritual formation (prayer, listening, meditating on the Scriptures, etc.) and social transformation. "Saint Ignatius was a mystic," wrote William James, the American philosopher, "but his mysticism made him one of the most powerfully practical human engines that ever lived."[20]

There's a story told of Ignatius by Diego Laynez, one of his closest friends, that captures something of the man's true heart:

> At night he would go up on the roof of the house, with the sky there up above him. He would sit quietly, absolutely quietly. He would take his hat off and look up for a long time at the sky. Then he would fall to his knees, bowing profoundly to God. . . . And the tears would begin to flow down his cheeks like a stream, but so

quietly and gently that you heard not a sob or a sign nor the least possible movement of his body.[21]

This is a beautiful depiction of contemplation: an expression of prayer beyond words, fully yielded to the loving presence of God. It is, if you like, the intimacy of the elderly couple sitting together in contented silence or of a mother gazing down at her sleeping baby. It's that timeless moment at the end of an exceptional cinematic experience, when no one moves, no one speaks. It's the hearts of the couple on the Emmaus road "burning within" as they silently listened to Jesus.

Psychologist David G. Benner, who has written one of the best books on *lectio divina*, compares it to receiving a letter from the love of your life. You pore over every word, every phrase, reading it more than once and, as you do so, "the words initiate a reverie of love."[22] But then, imagine that your loved one suddenly walks through the door just as you are reading their letter. In that joyous moment, as you instinctively embrace, the love that was a reverie becomes the real thing. And the love letter is all but forgotten in the presence of your heart's desire. This helps me to understand the progression from reading, rereading, and reflecting on God's love letter in the Bible to actually enjoying God's loving presence itself in an encounter intimated and initiated by his written Word.

Perhaps this sounds a bit esoteric and unattainable, but it's really very simple. Having slowly, prayerfully read the Scriptures, you only need to wait—don't rush off. Enjoy the moment. There's nothing to say or do. Simply sit quietly for a few minutes, reflecting on what you've just read and what God has just said. Your lover won't always burst through the door! Sometimes you'll just sit in the afterglow of your time with his letter for a few minutes before getting on with your day.

But there will be other times when the author of the love letter will indeed surprise you with his presence. He'll step through the door and you'll become extraordinarily aware of his closeness. So much so that you'll lose your awareness of yourself, and even of time itself, as if you've stepped into eternity (which, in a way, you have). Like Ignatius on that rooftop, weeping under the stars, you will be *lost in wonder, love, and praise.*

Yielding like this at the end of your prayer time is not unlike pausing at the start (and, indeed, there is something cyclical about the entire process—see diagram). But your awareness of God's presence is going to be deeper, the silence easier, and your heart fuller this time around because of the things he's shown you through his Word. (For guidance on practicing contemplative prayer, see chapter 8 of *How to Pray: A Simple Guide for Normal People.*)

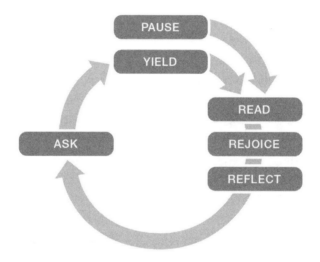

The sustained practice of *lectio divina*, and especially these closing moments of yielding, can be transformative in our lives, as God's Word migrates from our heads to our hearts, from wrestling to resting, from the Word to the Great Silence.

And this brings me to the thing I've been longing to tell you: the most wonderful secret superpower granted to those who practice *lectio divina* over weeks and months and years. By training ourselves to hear God's voice where it's easiest—in the Bible—we gradually learn to hear his voice everywhere else as well. We start to hear him in books that are not "sacred texts" and between the lines of newspapers and in conversations with colleagues who don't even believe God exists. When we root ourselves in Scripture, the whole of creation becomes God's mouthpiece.

By training ourselves to pray the Bible—embracing interruption, exercising intuition, and engaging imagination—we are, in fact, training ourselves by these very means to hear God's word in all of God's world. We start to make secular places sacred, simply by the way we listen to them. And, of course, wherever in the world God's word is received by faith, his kingdom has already come. In the words of the Jesuit paleontologist Pierre Teilhard de Chardin, "The world has little by little caught fire in my sight until, aflame all around me, it has become almost luminous from within."[23]

Pause & Pray

Sitting comfortably, I *Pause* and invite the Holy Spirit to come. Opening my Bible, I *Read* John 15:9–17 twice through, slowly, imagining the scene and noticing which word or phrase particularly stands out to me. Taking that word or phrase, I discuss it with the Lord and *Ask* for his help. Finally, I *Yield* myself afresh to abide in his love.

* * *

Over the last two chapters we have explored how to hear God's voice in and through the Bible by listening attentively with both our heads and our hearts, remembering the way Jesus himself applied Scripture on the Emmaus road. There's a beautiful old collect from the Book of Common Prayer, written by Thomas Cranmer almost five hundred years ago, that draws all these threads together:

Blessed Lord, who hast caused all holy Scriptures to be written for our learning;

Grant that we may in such wise hear them, read, mark, learn, and inwardly digest them,

that by patience and comfort of thy holy Word,

we may embrace, and ever hold fast, the blessed hope of everlasting life, which thou hast given us in our Saviour Jesus Christ. Amen.

Every word in this exquisite prayer is clearly carefully chosen. None of it is unconsidered. Cranmer's five verbs—*hear, read, mark, learn,* and *inwardly digest*—must all be significant.

In the previous chapter we picked up a few tools to help us hear, read, mark, and learn the Bible using our heads. And now in this chapter we have considered the call to "inwardly digest" God's Word through meditation, using our hearts. The poet and priest Malcolm Guite tells a moving story about visiting a very old lady on her deathbed:

She was suffering equally from dementia and neglect and the nurse told me that she couldn't speak three words of sense together. At a loss as to how to pray I began to recite the 23rd psalm, in the Prayer Book version. Suddenly I became aware of a voice beside me, faint at first but growing stronger. It was the old woman joining in through laboured breath. I had a strong sense that the person speaking these words was not the wandered old lady but the little girl who had learnt them all those years ago. We made it to the end of the psalm together and she died peacefully as I was saying the Gloria. "I will dwell in the house of the Lord forever" were the last words on her lips.[24]

How very wonderful to have absorbed God's Word so deeply into your very being, through a lifetime of hearing, reading, marking, learning, and digesting its truth, that it speaks at last when nothing else, and no one else, can. "I will dwell in the house of the Lord forever." With these words, that old lady died. And her story reminds me, as I often need to be reminded, that all the other ways in which God speaks are transient—dreams and visions will pass away, prophetic utterance speaks for a season, "the grass withers and the flowers fall, but the word of the Lord endures forever" (1 Pet. 1:24–5).

Living Word: Ignatius of Loyola (1491–1556)—Hearing God through Prayerful Reflection

Few people have done more than Ignatius of Loyola, the sixteenth-century founder of the Jesuits, to popularize the kind of subjective, imaginative ways of hearing God in the Bible that we've been exploring in this chapter. He particularly championed the use of *lectio divina*. Ignatius wrote:

> If one finds . . . in one or two words [of Scripture] matter which yields thought, relish, and consolation, one should not be anxious to move forward, even if the whole hour is consumed on what is being found.[25]

There's an old joke about a Franciscan, a Dominican, and a Jesuit who were praying, when the lights went out. The Franciscan said, "Oh, this is a wonderful opportunity to live more simply." The Dominican launched into a sermon about the significance of darkness and light. And the Jesuit went off to change the fuse.

The Jesuits (sometimes called Ignatians after their founder Ignatius of Loyola) are a worldwide religious order renowned for the practicality of their spirituality. Their motto, *Ad maiorem*

Dei gloriam, abbreviated AMDG, means, "For the greater glory of God." Jesuits are interested in finding God in all things and giving him glory through all things.

The practical tools developed by the Jesuits over the last 450 years continue to help millions of people today to pray and hear God in the midst of ordinary life. These tools include the Spiritual Exercises—a four-week, in-depth journey of spiritual formation, written by Ignatius himself, combining intensive Bible study, reflective prayer, and spiritual direction. Other tools include the *lectio divina*, to which the Jesuits have added their own particular emphasis around the role of the imagination in hearing God (see p. 87). Also, the examen, a reflective model of prayer designed to help identify God's voice (and our own sin) in the midst of normal life. (For those wishing to practice these forms of prayer, the Lectio 365 devotional from 24-7 Prayer offers the *lectio* every morning and a form of the examen every evening.[26])

Ignatius of Loyola is probably the only saint with a notarized police record: for nighttime brawling with an intent to inflict serious harm. Born in the Basque region of northern Spain, the young Íñigo López de Loyola was focused entirely—as it says in the first sentence of his autobiography—on "the vanities of this world" and "a great and foolish desire to win fame."[27] He became a soldier, but at the age of twenty-eight, his leg was shattered by a cannonball in battle, which left him limping for the rest of his life. While convalescing at his family castle in Loyola, he was dismayed to discover that the only books available to him were religious: one on the life of Jesus and others on the lives of saints. Reluctantly, he began reading but quickly became enamored by the beauty of Jesus and the heroism of these great men and women of faith. Through these books, Ignatius found himself enthralled with a new vision: to be a knight serving the King of kings.

Upon recovery he went to the monastery at Montserrat, where, with typical swagger, he removed his armor, laid down his sword, stripped off his finery, and gave his clothes away to the first beggar he met. After that, for a year he himself became a beggar in the nearby town, devoting as much as seven hours a day to prayer in a cave by the Cardoner River. Sitting there one day, he experienced "an enlightenment so strong that everything seemed new."[28] He perceived with "a very great clarity"[29] that the true destiny of humanity is to return home to God, in whom alone our souls find peace and joy.

The aspiring saint changed his name, moved to Paris, and gathered a group of six lifelong friends who together formed The Society of Jesus. The longevity of these friendships speaks volumes, I believe, about Ignatius' true character. As does the depth of spiritual insight revealed in his writings and the passion at the heart of his prayer life, from those early days in that cave by the Cardoner River to his latter years praying under the stars on the rooftop of his monastery in Rome.

We find in the life of Ignatius the genetic code for the entire Ignatian way to this day. It took a soldier who became a mystic to father a movement of "contemplatives in action." And it took a highly ambitious young man, his head filled with dreams of glory, to establish an organization committed to the greater glory of God. And it took the kind of dreamer who finds his calling in books about the heroism of others to pioneer a spirituality that is unafraid of the power of human imagination. This last insight is probably his greatest gift to those of us seeking to hear God's voice. It is the permission to open our imaginations to God, as a vehicle by which we may hear him speak, through the Bible *ad maiorem Dei gloriam*—to his greater glory.

Anima Christi (A Prayer from the Start of the Ignatian Spiritual Exercises)

Soul of Christ, sanctify me.

Body of Christ, save me.

Blood of Christ, inebriate me.

Water from the side of Christ, wash me.

Passion of Christ, strengthen me.

O Good Jesus, hear me.

Within your wounds hide me.

Permit me not to be separated from you.

From the wicked foe, defend me.

At the hour of my death, call me

and bid me come to you

That with your saints I may praise you

For ever and ever. Amen.

Listening Exercise: *Lectio Divina*

The nature of water is soft, that of stone is hard; but if a bottle is hung above the stone, allowing the water to fall drop by drop, it wears away the stone. So it is with the word of God; It is soft and our heart is hard, but the [one] who hears the word of God often, opens his heart to the fear of God.

—Abba Poemen (340–450)

In this chapter we've been learning how to pray the Bible, turning God's Word into a living conversation. It's been quite practical, so you should hopefully now feel able to practice *lectio divina* for yourself, engaging with the text slowly and intuitively using the simple P.R.A.Y. process: *P*ausing, *R*eading and *R*eflecting, *A*sking in prayer, and *Y*ielding to the things the Lord has shown you. These principles can be applied in numerous ways. Here are four suggestions:

Four Approaches to *Lectio Divina*
Inflective Reading

When reading and rereading a particular verse, experiment with changing the emphasis on different words. This sounds simple but can be a surprisingly powerful way of meditating on a text. For instance, let's take just the first six words of the most famous verse in the Bible:

- *"For **God** so loved the world..."* The greatest lover of life in the universe is God himself. He is love! I focus on him in praise.

- *"For God **so** loved the world..."* This tiny little adverb—*so*—takes on enormous weight. He didn't just love us a bit, with his fingers crossed behind his back, he loved us a lot! God "so" loves me. He "so" loves my family. He "so" loves people who don't love him back. Do I ever ration or restrict my love, as if it's a limited resource?

- *"For God so **loved** the world..."* His heart toward us is not anger, frustration, or disinterest but wholehearted, all-consuming love. Is this my primary attitude toward the world? Whom do I struggle to love in this way?

• *"For God so loved **the world** . . ."* Wow! Not just Christians.
  Not just humans. God loves the world of molecules and
  mountains, businesses and cultures, the places and people
  he has made. How might my attitude change if I were to
  live with a greater awareness of God's overwhelming love
  for everyone I meet?

Reading with the Senses (the Gospels)

Taking either a parable or a story about Jesus from John's
gospel (the most visual of the gospels), use your five senses to
examine and explore the scene. You might ask, "What am I seeing here?" "What am I hearing?" "Am I tasting or smelling anything?" "What am I feeling?" You might also wonder, "Where
am I in this story? What's my viewpoint? Am I in the crowd?
Among the disciples? Alongside the Pharisees? The person
being healed?" Now try rereading the story from an alternative
perspective, identifying with another person. As you circle the
story in this way, bringing it to life by working the angles and
reading between the lines, you will prime new possibilities
within yourself, creating space for God to speak in ways that
will sometimes exceed anything you could have conceived without him.

Reading in Groups

One of the simplest and most effective ways of practicing
the *lectio divina* in groups is to take turns reading a short passage of Scripture aloud, reading a verse or two each. Having
read the text in this way, go round the circle inviting each
person to identify a word or phrase that struck them, without
explaining why. (Inevitably some people will notice the same

phrase, which is fine.) Now repeat the process, reading the same passage before naming its highlights once again. You will easily be able to turn this meditation into a rich time of open prayer.

Reading Icons

The principles of *lectio divina* can be applied to the "holy reading" of any sacred text—not just the Bible—and even to icons, which are such an important aspect of prayer in Eastern Christianity. These highly stylized depictions, mostly of biblical figures and scenes, adhere to a set of signs and symbols. Two of my favorite icons, through which God has certainly spoken to me in prayer, are *The Hospitality of Abraham* (fifteenth century, Russian) and the lovely *Christ and His Friend* (eighth century, Egyptian).

Icons are visual sermons, with their own language, correctly described, therefore, as being "written" (not painted) and "read" (not viewed). So it's certainly appropriate to apply the principles of *lectio divina*—holy reading—to the way we interact with them. The P.R.A.Y. process works well. Approaching the icon prayerfully, we *P*ause to *R*ead and *R*eflect on its meaning, listening out for the whisper of God and turning our reflections into prayerful *A*sking, before *Y*ielding ourselves to the Lord in worship.

To read icons correctly, it is necessary to understand their symbolism. Colors are always significant. For example, blue represents heaven, and red refers to life and blood. Thus, if Jesus is dressed in both blue and red, we are reminded that he is both human and divine. Similarly, you will see a lot of gold, which represents uncreated light, God eternal. Icons are two-dimensional because they are meant to be signs pointing beyond themselves to a greater, fuller reality and are not meant to be admired in themselves as works of art. One iconographer explains it like this: "By employing classical concepts of idealized beauty and changes in perspective, icons speak to us of reality transformed and transfigured, both in and through God's presence. They speak of transcendence and mystery."[30]

Some people remain wary of icons, worried about idolatry and the distance they may create between us and the Lord, who needs no intermediary. It's appropriate to share such concerns, which were much debated in the early church. (Icons were only finally accepted as legitimate means of worship at the Second Council of Nicaea in 787.) No one should feel any pressure to use icons in prayer. But if you are visual and find it helpful to focus on something physical in a time of prayer, an icon can be helpful and is arguably more meaningful than, say, staring at a candle or a sunset or lyrics on a screen.

Richard Foster writes:

> As we lovingly behold the icon, we seek to pass beyond the image in wood or paint to the person of Jesus himself, and from the person of Jesus into the very presence of the triune God. It is much like when we lovingly touch the photograph of a loved one; we seek to somehow pass beyond the paper to the person himself or herself.[31]

For Further Reflection

Lectio 365—a daily devotional app based around the *lectio divina*, which I cowrite and cohost with a team from 24-7 Prayer.

The *Lectio Divina* Course from www.prayercourse.org.

David G. Benner, *Opening to God: Lectio Divina and Life as Prayer* (Downers Grove, IL: IVP, 2010).

Michael Casey, *Sacred Reading: The Ancient Art of Lectio Divina* (London: HarperCollins, 1996).

The New Testament uses two Greek terms to describe the word of God: *logos* and *rhēma*. *Logos* refers to the expressions we've studied so far: God's living word in Jesus (chapter 1) and God's written word in the Bible (chapters 2 and 3). But the other term, *rhēma*, describes God's *spoken* word, living and active today, in prophecy. As the apostle Paul says, "The one who prophesies speaks to people for their strengthening, encouraging and comfort" (1 Cor. 14:3). In this chapter I set out some keys to help you grow in this important spiritual gift and some simple principles for handling it appropriately.

4

Hearing God's Word in Prophecy

Were not our hearts burning within us while
he talked with us on the road?

—Luke 24:32

Follow the way of love and eagerly desire . . . prophecy.

—1 Corinthians 14:1

I meet so many people—especially young people—who are sick and tired of the way that prophecy has been used and abused in recent years. God's voice has undoubtedly been claimed falsely in scandalous ways. I understand that you may be deeply wary of so-called prophets and their "prophecies." But one of my great passions in writing this book is to beg you not to give up on this important and wonderful gift of the Holy Spirit, which is perhaps needed now more than ever. Instead, let's return to the biblical guidelines and common-sense protocols underpinning the appropriate use of the gift of prophecy in the church today.

I'm also aware that you may be wary of prophecy simply because it's unfamiliar, or considered risky, in your own Christian tradition. In this chapter, therefore, we are going to seek to understand what prophecy is and how it works and some simple principles for how to do it.

* * *

It's hard for me to put into words the extent to which my life has been shaped and directed by the wonderful supernatural gift of prophecy.

I'm sixteen, maybe seventeen years old, and a guy with an infectious smile is standing in a prayer meeting, describing a mental impression he says he's received from God. It's a sword with the word *envy* written on it. Simple enough. Except that I'm astonished. Flummoxed and floored. For two reasons: first, I've never experienced anything like this before; and second, I know that it's specifically and embarrassingly for me. I'm suddenly gripped by an awareness that the living God is in the room, that he's eyeballing me, and that I need to sort out my attitude.

And now I'm at university, and a bunch of us have jumped in a minivan and driven ourselves out of London to visit a church two hours south on the coast. The preacher singles me out, asks me to stand, and proceeds to read my mail. He describes details of my life he has no earthly way of knowing.[1] My heart is beating fast. I'm shaking in my boots. In fact, this experience has such a deep impact on me that I will relocate here, to this backwater, from the capital, just as soon as I graduate. And it's here in this church that I'll meet my wife, start the first 24-7 Prayer room, and step into the very things that are being prophesied over my life tonight.

Sammy and I are now married, and 24-7 is in full swing. We've been viewing a large property with two other couples, wondering about buying it together as a center for family, hospitality, and mission. But now my phone is buzzing. It's a text from someone in South Africa who knows nothing of our plans: "I'm sensing that you are considering a new project—entering into some kind of partnership— and the Lord says be careful. I don't think it's right."

Sammy and I are still trying to process this bolt out of the blue when one of the other couples calls. "So what did you think of the house, Pete? Shall we put in an offer?"

Calmly but firmly I say, "No, I don't think it's right. I don't think God is in this."

With hindsight, it's a narrow escape for us all.

And now I'm in the pub with David. He's a brilliant young leader I'm mentoring, and I'm trying to work out how to challenge him about his unhealthy intensity without being, well, too intense. There's a line going round in my head about the fruit of the Holy Spirit being joy, not intensity, but David interrupts my thoughts, saying he's got something to discuss. I say, "Me too," and he says, "You first."

So I take a deep breath and decide to cut to the chase. "David, you need joy in your life."

He gasps and stares at me. "Say that again."

"I think you need joy in your life."

"I need joy in my life?"

"Yes." He's still staring at me. His mouth is open but there's no sound.

"Pete, the thing I was wanting to discuss," he says eventually, "is a girl I met online. I'm wondering if we should date, and, well, I'm freaking out here because *her name is Joy*!"

David does indeed get Joy in his life. In fact, he marries her. And together they have two beautiful children, serving God today on the frontlines of cross-cultural urban mission.

Clearly, sometimes God speaks prophetically in spite of us. And this can be quite a relief.

It's a few years later, and my friend Bill has texted me: "If you keep prioritizing the poor, God says he will give you the palaces too." Not knowing anyone with a spare palace, I figure it's metaphorical, a nice alliterative way of saying that we should continue doing what we're doing with the poor: scraping drunks off the street in Ibiza, loving gangsters on the Cape Flats, putting shoes on the feet of Roma children in Macedonia, fighting racism in America, and so on. Prayer and the poor: that's us. Palaces? Not so much. I thank Bill and forget about it. Until I get a phone call from the office of Cardinal Schönborn, the archbishop of Vienna, a few days later.

"The cardinal would like to extend a warm invitation to the 24-7 Prayer movement to convene in Saint Stephen's Cathedral."

"Wow!" I say. It's not every day that one of the most senior Catholics in the world cold-calls a maverick prayer movement to offer them the keys to his cathedral. "That's incredibly generous. Please thank the cardinal, sincerely. It's very kind, but I don't think it would work. Our guys are more at home in nightclubs with sticky floors, not world heritage sites. We'll break something."

I detect a slight chuckle from Vienna. "Well, that's a shame because the cardinal also told me to offer you the use of his palace."

The word *palace* hits me like a jet of icy water. Never before or since have I been offered one. Never before or since have I received a prophetic word about one. And so it is that we celebrate fifteen years of 24-7 Prayer in a Viennese palace and a fifteenth-century cathedral where Mozart once sang in the choir. And we do so, I should add, without breaking a single thing.[2]

You can dismiss things like this as lucky coincidences if you really have that much faith in fluke, but I honestly find it easier simply to believe in a living, loving God who still speaks and acts today, sometimes in quite extraordinary ways through very ordinary people like you and me.

Prophet Motive

The New Testament uses two Greek terms to describe the word of God: *logos* and *rhēma*. *Logos* refers to the *written* word of God found in the Bible (Heb. 4:12). It is also used to describe the living word of God found in Jesus (John 1:1). These are the expressions of God's word we've explored so far in this book: Jesus (chapter 1) and the Bible (chapters 2 and 3).

But the other word, *rhēma*, describes the *spoken* word of God expressed in prophecy (1 Cor. 2:13), and this is where we turn our attention now, seeking to understand, receive, and handle this gift in our own lives today. Many of the passages we traditionally apply to the Bible actually refer to prophetic utterance. For instance, in the wilderness, Jesus tells Satan, "Man shall not live on bread alone, but on every [*rhēma*] that comes from the mouth of God" (Matt. 4:4). What's more, the original Greek word translated here as "comes from" is *ekporeuomenō*, which literally describes speech "continually coming out from" the mouth of the Lord. Jesus is saying that we are sustained not just by studying the things God has said in the past as revealed in the Bible (*logos*) but also by feeding on the things God is continually speaking to us here and now (*rhēma*).[3]

Our focus thus far has been on learning to hear God for ourselves, personally through Scripture, but prophecy shifts the focus to hearing his voice for other people. The apostle Paul describes it like this: "The one who prophesies speaks to people for their strengthening, encouraging and comfort. . . . The one who prophesies edifies the church" (1 Cor. 14:3–4). It couldn't be clearer: by way of prophecy, God speaks through us into the lives of others. That's what the guy with the infectious smile was doing when he shared the picture of the sword carrying the word *envy*, it's what the preacher did when he pulled me out of the crowd and read my mail, it's what the South African did when she texted me the warning about buying that house, and it's what Bill did when he sent me the message about the poor and palaces. It's even what I managed to do (completely unwittingly) that day with David in the pub.

So the primary *focus* of prophecy is others, and the primary *purpose* of prophecy is their strengthening, encouraging, comfort, and edification. In other words, it is not, as is often supposed, a way of exposing, criticizing, or pulling people down, and it's only rarely a way of pronouncing judgment. Neither is it primarily about predicting the future. In both Old and New Testaments, prophecy is predominantly a means of declaring God's will and powerfully communicating his heart.[4]

This fundamentally loving motivation is mapped out quite clearly by the apostle Paul in his first letter to the church in Corinth.

In chapter 12 he lists the "gifts of the Spirit" (including various types of prophecy). In chapter 13 he pens his great hymn to the preeminence of love: "Love is patient, love is kind . . ." And then, in chapter 14, he draws the previous two chapters together, saying, "Follow the way of love [chapter 13] and eagerly desire . . . prophecy [chapter 12]," and proceeds to provide detailed instructions on how to exercise the prophetic gift. In other words, chapter 13 is not an anomaly. It isn't a deviation from the prophetic theme of these chapters. When people say they prefer 1 Corinthians 13 about love to the bit about weird spiritual gifts, they completely miss the point! This is not an either/or. There were no chapter divisions in Paul's original letter. He is urging us to "eagerly desire gifts of the Spirit, especially prophecy" (1 Cor. 14:1) precisely *because* we love other people and therefore want them to be strengthened, encouraged, comforted, and edified by God's Word. And he is also telling us that spiritual gifts are useless— "only a resounding gong or a clanging cymbal" (1 Cor. 13:1)—unless they are administered with love.

The original Greek word translated here as "eagerly desire" is *zéloó*, from which we get words like *zealot* and *jealous*. It literally means to "covet" or "burn with zeal" for a person or a thing. On three separate occasions Paul chooses to use this forceful word to describe the attitude we should have toward spiritual gifts (1 Cor. 12:31; 14:1, 39). People who are ambivalent toward prophecy, saying, "Oh, well, I guess God can give me that gift if he wants, but I'm not going to get worked up about it," may not realize that their attitude is unloving and at odds with Scripture.

Pause & Pray

Is prophecy a spiritual gift that I "earnestly desire"? I take a moment now to ask the Holy Spirit to give me a passion to hear and speak his word.

Thus Spake the Prophet Kermit

Before I was born the L<small>ORD</small> called me;
from my mother's womb he has spoken my name.
—Isaiah 49:1

I'm talking to a man who looks a lot like the skinny younger brother of Santa Claus. Snow-white beard, twinkly eyes, a ready laugh, abuzz with nervous energy. Ken Helser is telling me the stories of his hippy days touring America, signing record deals, doing drugs, and all the rest. It was 1970. He was sitting in a yoga position, smoking a massive joint, and reading a Bible when he heard a voice: "Hear God," it said, "and you will live." It was an experience that set Ken on a spiritual quest, traveling from church to church in his native North Carolina, asking the same questions wherever he went: "Does God really speak today? If so, how does he speak? And how do you know it's him?" For three months, he says, no one anywhere could answer him.

At last he found a Baptist pastor who knew what he was talking about. He seemed to have countless thrilling stories of hearing God's voice for himself. "So can you teach me to hear God?" Ken asked eagerly, sensing that his twelve-week pilgrimage might finally be coming to a conclusion.

"No!" snapped the pastor. "You are bowing down to an idol. Music is your god. If you want to hear God, you need to make Jesus Lord."

Longing to "hear God and live," Ken Helser made Jesus Lord. He repented of his sins, kicked drugs, quit the band with its promise of fame, and solemnly recommitted himself to be faithful to his wife and two daughters. "I began to discover," he says, with his eyes twinkling, "that in *everything* God has a voice." I would go about my day talking to him, asking, "What are you saying in this situation? Where are you at work in this place? What was that encounter all about?"

A few years later, a retired school teacher by the name of Kermit came to see Ken. They'd only met once before, but Kermit announced that he had a message from God and proceeded to describe an encounter with God he'd had one evening while praying on the baseball field. The Lord had appeared to him and said, "Tell my servant Ken Helser that I have healed his seed. He's going to have a son who is to be called Jonathan David. He'll play the harp and sing like an angel. He'll write prophetic songs for his generation, and his music will go out all over the earth."

What Kermit didn't know as he delivered this message was that Ken's wife Linda had cancer of the uterus. She was just two weeks away from a scheduled hysterectomy, which was going to make conceiving another child medically impossible. Neither did he know that Ken was hiding a secret fear that his years of hard drug abuse had damaged "his seed." He hadn't told Linda, but this was the real reason he'd always resisted the idea of having a third child.

But now, with his faith turbocharged, Ken rushed home to pray for Linda's healing before persuading their gynecologist to conduct just one more preoperative test, explaining that they had prayed. The results came back, and the pathologist was baffled. In fact, he kept checking that this really was the same woman, because there was no longer any sign of the cancer. As for the gynecologist, when he came down the corridor to break the good news to Ken and Linda, he was whistling. "That's gotta be a good sign!" chuckled Ken.

"I've been in practice thirty years," the doctor said, "and I think I just witnessed my first miracle." He paused to let the words sink in. "Ken, your wife is two hundred percent okay!"

Jonathan David Helser was born the following year, the fruit of a miracle attested by science and promised by God. But growing up, he showed no interest at all in music; his sole obsession was sports. Wisely, Ken and Linda never put any pressure on him, never shared the details of Kermit's prophecy. And then, at the age of nineteen, he finally asked his dad to teach him a few chords on the guitar and went off to the UK to train with Youth with a Mission at its base in

Nuneaton. Ken went to visit and listened in awe as, for the first time ever, he heard Jonathan David play one of his own songs—a call upon his generation to rise up and take back the land.

Today, Jonathan David Helser makes music with his wife Melissa that truly circles the earth, just as the prophet Kermit predicted all those years ago. In fact, I was with him the day he heard the news that his song "Raise a Hallelujah" had reached number 1 on the airplay charts.[5] And as for his award-winning anthem "No Longer Slaves," it contains some especially poignant lines:

> From my mother's womb
> You have chosen me
> Love has called my name
> I've been born again
> Into Your family
> Your blood flows through my veins
>
> I'm no longer a slave to fear
> I am a child of God[6]

Simple Keys to Growing in the Prophetic Gift

Stories like these are clearly inspiring, and I hope they leave you in no doubt that God still speaks prophetically today. But they can also be a bit intimidating for those of us who sometimes struggle to discern the voice of God even in the simplest of ways from day to day. Obviously, it's not possible to engineer the kind of encounter with Jesus that Kermit had that evening on the baseball field. (He himself had never experienced anything like it before and was simply being faithful in prayer when it happened.)

So how do we actually, practically, begin to exercise the spiritual gift of prophecy?

Let's turn to another story about another boy born miraculously and called by God even in his mother's womb:

The boy Samuel ministered before the LORD under Eli. In those days the word of the LORD was rare; there were not many visions.

One night Eli, whose eyes were becoming so weak that he could barely see, was lying down in his usual place. The lamp of God had not yet gone out, and Samuel was lying down in the house of the LORD, where the ark of God was. Then the LORD called Samuel.

Samuel answered, "Here I am." And he ran to Eli and said, "Here I am; you called me."

But Eli said, "I did not call; go back and lie down." So he went and lay down.

Again the LORD called, "Samuel!" And Samuel got up and went to Eli and said, "Here I am; you called me."

"My son," Eli said, "I did not call; go back and lie down."

Now Samuel did not yet know the LORD: The word of the LORD had not yet been revealed to him.

A third time the LORD called, "Samuel!" And Samuel got up and went to Eli and said, "Here I am; you called me."

Then Eli realized that the LORD was calling the boy. So Eli told Samuel, "Go and lie down, and if he calls you, say, 'Speak, LORD, for your servant is listening.'" So Samuel went and lay down in his place.

The LORD came and stood there, calling as at the other times, "Samuel! Samuel!"

Then Samuel said, "Speak, for your servant is listening." (1 Sam. 3:1–10)

According to Josephus, the first-century Jewish historian, Samuel was just eleven years old at the time of this dramatic, life-defining encounter. We know that his hair would have been very long, having never been cut, in line with the Nazirite vow by which his mother had dedicated him to the Lord as a baby (see Num. 6:1–21). And, interestingly, we are told that he was living at a time when "the word of the LORD was rare" (1 Sam. 3:1).

Words in Season

It's easy to assume that people in the Bible found faith easier, and certainly that they found hearing God's voice simpler than we do. But Samuel was living at a time when God's voice was far rarer and more unfamiliar than it is for us today. No wonder it took him a few attempts to understand.

In chapter 2 of this book, I recounted the dramatic way God answered our prayers for rain on the island of Ibiza. And elsewhere, in my book *Dirty Glory*, I've described the equally remarkable story of how God called Brian and Tracey Heasley to move to Ibiza in order to head up our work there. Honestly, it's one of the most extraordinary examples I know of God speaking today. But our mission to Ibiza has been running now for twenty years, and it isn't like that all the time! In fact, it would be thoroughly unhealthy and weirdly intense if it were a daily display of signs and wonders.

At the start, God spoke dramatically and directionally in order to confirm and commission what we were launching. There were "signs following" (Mark 16:20 KJV), because we needed them to know which way to go. As Jack Deere says, "The clearer the revelation, the harder the task. . . . In fact, the clarity of the voice may well be the main thing that gives you the power to endure the subsequent testing."[7] These days in Ibiza, God generally speaks to our team less obviously, more quietly, leaving them to exercise common sense and to be faithful to all the things he's previously made clear.

God does not speak indiscriminately like a relentless radio station. The atmosphere around us is not abuzz with his continual chatter, accessible to anyone who happens to tune in. God's specific words tend to be targeted and seasonal. Of course, his *logos* word (in Christ and in Scripture) remains consistently and wonderfully available, but there are times in all our lives—as there were in Bible times—when God's *rhēma* word is rare. Perhaps this is because he is simply not in a hurry. But also because our Creator understands that we are seasonal beings, living in a seasonal world, and we don't thrive and mature in a mode of continual harvest.[8] Just as a farmer knows when to sow, when to wait, and when to harvest, so God waits for the seeds of prophetic revelation to bear fruit in our lives. He may also withdraw for a while when there is particular sin in the land or if he is awaiting our obedience to an earlier word. Mature disciples learn not just to celebrate the seasons of abundant revelation but also to wait patiently and watch diligently during the in-between seasons when "the word of the LORD [is] rare" (1 Sam. 3:1).

Finding Your Eli

Samuel learned to recognize God's voice through the counsel of Eli, his spiritual father. It wasn't enough for him to hear the audible voice of God; he also needed human wisdom and advice. We all need someone like Eli who can coach us in discerning God's word. Who is your Eli? Is there someone you know who hears God better than you do? I'd encourage you to ask them to help you. Even now, I often ask people very simple questions, such as, "How do you know what God is saying?" And if they use phrases like, "God told me," or, "the Holy Spirit spoke," or, "I just sensed," I will ask, "How?"

I'm not being cynical. I'm being teachable—seeking to learn and grow. The prophet Elisha was mentored by the prophet Elijah. Eventually he even received a double portion of his mentor's gift and authority (2 Kings 2:9). Elisha also led his own network of prophetic training schools located in various cities such as Bethel, Jericho, and Gilgal.[9] As for the prophet Samuel, having been mentored as a boy by Eli, he also developed prophetic schools. On one occasion when King Saul's soldiers approached Samuel's company of prophets, "the Spirit of God came on Saul's men, and they also prophesied" (1 Sam. 19:20).

Certain people today seem to be contagious with the Holy Spirit in a similar way. When I spend time with them, my faith grows and I find myself wanting to walk and talk with God in greater intimacy. It's important to honor such people (they won't be perfect) and to prioritize time with them.

I'm aware that some people reading this will struggle to think of anyone who could be their Eli. Perhaps, like Ken Helser, you will have to look for many months before you find someone who can really help. When I became serious about my faith, I approached a number of older men, hoping that one of them would be my Eli. Each one of them said they would be happy to help, but none of them knew how to disciple a younger Christian because, I think, it had never been done for them. It took me two years to find my Eli. I hope it's easier and quicker for you!

In the meantime, you can also get personal coaching from great heroes of the faith by reading about their lives. I have always found it the most extraordinary privilege to sit at the feet of such remarkable men and women as Frank Laubach, Teresa of Ávila, George Müller, and Billy Graham by reading their biographies.

Happy Eater

It's such a relief to see in the story of Samuel that God doesn't give up on him when he fails to recognize his voice. The Lord keeps calling until finally Samuel recognizes and responds. Similarly, on the road to Emmaus, Jesus is gracious with his traveling companions. He remains with them for just as long as it takes for them to realize it's him. As we seek to grow in our ability to discern God's voice, he understands our dullness and doesn't seem to mind that we often get it wrong. When we miss the moment, he doesn't say, "Tough, you've had your chance, I'm off to speak to someone sharper." He keeps knocking at the door, speaking our name, until at last we comprehend and respond.

When I first started taking my faith seriously, a Christian friend explained that God sometimes speaks through mental impressions he called "pictures." To me, as someone with a fairly visual imagination, this sounded terrific, so I decided to give it a try. I knelt by my bed and before long found myself thinking about the Happy Eater logo. Happy Eater was a chain of roadside diners that finally, mercifully, died out in the 1990s. Its logo depicted a bright red smiling face in profile, with its hand actually in its own mouth. It wasn't a great logo. I began to wonder if this was the sort of heavenly vision my friend had told me to expect.

There was obviously only one way to find out, so I drove five miles to my nearest Happy Eater with mounting excitement, feeling like a man on a mission. Perhaps the restaurant was on fire and I was being dispatched to save it. Someone might be weeping into their instant coffee, crying to the Lord for help, and I was going to be the answer. Maybe the next Great Awakening was about to kick off in a diner near Dorking.

And so I stepped into that restaurant like an international man of ministry on a mission from God. "Thank God you've come!" screamed the waitress. I half expected her to ask, "What must I do to be saved?" But instead, what she actually said was, "Table for one?"

Undeterred, I took a seat and began to survey the diner for signs of a red-hot spiritual opportunity. I was disappointed to note that no flames were emanating from the kitchen and no one seemed particularly suicidal. In fact, there was no hint anywhere of anything unusual at all. But then I remembered how the apostle Philip had been supernaturally redirected by the Holy Spirit to witness to an Ethiopian eunuch in the desert, and it occurred to me that perhaps I'd been sent here to share my faith. At that precise moment another waitress appeared to take my order. I took a deep breath, looked deeply into her eyes and asked if she would like to know the love of God.

"No, I'm alright, thanks," she said, a little too quickly.

I felt deflated and asked for tea instead.

Over the course of an hour, my excitement cooled at a similar speed to my cup of tea. Gradually I began to wonder if I'd simply got it wrong. Eventually, dejectedly, I paid for my tea, left a tip, and drove home feeling dumb and resolving never, under any circumstances, to tell another living soul about this embarrassing nonevent. There had been no flaming inferno, no suicidal trucker, no hungry soul seeking eternal salvation. Why, I wondered miserably, was my life so unlike those of the spiritual giants I read about in books? Why was I so bad at hearing God's voice? And why on earth was I fantasizing about the Happy Eater logo in my time of prayer?

But here I am now, a few years on, and I've got a theory about that day. Somewhere in the courts of heaven I imagine the Father turning to the Son and asking what I was doing, and the Son turning to the Spirit and asking the same question. And maybe the Spirit said that I'd been trying to learn to discern his voice, but I wasn't very good at it yet, so I'd just been on a wild goose chase to one of the worst diners in England under the false impression that the Father had a mission for me there. And maybe, when he heard this, the Father chuckled and leaned back in his throne and said, "Okay, I like that kid. Let's give him a break."

We all have to start somewhere in learning to discern the voice of God, and a few well-intentioned mistakes along the way are probably okay. In fact, they're probably essential. At the start of any relationship, it takes a while to recognize the other person's voice, but before long, their name flashes up on your phone, and eventually all you have to do is say, "Hi, it's me!"

Growing Your Prophetic Muscles

As Samuel grew in years from his initial moment of calling, he also grew in spiritual stature so that eventually "all Israel from Dan to Beersheba recognized that Samuel was attested as a prophet of the LORD" (1 Sam. 3:20). What began as a one-off prophetic encounter at the age of eleven became a lifetime of listening to God's word and speaking it out to other people.

The gift of prophecy grows like a muscle with regular exercise. In fact, the apostle Paul tells us to "try to excel in those [spiritual gifts] that build up the church" (1 Cor. 14:12). This is unfamiliar language. We don't talk a lot about trying "to excel" in anything spiritual, perhaps because we worry about it becoming a legalistic work of the flesh. But Paul clearly doesn't think that the gifts of the Spirit just get beamed down on us indiscriminately. Those who work hard at developing their prophetic muscles, the way an athlete might train at the gym, will inevitably grow like Samuel in spiritual stature and strength. We do this by walking closely with Jesus from day to day. We do it by acquainting ourselves with the sound of his voice through the quiet discipline of prayerful attentiveness toward his presence. We do it by finding our own Eli to encourage and coach us in hearing God's voice. We do it too by welcoming feedback and learning from our mistakes. We also exercise the prophetic by diligently delivering the things God gives us to say with increasing levels of confidence, competence, and consistency.

Exercising a prophetic gift: Since all believers can be filled with the Holy Spirit (Acts 2:4; 19:6; Eph. 5:18), we can (and should) all receive and exercise his gifts, including prophecy. But our first attempts at prophecy can be scary, so it's helpful to ask yourself, "Will the thing I think I'm seeing, hearing, or sensing bring encouragement if I share it? Will it be edifying?" And most important of all, "Does it sound like Jesus?" A simple, memorable rule of thumb is therefore to apply the ABC filter:

- **A**ffirming: Does this word fulfil the criteria of 1 Corinthians 14, by being *strengthening, encouraging, comforting, edifying,* and *upbuilding*?
- **B**iblical: Is this word consistent with the broad teaching and witness of Scripture (not just a specific verse taken out of context—see chapter 2)?
- **C**hristlike: Is this word consistent with the character, mission, and message of Jesus?

The ABC filter is not perfect. There are times when a word from God may be deeply disruptive and not comforting at all (I'm sure you can think of examples in the Bible). But for those taking their first faltering steps in this area, it's much less scary to start with encouraging and affirming words before moving on to the more challenging ones.

It's also a good idea to ask, "What's the worst that could happen if I get this wrong?" If, for example, you receive a mental image of a waterfall, and you sense that it might be a message about spiritual refreshment for someone, it's clearly *a*ffirming. It also lines up with a major *b*iblical theme around cleansing and refreshment. And it certainly reflects the character of *C*hrist, who said, "Let anyone who is thirsty come to me and drink" (John 7:37). The worst that could happen if you get this wrong is a mild moment of slightly unanointed encouragement! There's really nothing to lose by sharing it.

But if, on the other hand, you were to receive a disturbing dream about someone committing adultery, you would need to think very carefully indeed before sharing it publicly for fear of falsely accusing and deeply hurting the couple involved. Instead, you might harness your concerns in private prayer for those involved, and then, if your concerns persist, you might quietly and humbly flag them with a pastoral leader "just in case." I say "humbly" because, as the apostle Paul says, "we know in part and we prophesy in part" (1 Cor. 13:9). Everyone sometimes gets it wrong. No one hears perfectly from God—no matter how supernatural the moment of epiphany may be. Over the years in pastoral ministry, I have seen several marital affairs exposed by prophetic dreams, but I have also, more often, had to protect innocent people from the trauma of false accusations that might otherwise have been made "in the name of God."

Moving in a prophetic ministry: As we get better at hearing God and more seasoned in sharing his words with other people, our gift, competence, and character may become recognized and trusted within the local church. This isn't an inevitable progression. While everyone can receive and learn to exercise the gift of prophecy, relatively few develop a trusted ministry in this area. We often make space in our local church services, and at 24-7 Prayer gatherings too, for people to share what they sense God saying. Sometimes the most powerful contributions come from children, young people, or those who are very new to faith. But there are certain people who always have my particular trust. If I see them walking toward the front, I am highly likely to let them share. These are people I will also often approach when seeking the Lord for wisdom, asking them to be attentive to the Lord because I recognize their ministry in this area.

Holding a prophetic office: In Ephesians 4 as well as 1 Corinthians 12, the apostle Paul makes a list of the roles required at the heart of church leadership teams to "equip his people for works of service, so that the body of Christ may be built up" (Eph. 4:12). These are "the apostles, the prophets, the evangelists, the pastors and teachers" (v. 11). When people with a trusted ministry in any of these five areas step into a recognized leadership position within the church, carrying all the necessary responsibilities and accountabilities associated with such a position at either a local or translocal level, they may be considered to carry the "office" of prophet, evangelist, teacher, etc. One of the additional requirements incumbent upon a person carrying such an office is that they will use their position to "equip his people" so that the church "may be built up." In other words, as well as prophesying *to* people, they will prophesy *with* people, nurturing a prophetic culture, multiplying their gift by training others to hear God and to share it appropriately.

Rediscovering the Natural in the Supernatural

Isn't it interesting that Samuel mistook God's audible voice merely for that of the man next door? This is not what we expect God to sound like. Hearing him speak should surely be unmistakable and unmissable: a booming voice from the heavens, an angelic appearance at night, that sort of thing. But sometimes (actually, most of the time, in my experience) his voice is entirely mistakable for something or someone else. Most of the time we miss the voice of God not because it's too strange but because it's too familiar. He sounds like a song on the radio, a fleeting thought, the old man next door. The God of the universe is rarely weird. He is the very one who has predetermined and defined that which we consider "normal," so it would be ludicrous if he had to somehow banish himself from his own norms whenever he wanted to communicate with his own creation. He speaks in a familiar accent. He impregnates the natural with the supernatural and makes the mundane holy. Again and again he comes to us, as one mystic puts it, disguised as our own life.[10]

This was certainly the experience of the couple on the Emmaus road, who managed to walk for more than an hour in the company of the resurrected Jesus, even welcoming him into their home, without realizing that it was him! Perhaps this is why artists in many traditions have felt the need to add halos to their depictions of the Lord, worrying that we might fail to distinguish divinity from mere humanity when we see it.

*   *   *

It was a cold, wet Sunday in the weeks before Christmas, and I was expounding Philippians 2, challenging one of our congregations to live more humbly in the way of Jesus. At the end of my talk, I invited people to stand if they wanted to receive prayer. One of those who stood was Benjamin, dressed in civilian clothes, with nothing to indicate that he was a major in the British Army. And then, only a few moments later, I was surprised to see this athletic young officer, normally so positive and impressive, doubled up and weeping profusely. I made a beeline for him at the end of the meeting and asked if he was okay.

"More than okay!" he said, beaming and drying his eyes. "God has just spoken to me more clearly than ever before!" He stood, he said, because he felt the need to humble himself. He'd been working too hard and realized the danger of worshiping his career. He'd also been feeling frustrated at work—unrecognized by his superiors—and knew that he needed to trust God, not human beings, for military advancement. And when he stood, a stranger had sidled up to him with what he thought might be a word from God. The phrase he had in his head, he said rather apologetically, seemed random, and he honestly didn't know what on earth it might mean. Pausing, he cleared his throat and said three words: "Glasgow is irrelevant."

And that was the moment Benjamin broke down, weeping uncontrollably. Even as he recounted it to me, he started filling up again. I began to wonder if something terrible had happened to him in Scotland's most populous city. Perhaps there was a difficult relationship with someone up there?

Seeing my puzzlement, Benjamin started to explain. "Glasgow is shorthand," he said. "It's an expression we all use. Every soldier in the British Army knows what Glasgow means because it's where our Army Personnel Centre is based. Glasgow is where our pay comes from. It's where our deployments are determined. It's the administrative center for our entire careers."

Slowly, I began to nod.

"We'll often say, 'Glasgow has given me orders,' or, 'I need to talk to Glasgow.' That man may not have known what it meant, and I certainly don't know who he is, but God just spoke to me in army language. I was standing to humble myself, to relinquish control of my military career, to tell God that I would trust him for promotion at the right time. It wasn't easy. And a complete stranger—literally, someone I've never seen before—just told me three words that could not have been more apt: *Glasgow is irrelevant.* I must trust God more than the Army Personnel Centre!"

We looked around the room but couldn't see the covert prophet anywhere. To this day I wonder if he knows how powerfully God used him that day. Seeing that Benjamin was still churned up, I offered to pray for him, and, as I did so, I received a simple mental impression of a ladder missing a rung. Remembering that he'd decided to trust God for promotion, I suggested that perhaps there was a promotion coming that would "miss a rung": a double promotion. It was very simple—nothing dramatic—I couldn't be sure I hadn't crafted the image in my own imagination. But it passed the ABC filter, being *affirming*, *biblical* (based on the passage I'd been expounding that day), and it certainly seemed to be the sort of thing *Christ* would say and do.

A few days later, Benjamin was deployed to an American airbase in Western Iraq. On paper it was an easy deployment—no one had ever died from enemy attack at this particular base—but it was a tough time to be sent away, leaving his wife and young children just before Christmas. But thanks to the way God had spoken that Sunday, they parted with a sense of his presence and protection.

After a few weeks in Iraq, Benjamin caught the attention of his commanding officer and was promptly and unexpectedly promoted to Battle Group Chief of Staff, effectively his number two, and certainly a couple of rungs ahead of anything he might reasonably have hoped for at that stage in his career. The promotion had bypassed "Glasgow" because he was on tour in active service. Quietly, Benjamin remembered the words about Glasgow being irrelevant, and about the missing rung, and thanked God for this unexpected favor.

Then, on January 3, 2020, a US drone strike assassinated General Qasem Soleimani, one of the most senior commanders in the Islamic Revolutionary Guard, considered to be the right-hand man of Iran's supreme leader, Ali Khamenei. A week later Iran retaliated by launching a targeted rocket attack on the Camp Taji airbase north of Baghdad, where Benjamin was now the chief of staff. It was terrifying. Twenty-eight rounds landed in two minutes. There was a great deal of indirect fire. The compound was hit by multiple rockets. A medic was killed. A hundred and ten men were injured. They were sitting ducks. Everyone was on pins and needles. No one knew where the next missile might land.

And yet Benjamin felt completely calm. He found that he was able to bring peace and clarity, even arranging a funeral and sharing his faith, knowing for sure that he had been stationed here for this very moment of grave crisis and had been raised up to lead—not by Glasgow but by God himself.

Whoever it was that gave Benjamin those three words, I suspect he'd be very surprised indeed to discover how powerfully God honored his simple faith that day. A phrase must have entered his mind, notable only for its peculiarity, and it must have been tempting either to ignore it or to embellish it into something that sounded more spiritual. But by acting simply, quickly, and faithfully, he brought unquantifiable "strength, encouragement and comfort" to a humble soldier preparing himself to leave his family at Christmas, bound for a military compound in the desert of western Iraq.

When a thought, a phrase, or a picture comes into our heads, those seeking to grow in the prophetic will often wonder, "Is this just me, or is it God?" I'd be very surprised indeed if that man prophesying to Benjamin that day didn't ask himself this question. And at the point of such uncertainty, the ABC filter helps to eliminate impressions that probably aren't from the Lord. Having run that simple check, it's easy enough to ask the subsequent question: "What's the worst that could happen if I get this wrong?" I'm sure you'll agree that a few mistakes—an occasional moment of mild embarrassment such as mine at the Happy Eater in Dorking—are a small price to pay for anyone whose "earnest desire" is to grow in this wonderful, life-changing gift.

It's entirely possible—indeed, it's entirely probable—that God already speaks to you more than you realize. This is why you need ears to hear him and the Spirit's help in discerning his voice amid all the other noise of life. As Ken Helser said, "In *everything* God has a voice." Our task, therefore, is to keep asking in every situation, "Where are you at work here?" And, "What are you saying in this situation?" Our attentiveness to God's voice in this way, and our willingness to obey, can determine destinies, as Jonathan David Helser knows, and as Benjamin found out on that cold, wet Sunday just before Christmas.

Pause & Pray

Is it possible that God is already speaking to me through some-one familiar or some circumstance in my life right now?

How to Handle the Prophetic

I've talked in this chapter about how to speak God's *rhēma* word lov-ingly into the lives of others by paying attention to ordinary thoughts, words, and pictures using the ABC filter. But having considered these rudiments of *giving* prophetic words, we also need to think about the art of *receiving* prophetic words from others. The apostle Paul teaches very clearly that we must filter prophecies with discernment and discretion because they are invariably only partially right, or at least limited in their insight (1 Cor. 13:9). There are three keys to doing this well: *weigh it*, *wait on it*, and *walk in it*.

Weigh It

Paul says that prophetic words need to be weighed (1 Cor. 14:29). Don't accept them indiscriminately. Weigh them against the witness of Scripture and against the character of Christ. Elsewhere he warns, "Do not treat prophecies with contempt but test them all; hold on to what is good, reject every kind of evil" (1 Thess. 5:20–22). Prophecies will be a blend of "what is good" mixed with "every kind of evil." We must therefore exercise careful discernment, neither accepting nor rejecting them wholesale. Treating prophecies with respect means making the effort to prayerfully filter out the bad and hold on to the good.

Weighing prophecies also involves weighing the prophets them-selves! Ask yourself, "Do I trust them?" Jesus says, "Watch out for false prophets. They come to you in sheep's clothing, but inwardly they are ferocious wolves. By their fruit you will recognize them" (Matt. 7:15–16). A good life will bear good, sweet fruit. Some people will abuse the gift of prophecy with sinister motives. If you receive a prophetic word that seems particularly significant, or that troubles your common sense, or that is directional for your life, it's important to seek the discernment and counsel of a third party whom you trust.

Wait On It

A prophecy can often be the right word at the wrong time. Our tendency is always to assume that prophetic words apply imminently or immediately. But the Bible is full of examples of prophecies that took years or even generations to be fulfilled. It's often appropriate, therefore, to adopt a "wait and see" approach when you receive a word that doesn't have an obvious or immediate outworking. You might decide to keep such words on the back burner, neither doubting their veracity nor trying to force them to happen.

Many years ago, Sammy and I received a prophetic word about helping famous musicians and political leaders. Our hearts leaped with excitement, but at the time we didn't know any famous musicians or political leaders! Somehow that word, which seemed impossible when it was first given, is now coming to pass, but it has certainly spent many years on the back burner.

A respected American prophet once addressed a church in Lincoln, England, predicting a massive movement of the Holy Spirit on the city's university campus. Those listening were too polite to point out to the ill-informed American that there was not a university in town. But then, a few years later, much to everyone's surprise, a brand-new campus was indeed built in the city, whereupon the church revisited this word with excitement. The prophet had foreseen something after all, fresh faith was released, and today that church has a thriving ministry among students.

Walk in It

There's a story about an elderly man accosting a preacher at the end of a church meeting. "Many years ago, you prophesied that I would go to Africa, but," he said, shaking with indignation, "it's never happened!"

Quietly, the preacher replied, "Did you ever buy a ticket?"

Having weighed a word, if you sense it's right, both in content and timing, you need to get practical. Ask yourself, "Is there anything practical I need to do? How should I act in order to activate this thing the Lord seems to be saying?"

When Samuel finally realized that it was God speaking to him, his response was one of humble submission, saying, "Speak, for your servant is listening." Few things maintain and increase the flow of God's word like a willing spirit. Jesus says, "Blessed rather are those who hear the word of God *and obey it*" (Luke 11:28, italics mine).

Talk to people who hear God in extraordinary ways and you will invariably discover lives of extraordinary sacrifice. There's a sort of holy dance between God's word and our response. He speaks and we obey, and the more we obey, the more he seems to speak. When it comes to prophecy, our action often activates something more. Conversely, there are few things that stop the flow of divine revelation in our lives as effectively as a sense of entitlement and apathy. Sometimes God pauses from speaking simply because he is waiting for us to act on the things he has already revealed to us.

There's a story about this in 2 Kings 6. Elisha's company of prophets have outgrown their meeting place, so they've gone down to the river Jordan to fell trees for the construction of a bigger venue. One of them drops an iron axe-head in the water and cries out to Elisha in dismay. "Where did it fall?" the prophet asks. And "when he showed him the place, Elisha cut a stick and threw it there, and made the iron float. 'Lift it out,' he said. Then the man reached out his hand and took it" (vv. 6–7).

Loren Cunningham, the founder of Youth with a Mission (YWAM), teaches that when "the word of the Lord [is] rare," it's a good idea to return to the last thing God said to you, just as that prophet returned to the spot where he had dropped his axe.

Ask yourself, "Have I been faithful to the revelation God has already given me?" And ask the Lord if there's anything new he still wants to show you through this previous word. By being faithful to the last thing he said, you position yourself to receive your next assignment from God.[11]

*   *   *

I was leading the first meeting of the first Wildfires Festival when I recognized an old friend called Jono, whom I hadn't seen for many years. He'd just been receiving prayer, so I went over, said hi, and asked if he was okay. He told me that he hadn't been to any big Christian event for more than ten years, so this was a big, scary deal for him even to be there. He'd been knocked off his bike and suffered a serious brain injury, which had left him struggling with neurological pain and vertigo, and he'd been in a very dark place ever since. In fact, he'd been hesitant to come to the meeting, let alone to ask for prayer. But when he did, someone had shared with him a picture of a bike going down a hill, then suddenly everything had gone dark. It could hardly have been a more accurate description of his accident. Jono was blown away. He felt seen and known by God. Here he was at his first big meeting in years, daring to respond, and immediately God's amazing grace had been poured out through that single, simple word.

He agreed to share this story from the stage, and everyone whooped and applauded. I asked if the man who'd received this prophetic word was in the crowd, and a guy called Mike stepped shyly to the front. "So how on earth did you get such an accurate word of knowledge for a complete stranger?" I asked.

"Oh, um, it was just a picture that flashed into my head as I walked toward him, and it seemed so weird that I wondered if it might have come from God!"

"And how sure were you," I asked, "that it was prophetic?"

Mike paused, chuckled, and said, "About ten percent."

"You were only ten percent sure?" I checked. "There was a ninety percent chance it was wide of the mark?"

"I suppose so," said Mike, "but I figured there was nothing to lose if I was wrong."

I turned to Jono. "And how glad are you that Mike took that ten percent chance?"

"One hundred percent!" he beamed.

In this little encounter we see so many of the prophetic principles I've sought to outline in this chapter. First, Mike's motive was love. His prophecy—humbly and sensitively delivered—undoubtedly brought "strengthening, comfort and encouragement." Second, it was a *rhēma* word for Jono. Mike didn't just quote a Bible verse about light out of darkness; he spoke accurately into a very particular situation inspired by the Holy Spirit. Third, Jono had waited many years for this moment. It was "a word in season," but that season had taken a long time to come. For many years until that moment, "the word of the LORD was rare." Fourth, both Jono and Mike were obedient. It took courage for Jono to come to the festival and to respond at the end of the meeting to request prayer, but that was what primed him to receive such a remarkable encouragement. I don't think he'd have received it if he'd stayed at home or even just stayed at the back of the meeting. Finally, Mike took a 10 percent risk for which Jono is 100 percent grateful. He wasn't sure. He didn't have a particularly dramatic, unmistakable revelation from God—just a fleeting mental impression—and yet its impact could hardly have been more dramatic. He asked himself, "What's the worst that can happen if I get this wrong?" and the answer was, "Not very much." So he took a calculated risk.

I hope this chapter has inspired you to take a few more 10 percent risks in learning to prophesy, because if you do so, sooner or later someone somewhere will be 100 percent grateful for your diligence in listening and your willingness to speak God's word into their lives. The more you practice, embedded in community, the sharper your discernment and the stronger your prophetic muscles will grow.

Living Word: Heidi Baker— Hearing God through Prophecy

How do you choose just one life to feature as an illustration of the power of prophecy, when there are so many extraordinary examples throughout history? I was tempted to focus on one of the desert fathers in fifth-century Egypt and Syria, or on Joan of Arc in fifteenth-century France, or on C. H. Spurgeon in nineteenth-century America. I was also tempted to recount some of the remarkable prophecies of sixteenth-century Scottish Reformers such as John Knox and Samuel Rutherford because Presbyterianism today seems to have forgotten the remarkable role that the gift of prophecy played in the lives of its founding fathers.[12]

But in the end I decided to feature Heidi Baker because she is a contemporary woman (so far we've looked at two men and one woman, all from centuries past) and because her story dramatically demonstrates the life-changing power of prophecy today.

Heidi Baker is a glorious iconoclast. She is a Californian from Laguna Beach who moved with her husband Rolland to Mozambique when it was registered as the poorest nation on earth. She is a Pentecostal pastor who spends herself on behalf of the poor, and a doctor of systematic theology who has planted hundreds of churches and witnessed countless miracles along the way. The gifts of the Holy Spirit, and especially prophecy, continue to mark her extraordinary ministry.

Heidi became a follower of Jesus through a Navajo evangelist while living on a Native American reservation in Mississippi. Several months later "she was taken up in a vision for several hours and heard Jesus speak audibly, telling her to be a minister and a missionary to Asia, England and Africa."[13]

In obedience to this vision, Rolland and Heidi Baker founded Iris Global and moved first to Asia, then to England, and finally to Mozambique in 1995, where they began developing homes for orphans first at Chihango and later at Machava. There was fierce persecution of their work, and Heidi became seriously ill with double pneumonia and blood poisoning. Against the orders of two doctors, she flew thirty hours to a conference in Toronto in a state of complete exhaustion, carrying the burden of responsibility for more than three hundred children.

At the start of the event, God opened up Heidi's lungs and allowed her to breathe freely. Each day after that, in an environment of worship, teaching, and prayer, she felt her strength returning until she had an encounter with the Lord that continues to define her ministry to this day:

> One night I was groaning in intercession for the children of Mozambique. There were thousands coming toward me, and I was crying, "No, Lord. There are too many." Then I had a dramatic, clear vision of Jesus. I was with Him, and thousands and thousands of children surrounded us. I saw His shining face and his intense, burning eyes of love. I also saw his body. It was bruised and broken, and His side was pierced. He said, "Look into My eyes. You give them something to eat." Then he took a piece of His broken body and handed it to me. It became bread in my hands, and I began to give it to the children. It multiplied in my hands.
>
> Then again the Lord said, "Look into My eyes.

You give them something to drink." He gave me a cup of blood and water, which flowed from His side. I knew it was a cup of bitterness and joy. I drank it and then began to give it to the children to drink. The cup did not go dry. By this point I was crying uncontrollably. I was completely undone by His fiery eyes of love. I realized what it had cost Him to provide such spiritual and physical food for us all. The Lord spoke to my heart and said, "There will always be enough, because I died."[14]

Heidi returned to Mozambique from that extraordinary encounter supernaturally healed, reenergized and renewed in faith for God's commission and provision. Today, Iris ministries cares for 14,600 children in all ten regions of Mozambique. It treats more than 30,000 people per year in its clinics, builds houses, runs schools, drills wells, dispenses disaster relief, and plants literally hundreds of churches every year, especially among the Makua, a people group once listed by missiologists as "unreached and unreachable." Again and again, day by day, in multiple locations, Heidi and Rolland Baker continue to demonstrate that "there will always be enough."

Listening Exercise:
Growing in Prophecy

Prophets, though human, spoke from God as they were carried along by the Holy Spirit.
—2 Peter 1:21

Prophetic Exercises
Journaling Prophetic Words

We can honor and nurture the gift of prophecy in our lives by carefully recording the things we sense God telling us, whether they come through others or through our own personal times of prayer. I have a folder full of such prophetic words that I dig out whenever I'm seeking God's guidance or struggling to hear his voice. It's amazing how often a prophecy I've half-forgotten, or taken only half-seriously, suddenly comes alive and speaks directly into my situation months or even years after it was first received. Sometimes I look back on words that seemed to have missed the mark at the time they were given, only to discover that they've become more accurate than I could ever have originally anticipated. For example, I remember receiving a prophecy about being an entrepreneur at a time when I was focused on becoming a pastor. I didn't just disagree with this word—I hated it! (An entrepreneur was, in my mind, someone like Richard Branson or Elon Musk.) I didn't want to be rich, and I didn't feel called into business. I left that meeting thinking, "Wow, those guys could hardly have got that more wrong!" But I return to that word now and realize it's an excellent description of my gifting. For almost thirty years I've been pioneering, experimenting, starting things from scratch—churches, ministries, and, yes, even a couple of business ventures along the way. This kind of remembering and reevaluating of prophetic words is essential to obedience, but it is only possible if we are diligent in recording them at the time.

Prophetic Workshop (Groups)

This exercise is a great, simple, interactive way of helping people of all ages to listen to God and to share his words with others. Start by handing out photographs cut from newspapers and magazines to each member of your group (the pictures don't have to be religious in any way, and it's probably better if they aren't). With each person holding their picture, ask the Holy Spirit to speak. Having prayed, everyone should take time to study the image in their hand, asking the Lord to reveal his heart in some way through it. Some people will find this very easy, but others will struggle at first. Take your time. There's no hurry. If anyone wants to choose another picture, that's fine, so have some backups. Once everyone seems ready, remind them of the four positive guidelines listed in 1 Corinthians 14:3–4: prophecy should aim to strengthen, encourage, comfort, and edify. Then invite each person to share what they sensed God saying, whether it was for themselves or someone else in the circle. This simple exercise can be surprisingly effective in opening ears to listen to the Holy Spirit in the ordinary stuff of life and in boosting confidence to share words from God with other people.

Questions for Personal Reflection and Group Discussion

- Have I ever been hurt by someone claiming to be speaking on behalf of God?
- What is the last thing I'm sure God said to me? Is there anything I still need to do to respond?
- In what ways does God tend to speak to me most?
- Paul tells me to "eagerly desire gifts of the Spirit, especially prophecy" (1 Cor. 14:1). How hungry am I to hear God—and to speak God's words—in this way?

For Further Reflection

Graham Cooke, *Developing Your Prophetic Gifting* (Lancaster: Sovereign World, 1994).

Christine Westhoff, *ReFraming the Prophetic* (online Bible study), www.reframingtheprophetic.com.

Mark and Patti Virkler, *Dialogue with God: Opening the Door to Two-Way Prayer* (Newberry, FL: Bridge-Logos, 1986).

PART 2

GOD'S WHISPER:

VOX INTERNA

Caravaggio, *Supper at Emmaus*
incamerastock / Alamy Stock Photo

Were not our hearts burning within us?
—Luke 24:32

As we turn from *God's word* (his voice external) to *God's whisper* (his voice internal), we come to the heart of the problem that many millions of Christians have with hearing God, namely, their presumptions about what God sounds like and their expectations about how they think he should speak. His voice is relatively easy to hear when it comes to us loud and clear—through an encounter with Jesus (chapter 1), through the Bible (chapters 2 and 3), and through supernatural prophetic utterance (chapter 4). But it's easy to miss when it comes, as it mostly does, in a voice hushed to "a gentle whisper" (1 Kings 19:12).

5

Hearing God's Whisper

Jesus himself came up and walked along with them;
but they were kept from recognizing him.

—Luke 24:15–16

And after the fire came a gentle whisper.

—1 Kings 19:12

As we turn from *God's word* (his voice external) to *God's whisper* (his voice internal), we come to the heart of the problem that many millions of Christians have with hearing God, namely, their presumptions about what God sounds like and their expectations about how they think he should speak. His voice is relatively easy to hear when it comes to us loud and clear—through Jesus (chapter 1), through the Bible (chapters 2 and 3), and through supernatural prophetic utterance (chapter 4). But it's easy to mistake when it comes, as it frequently does, in a voice hushed to "a gentle whisper" (1 Kings 19:12).

And so in this chapter, at the start of this second section of the book, I want to show you from the Bible how subtle, how quiet, and how easy to miss the Creator of the universe has almost always been. My hope, if I can convince you, is that a thrilling new vista will open for you: the possibility—no, the probability—that God is speaking to you more than you realize and that you can truly converse with him at a level of intimacy you may never have previously imagined possible.

*   *   *

One of the greatest discoveries of my life—one that has quietly revolutionized my relationship with the Lord—is that the Creator of the universe whispers. I used to think that if God showed up in my life, he'd do it in style. There could be no doubt about it. He'd kick down the door in steel-toed boots, speak in a booming voice, use a little dry ice, tricks of the light, that sort of thing.

Perhaps you remember the story of Jesus walking on the water. "Shortly before dawn [Jesus] went out to them, walking on the lake" (Mark 6:48). Boom! This is precisely the kind of thing we expect God to do. Hail the CGI Jesus. Say hello to the Marvel movie Messiah. But then, when Jesus nears the boat, we are told the strangest thing: "He was about to pass by them."

What?

Having gone to all the effort of walking halfway across an inland sea on a stormy night, Jesus is "about to pass by"? Playing it cool. Feigning disinterest. Pretending he's got some place else to go, some other boat to visit. I imagine him giving the disciples (who are understandably *freaking out*) one of those little nonchalant waves. A casual "hi." The kind of absent-minded nod you reserve for acquaintances in the street when you don't want to stop and talk.

If this were just a one-off, it would be a fascinating, playful, quirky little footnote in the Gospels. But the thing is this: it's not a one-off at all. Jesus does similar things, plays similar games, on several occasions, which leads me to wonder if there's something here to learn about the character of God.

The encounter on the Emmaus road is another example. First Jesus conceals his identity, and then, "as they approached the village to which they were going, Jesus continued on as if he were going farther" (Luke 24:28). Here he is, playing exactly the same trick! Making out he's got somewhere else to be.

We can be fairly sure that, having risen from the dead, Jesus has all the time in the world. You might say that his schedule is wide open. And the couple with whom he's been walking still haven't realized his true identity because he hasn't revealed it yet. He's been stringing them along, hiding himself from them all this time. (How many others were there who met the resurrected Jesus but let him pass by, because they failed to invite him in?)

We see something similar described in the gospel of John when it says of Jesus, "Though the world was made through him, the world did not recognize him" (John 1:10). Isn't that extraordinary? And we see it again when "Jesus stood on the shore, but the disciples did not realize that it was Jesus. He called out to them, 'Friends, haven't you any fish?'" knowing full well that they'd had a fruitless and frustrating night (John 21:4–5).

There's something delightfully playful here. Something smiling and unassuming about the King of kings. A wry humor and a coy twinkle in his eye. But it's more than that. There's also a glimpse in all these stories of a set of qualities we never ever expected to find in the demeanor of God. Could it be that the Creator of the cosmos is meek and not pushy? Humble and not presumptuous? Unassuming and not intrusive? (Even the asking of these questions feels a bit like a kind of blasphemy, but how else are we to make sense of the evidence?) Jesus wears his charisma lightly. He seems perfectly content to walk away from the spotlight of human attention and adulation.

All this is so far from our experience of human power that we struggle to equate it with any kind of God. And yet it is simultaneously precisely our actual experience of God every day. Looking back on our lives, we can see pretty clearly where he was present, even if we hardly realized it at the time. Of course, we want him to be unmissable and unmistakable. We expect him to flash around his all-access pass, to kick down the door of our lives, but instead he waits for us to invite him into our boat or our house or our heart. In the words of Emily Dickinson, he "tells it slant."

Tell all the Truth but tell it slant—
Success in Circuit lies
Too bright for our infirm Delight
The Truth's superb surprise

As Lightning to the Children eased
With explanation kind
The Truth must dazzle gradually
Or every man be blind—[1]

You know this is true, and so do I: "The truth must dazzle gradually." Angels tend not to turn up in medical research labs to announce the cure for cancer. But God does quietly call, equip, and inspire medical researchers to make extraordinary discoveries. Evil people get away with murder, and for the most part the Lord does not intervene dramatically to stop them. But, gradually, justice prevails. Instead of turning up in your living room every Thursday at nine, God waits for you to make the effort to read a book like this.

Billions of people wake up each day precariously balanced on a rock traveling at 66,627 miles per hour around the sun in a galaxy that is itself moving at 1,342,160 miles per hour in relation to extragalactical frames of reference. Quietly these people make themselves coffee, stare out at the dawn breaking, the dew glistening and, for the most part, barely give the maker of so much mystery a second thought. Their three-pound brains churn through eleven million bits of information per second, and their ten-ounce hearts pump five liters of blood through 100,000 miles of tubing, and yet the great Giver of Life demands neither allegiance, acknowledgment, nor thanks. "The Lord is not slack . . . but is longsuffering toward us, not willing that any should perish' (2 Pet. 3:9 NKJV).

The one who walks on water to meet us appears perfectly prepared to walk on by when he finally reaches the boat. Resurrected from the dead, he goes incognito among the commuters heading home to Emmaus, walking the dusty road like everyone else, secretly hoping—but politely waiting—for an invitation to dinner.

The Abbreviated Word

These divine qualities of meekness and gentleness, so evident in Jesus, are laced through the whole of Scripture. Drawing on the Latin translation of Isaiah, the church fathers used to speak of the "abbreviated word," *verbum abbreviatum*, as if "the divine word trimmed itself to our capacities. It did not appear in overwhelming power and splendour but in accessible human form."[2]

This is the great epiphany of Elijah on Mount Horeb. Having conquered the prophets of Baal in the foothills of Mount Carmel with fire falling from heaven to consume his offering, and having prayed until rain fell to end three years of drought, Elijah is experiencing the kinds of miracles we tend to ask of God. But they haven't made any difference. Jezreel hasn't turned back to Yahweh. Ahab and Jezebel haven't repented. In fact, they have issued a death threat against Elijah, who is now fleeing for his life. God has played his strongest hand, and it simply hasn't worked. Elijah is understandably depressed. He had hoped to be a national hero, but instead he's hunted and scared. "I have had enough, LORD," he prays. "Take my life" (1 Kings 19:4). God is far too gracious to ask why he's bothered fleeing for his life if he's really so keen to die and instead tells him to "stand on the mountain . . . for the LORD is *about to pass by*" (1 Kings 19:11, italics mine). It's precisely the same phrase used centuries later of Jesus on the Sea of Galilee: "he was *about to pass by*."

Elijah must have climbed Mount Horeb with great expectations. He knew very well that this was where Moses had received the Ten Commandments. Stone tablets had been inscribed by the very finger of God amid howling winds, burning trees, and boulders split by lightning. And sure enough, these same signs do indeed break loose. We are told that "a great and powerful wind tore the mountains apart and shattered the rocks" (1 Kings 19:11) and that after that there was an earthquake, and finally there was a fire. These were exactly the kinds of phenomena Elijah had anticipated as hallmarks of God's presence, and yet after each one a very surprising thing is said: "The LORD was not in the wind. . . . The LORD was not in the earthquake. . . . The LORD was not in the fire" (vv.11–12).

Where, then, is God? The answer, of course, is that his presence is manifest in the dullness after the drama. The Great Elemental Force shows himself gentle and makes himself personal in "a still small voice" (1 Kings 19:12 KJV) or, as a more literal translation of the original Hebrew says, "the sound of gentle silence."

We expect the King of kings to shout with primal power in earthquake, wind, and fire. Of course we do! From the origins of time, God has been the Great Explanation of nature's many mysteries, the ultimate power that changes seasons, hurling thunderbolts and rumbling from the heavens in rolling thunder. Elijah knew very well, and so do we, that Yahweh is absolutely able to speak in dramatic ways; through miracles, calamities, and natural phenomena; through shaking rooms (Acts 4:31), blinding lights (Acts 9:3), and astounding prophetic revelations (Rev. 1:10). But perhaps the problem with such displays of power, and the reason God patently refrains from speaking in such ways most of the time, is that they belie the fundamental gentleness and intimacy of his heart. Dramatic revelations impress, for sure, but they can also intimidate, dominate, and alienate those on the receiving end. And so the "Potentate of time, Creator of the rolling spheres, ineffably sublime"[3] chooses to whisper in our ear way more often than he shouts from the skies.

This is important. If we are ever to feel fully safe and truly loved by the Lord of all the earth, we must eventually—like Elijah on Horeb and that couple on the Emmaus road—learn to listen for his voice in the anticlimax of life's nonevents.

> **Pause & Pray**
>
> Breathe through the heat of our desire thy coolness and thy balm;
> Let sense be dumb, let flesh retire;
> Speak through the earthquake, wind and fire,
> O still, small voice of calm.[4]

The couple with Jesus on the road to Emmaus were, we are told, "kept from recognizing him" (Luke 24:16). Isn't that an intriguing phrase? It's not just that Jesus was being coy and gentle, "telling it slant" so that they *didn't* recognize him—it's that they *couldn't* recognize him. Something was keeping them from seeing the very thing right before their eyes. Why would this be? What on earth is going on? It seems to me that there are three possible explanations, each one relevant to us as we seek to learn to discern God's whisper. They are distracted *physiologically*, *psychologically*, and *spiritually*.

Physiological Distraction

The first and most obvious explanation is *physiological*: Jesus simply looked significantly different after his resurrection, and so, as a result, the couple did not recognize him. This, as we have seen, is entirely consistent with descriptions of his altered resurrection appearances elsewhere. Sometimes we miss God's presence because he no longer appears to us, or speaks to us, in the familiar ways of yesterday. I've often noticed that God tends to speak differently to me in different seasons of life. Sometimes when I think God has gone silent, it's actually that he is speaking differently, in a new dialect more appropriate to the new landscape I am about to enter. If I remain locked in the past by tradition, nostalgia, or a stale imagination, I will almost certainly miss the new thing that the "Now God" is forever saying (Ex. 3:14; Isa. 42).

Psychological Distraction

The second explanation for the couple's inability to recognize Jesus is *psychological*. Quite understandably, they had no possible expectation of meeting a dead man walking on the Emmaus road. There is a well-documented psychological condition known as *inattentional blindness*, in which our brains can fail to perceive a thing right in front of us when it flat-out contradicts our prior assumptions and expectations.[5] Perhaps the couple on the Emmaus road experienced a form of inattentional blindness when the stranger drew alongside them as they walked.

This is particularly plausible if we accept the strong possibility that one of them had been at the foot of Christ's cross when he died and would therefore have been carrying deep trauma from all that she had recently seen. I say "she" because we're told in John's gospel of four women standing near Christ's cross: "his mother, his mother's sister, Mary the wife of Clopas, and Mary Magdalene" (19:25). Can it really be coincidence that a man with an almost identical name, Cleopas, is found walking away from Jerusalem two days later, discussing this very tragedy with an unnamed companion? Isn't it possible that we might have here a simple typo by one of the gospel writers? That these two companions on the road to Emmaus are in fact Mary and her husband Cleopas/Clopas? Not two men (as painters and preachers with their usual subconscious bias have traditionally depicted them) but a married couple heading home to Emmaus having shared the Passover with friends in Jerusalem, where they'd become distressingly embroiled in the tragedy of Christ's crucifixion? Nothing can be proven for certain, but theologians from Eusebius of Caesarea in the fourth century to Tom Wright in the twenty-first century have held that this is indeed Mary and Cleopas.[6] If they are right, it would also help explain another detail often overlooked in this story—the fact that the travelers host Jesus jointly, in the same house, upon arrival in Emmaus.

We know that the couple were "talking with each other about

everything that had happened" when Jesus joined them on the road (Luke 24:14). We can easily imagine the deep emotion of this conversation as Mary sought to process her personal trauma with her husband as they walked. What's more, Jesus might well have been seeking Mary out—just as he'd sought out Mary Magdalene earlier that day—in order to pay a pastoral visit to a woman who'd been traumatized by the violence of his death. (And if so, mightn't he also have visited the other two women—his mother and his aunt—earlier that day between Mary Magdalene at dawn and Mary the wife of Cleopas now at dusk?) These four women were the last loving faces he'd seen before death. How deeply he would have longed to comfort them from the cross, and now, at last, he can! At the first possible opportunity, on the first day of his resurrected life, Jesus makes a beeline to tell Mary Magdalene, and perhaps these other women too, that they can stop grieving, that he's okay, to bind up their broken hearts.

Whether or not we accept the Clopas/Cleopas theory, there is another factor here that might also have contributed to the "inattentional blindness" of this couple toward Jesus, and that is the significance of their destination. Emmaus may not be mentioned elsewhere in the Bible, but it was certainly a highly significant place in the history of Israel. It had been there in 167 BC that the warrior-priest Judas Maccabeus defeated the invading Hellenist army in a daring surprise attack that ultimately led to the liberation of Israel from the Seleucid Empire. Having won such a critical battle for independence at Emmaus, Judas Maccabeus went on up to the temple in Jerusalem, probably along the very road the couple were walking now, and there he destroyed its Greek idols and reestablished the worship of Yahweh. This was a moment of such seismic significance in the Jewish psyche that it is celebrated to this day around the world in the festival of Hannukah. Under the leadership of Judas Maccabeus, Israel finally repossessed its own promised land, reestablished its own legitimate priesthood, and went on to enjoy relative freedom for almost a century. And the turning point, the critical victory in this moment of national liberation, had taken place at . . . Emmaus.

Many Jews at the time of Jesus were hoping and praying for another messiah like Judas Maccabeus, and another victory like Emmaus, to liberate them once again, this time from the Romans. You can see this in the way that they welcomed Jesus just a few days earlier with the political chant "Hosanna" as he rode into Jerusalem like the Messiah predicted by Zechariah: "lowly and riding on a donkey" (9:9). And this latent longing for a military messiah in the mold of Judas Maccabeus did not go away after Jesus' death. Listen carefully to the language used by his own disciples in Acts 1:6: "Lord, are you at this time going to *restore the kingdom to Israel*?' (italics mine). Similarly, here on the road to Emmaus, bound for the very place of this famous victory, the couple frame their disappointment in Maccabean terms: "We had hoped that he was the one who was going *to redeem Israel*" (Luke 24:21, italics mine).

The death of Jesus had been a significant political disappointment for thousands of ordinary Jews, including this couple here on the road to Emmaus. We can perhaps pick up some small sense of the sheer intensity of their disappointment by remembering the denial, dismay, and self-doubt that can paralyze voters today when their idolized candidate loses in a presidential election. How much deeper such disappointment must have been for those living far from democratic power, under an oppressive pagan dictatorship like Rome.

Spiritual Distraction

We have seen that there were a number of powerful *physiological* and *psychological* reasons why the couple on the road to Emmaus might understandably have failed to recognize Jesus that day. But the phrase used by Luke here suggests that there was also something *spiritual* going on. When we read that the travelers "were *kept* from recognizing" Jesus (italics mine), the original Greek word translated as "kept" is *krateó*. This is a very forceful word, literally meaning that their eyes were overruled, taken into custody, or seized. There is absolutely no sense that the couple were merely being a bit unobservant or a bit dumb. Instead, God himself seems to have curtailed their ability to recognize the features of Jesus' face. Why on earth would he do this? Doesn't God want the whole world to know the good news—especially now that Jesus has risen from the grave?

In our addressing this important question, it's helpful to note the clear pace and shape of the story as a whole. Here at the start God blinds their eyes from recognizing Jesus, but then at the end we read that "their eyes were opened and they recognized him" (v. 31). Luke seems to be saying that we can't recognize Jesus by ourselves. We need the help of the Holy Spirit. Hearing God, then, is not just a technique that you perfect but a grace that you receive. The things taught in this book will only be useful if the Spirit of God takes them and causes your heart "to burn within." If information is to become revelation, and cognition about Christ is to become recognition of Christ, you will need something supernatural to take place so that the Lord gives you eyes to perceive, ears to receive, and a heart to believe what he is saying.

Pause & Pray

Lord, I acknowledge that I need your help to hear your voice. I can't do this on my own. Unless you open my eyes supernaturally, I will not see. Unless you open my ears by the power of your Spirit, I cannot hear. As I read this book, would you make my heart burn just as you did for that couple on the Emmaus road? Override my inattentional blindness, and open my eyes to perceive your presence in my life. Give me ears, and still my soul, to hear your whisper more and more.

Our own struggles with recognizing the voice of God tend to mirror those of Cleopas and his wife Mary (as I shall henceforth assume them to be). We too may be distracted psychologically, emotionally, intellectually, or spiritually from hearing the voice of God. And so it's reassuring to see how meticulously Jesus unpicks each one.

Shock and awe is not what traumatized or confused people require. Jesus knew that the couple needed to come with him on a theological and intellectual journey at least as long as the physical one from Jerusalem to Emmaus and that there were no shortcuts in this process of rethinking reality.

First, he asks questions and listens as Mary and Cleopas express their deep disappointment and process a little of their pain. In doing this, Jesus recognizes and begins to address the reality of their emotional and psychological wound.

Next, he takes considerable time to unpack the Scriptures. In doing this, Jesus addresses the theological misconceptions that are blinding them to the walking, talking miracle right before their eyes.

Upon reaching Emmaus, he steps into their home, their safe space, and shares with them a meal. Having addressed their emotional and intellectual distractions on the road, Jesus knows that they are now at last ready to have their eyes opened. And so at the meal table he reenacts the Last Supper. Mary and Cleopas may not have been in that Upper Room the previous Thursday, but they would surely have heard about it from those who were. And then, when Jesus lifts his hands to bless the bread and the cup, all remaining doubt is dispelled as the scars on his wrists become visible.

At last, they understand. The veil finally parts. Their minds have been opened intellectually, their hearts have been comforted relationally, and now their eyes are opened spiritually.

It has taken Jesus several hours to get to this point, carefully, systematically addressing the various factors contributing to the couple's inattentional blindness. And if it takes this long for Mary and Cleopas to perceive Jesus when he is physically present, fully visible, right there by their side, we shouldn't be surprised if it takes us a while to see and hear Jesus by our side.

It's notable that children find it relatively easy to hear God. But then we grow up and steadily accumulate layers of doubt, self-deception, disillusionment, and disappointment. Slowly but surely the material world loses its inherent magic, life is demystified, and our senses become desensitized to the whisper of God.

I suspect that you are reading this now because Jesus has been whispering to your soul. Perhaps he has drawn alongside you in some unexpected way as he did for Mary and Cleopas. There may have been conversations he seemed to join, questions he asked that unsettled you, things that happened which confused and hurt you, moments when the Bible came to life and ignited something unexpected in your heart. He may have been knocking at the door for a little while, and in picking up this book you are inviting him into your life in a new and quite vulnerable way. Perhaps there have been moments when you became aware of his presence in your home and at your table. In whatever way the Lord has been whispering to your soul, don't be surprised if he takes his time and tells it slant, removing the veils of misunderstanding and unbelief you never knew you had, slowly dismantling your intellectual, psychological, and emotional resistance to the Word that whispers love.

> Who is the third who walks always beside you?
> When I count, there are only you and I together
> But when I look ahead up the white road
> There is always another one walking beside you.[7]
>
> —T. S. Eliot

Living Word: Nicolas Herman (1614–1691)— Hearing God's Still, Small Voice

There is not in the world a kind of life more sweet and delightful, than that of a continual conversation with God.
—Brother Lawrence

Nearly four hundred years ago, a teenage soldier was staring at a leafless tree in the middle of a battlefield when God spoke to him. Suddenly, unexpectedly, Nicolas Herman received an overwhelming assurance that the One who brings trees to bloom in spring could also be trusted to make his barren and rather unpromising life beautiful and fruitful in season.

Five years later, a serious injury forced him out of the army and into a new job as a footman, but it was work to which Nicolas was singularly unsuited. Still walking with a limp from his war wound, he was—in his own words—"a great awkward fellow who broke everything."[8]

By the age of twenty-one, Nicolas already had two professions behind him. His career in the military was over, and he had failed horribly in service as a footman. What did God want him to do with the rest of his life? How was that tree ever to become fruitful now? When would the seasons finally change? Feeling drawn to a deeper life, partly by that vision of the tree, Nicolas approached a priory in Paris, where he was given work serving up, clearing up, and washing up in the kitchen for its friars. But the long hours on his wounded leg caused great pain, and he was eventually transferred to the workshop so that he could sit down to make and repair sandals.

The priory boasted a magnificent chapel with the first (and, at that time, the only) domed roof in all of Paris. But

Nicolas was never "promoted" from the workshop to the chapel with its rarefied priestly duties. Instead, for more than fifty years, he simply, humbly continued fixing shoes, diligently learning to discern God's whisper in the ordinary stuff of life, turning his workshop into a sacred place of prayer.

And this is how Nicolas became fruitful beyond anything he could ever have imagined as a dejected sixteen-year-old soldier staring at that tree. Visitors to the monastery began to seek the counsel of its cobbler, making a beeline for its humble workshop rather than its grand chapel. And countless people to this day continue to thank God for the life of Brother Lawrence, as he became much better known. By training himself to "practise the presence of God" in the ordinariness of life, amid its many disappointments and distractions, he gained insights that have helped millions to develop a more conversational and joyful relationship with the Lord. "There is not in the world a kind of life more sweet and delightful," he said, "than that of a continual conversation with God."[9]

This, then, is the invitation extended to each one of us: to follow in the footsteps of Brother Lawrence and thousands like him, discovering the "sweet and delightful" reality of a continual, conversational relationship with the Lord Jesus Christ, discerning his whispers amid the ordinariness, the busyness, and even the setbacks of our mundane lives.

> I have ceased all forms of devotion and set prayers except those to which my state requires. I make it my priority to persevere in his holy presence, wherein I maintain a simple attention and a fond regard for God, which I may call an actual presence of God. Or, to put it another way, it is an habitual, silent, and private conversation of the soul with God. This gives me much joy and contentment.[10]

Listening Exercise:
Hearing God's Whisper through Silence, Solitude, and Sabbath

The friend of silence draws near to God.
—John Climacus (579–649)

In this chapter we've explored the whisper of God and the misguided assumptions we tend to make about how he prefers to speak. Just as Elijah stood alone on Mount Carmel to hear God's still, small voice, and as Jesus rose early to talk quietly with his Father, and as the early desert fathers and mothers entered the wilderness to pray, so we are invited into the unfamiliar terrain of silence and solitude in order to learn to discern God's whisper.

Exercising Silence and Solitude

> *Solitude is the place of the great struggle and the great encounter—the struggle against the compulsions of the false self, and the encounter with the loving God who offers himself as the substance of the new self.*
> —Henri Nouwen

Cultivating Silence

Just as a lake that is still can reflect the light, and as a room that is silent can amplify a whisper, so a soul that is quiet can hear the voice of God. At a time of perpetual distraction, busyness, and noise, it can seem almost impossible to nurture silence and solitude, especially if we live with children or in an urban context. In his classic work *The Celebration of Discipline*, Richard Foster advises us to make the most of all the "little solitudes" that punctuate our days.[11] It's surprising how many of these *selah* moments there actually are—early morning or late at night, driving in the car or sitting alone on a crowded train, in the bathroom or walking between meetings—and how carelessly and comprehensively we fill these moments with digital distraction.

We aspire to be more centered and less scattered, more peaceful and present, less reactionary and more attentive to the whisper of God. By honoring the "little solitudes" of each day with our undivided attention, refusing to reach for our phones the moment we find ourselves alone, we can easily turn these in-between times into oases of stillness before God. And, collectively, these little moments probably add up to at least an hour of your day!

Once you've trained yourself to do this (and it can be much harder than you think—a sort of existential panic can kick in the moment you find yourself alone), you may like to begin to expand these micromoments. Drive the long way home, take a bath instead of a shower, get up a few minutes earlier, choose to walk to the meeting, pause at the end of a meal, wander into an art gallery, take yourself for coffee with nothing but a book, try reading poetry instead of prose, switch off the music when your partner leaves the house. The cumulative effect of relishing these minutes will be a greater inner stillness that emanates into the rest of your day, a deeper awareness of God's presence, and a refined sensitivity toward his voice.

Taking a Silent Retreat

A twenty-four-hour silent retreat may seem intimidating, especially if you're an extrovert, but it won't be long before your little daily solitudes are not enough and you long for more!

Silent retreats require planning (especially if you're going to attempt one at home). Generally, it's best to get away to a place where you can be undisturbed. Personally, I find it helpful to bookend my retreats with some direction at the start in the form of a conversation to set expectations, with a friend or spiritual guide, and a debrief at the end.

During my retreat I tend to plan a very light structure incorporating six elements: exercise, sleep, meals, reading, journaling, and prayer. If I am in a monastic setting, I will attend some (but probably not all) of the seven daily offices, and if mealtimes are not silent (as they often are), I will make arrangements to take my meals in my room. In planning my schedule, I am careful to go easy on myself. My personal tendency is to place unrealistic expectations on myself and to become overly idealistic about the potential of my retreat. The fact is that I am not going to read more than one book, and I might not even read more than one chapter. And it's okay to take a siesta—even an involuntary one while trying to pray. And I certainly don't need to return from retreat with any great new epiphany.

Practicing Sabbath

Perhaps the most important spiritual discipline for cultivating the silence necessary for hearing God is a weekly day off. Let me say that again: if you are struggling to hear God, it may be because you are neglecting the Sabbath. I am ashamed to confess that for many years I failed to honor God in this way. In fact, I probably felt quite proud of the hours I worked leading a church, and a movement, and responding to constant needs. I have had to repent. Norman Wirzba writes, "The extent and depth of our Sabbath commitment is the measure of how far we have progressed in our discipleship and friendship with God."[12]

Whatever day you make your Sabbath, make it joyful, slow, analogue, and nonnegotiable. If you are married and have kids, build this delightful discipline into the heart of your family life together.

There is so much good material written about this important subject that I would simply encourage you to start by reading either Abraham Heschel's classic *The Sabbath* or John Mark Comer's *The Ruthless Elimination of Hurry*.

Questions for Personal Reflection and Group Discussion

- What "little solitudes" do I have in my day, and how do I currently tend to use them?
- What emotions do I experience when imagining being alone and silent without a phone for a prolonged period of time?
- Recognizing that it's possible to be outwardly silent and still but inwardly noisy and chaotic, what do I allow to distract my thinking and disturb my own inner peace?

For Further Reflection

Henri J. M. Nouwen, *The Way of the Heart: The Spirituality of the Desert Fathers and Mothers* (New York: Ballantine, 1981).

John Mark Comer, *The Ruthless Elimination of Hurry* (London: Hodder & Stoughton, 2019).

One of the main ways God communicates in the Bible—and in which he continues to speak today—is through the subconscious realm of intuition. In this chapter I offer guidelines for those seeking to hear God in dreams and underline the importance of honoring the conscience, which is an essential yet fallible mouthpiece for the Holy Spirit. I also explore the Ignatian prayer of examen, which can be such a powerful tool for connecting with our own inner worlds.

6

Hearing God's Whisper in Dreams and the Unconscious

They recognized him, and he disappeared from their sight.

—Luke 24:31

If we believe the Bible we must accept the fact that, in the old days, God and his angels came to men in their sleep and made themselves known in dreams.

—Abraham Lincoln

No one could possibly have been more surprised than Sean the first time he encountered Jesus. It was the start of the pandemic, during the first national lockdown in the UK, and he'd fallen asleep in bed as usual. But that night, in a dream, Sean experienced a completely unexpected, totally life-changing encounter with Jesus Christ, which he's given me permission to share.

Sean would be the first to admit that he didn't know much about the Bible and certainly didn't go anywhere near a church if he could help it. But in his dream he saw a brilliant light emanating from a chair at a table and a man he recognized as Jesus walking up a stone staircase toward him. Jesus approached Sean, placed a hand on his shoulder, and simply said, "I've got you." Feeling that touch and hearing these words, Sean experienced an overwhelming sense of God's power.

"Every single cell in my body exploded with love, pure love," he told me. "It was better than any drug I've ever done. Like having goosebumps all over my body, inside and out." And when he awoke, Sean felt completely different. The power of his addiction to pornography had been broken, and so had his desire to swear. Even his long-standing, deep-rooted fear of death had lost its terror.

Prior to this moment, Sean had been seriously considering a significant change in career, and now, inspired by this extraordinary dream, he decided to try asking for a little divine guidance. By trade he is a tiler, but he'd developed arthritis in his right knee that made kneeling excruciatingly painful. An opportunity had come along to open a shop, and he was seriously considering it as an alternative career. But he'd also been offered knee replacement surgery and knew it wasn't a good time to launch a business.

The day after Sean prayed this prayer, he was busy tiling a bathroom, lost in his own thoughts without the radio on, when he heard a word being repeated again and again: "Corinthians." "I didn't know what it meant. Definitely didn't know it was in the Bible," he laughs. "So I just scribbled it up on the wall of the bathroom where I was about to tile so I wouldn't forget it. And then I heard something else: "Seven." The number seven, so I wrote that up too. Finally, I heard "Twenty-six."

As soon as he got home, Sean recounted this strange experience to his wife, and she said she thought it might be something to do with the Bible. You can imagine his surprise when he discovered that it was indeed book, chapter, and verse. Barely breathing, he looked up 1 Corinthians 7:26 and laughed out loud at what he found. His prayer the previous day had been about remaining as a tiler versus branching out in business during the pandemic, and these are the words he now read: "Because of the present crisis, I think that it is good for a man to remain as he is."

Fluke

There are 31,102 verses in the Bible, and I doubt there is another one that could have spoken so precisely into Sean's predicament that day.

If he had merely opened a Bible at random and picked out the first verse he saw, there is an infinitesimally small likelihood—a 0.0032 percent chance—that it would have been this one. But, of course, the chances are even smaller than that because he didn't go to the Bible at all. Sean heard a voice repeating a sequence that he didn't even know was in the Bible!

Sean himself is in no doubt whatsoever. "It was as though God was speaking directly to me, answering my exact question using the Bible. The 'present crisis' was obvious—the pandemic was still raging all around—and God was speaking loud and clear, telling me to remain working as a tiler for now. So I turned down the shop opportunity, stayed tiling, and booked myself for knee surgery as soon as possible."

I'm sure some people would say that Sean's experiences were a series of psychological tricks and random flukes. But personally, I find it easier to accept that there is a God who still speaks today through dreams. In Bible times, dreams were one of the most consistent and powerful ways in which God communicated. This is particularly worth noting because they are perhaps one of the least respected and least practiced ways of listening to God in the West today.

In his book *Dreams and Healing*, priest and Jungian psychotherapist John Sanford mourns the damage done to our understanding of dreams by the Western church's absorption of rationalistic materialism.

> Every major figure of the early Christian Church through the time of St. Augustine cites dreams as an important way in which God spoke to mankind, and many of the Fathers of the Church wrote psychological treatises on dreams. . . . The church, as it became increasingly institutionalized, devalued and denied the reality of the individual soul and its dreams in favor of collectivized creeds, rituals and traditions [even though this] went against the views of the Bible and early Christianity.[1]

An old school friend of mine married a woman from Lahore, Pakistan. She arrived in England for their wedding day having never left her home city, let alone her own country. It was to be quite a culture shock! Early in their marriage, Andy and Farah were watching the news one night on television when there was a report of a terror attack on the exact part of Lahore in which Farah's family lived. Andy asked if she was okay—if she wanted to call her folks—but she just shrugged and said, "It's only the news!"

But a few days later, Farah received a vivid dream of a similar attack taking place in her home city and became quite distraught, remaining worried until eventually she could establish that her family was fine. The dream had undoubtedly carried more weight for Farah than the television news because her primary paradigm is religious rather than rationalistic. Farah is a bright woman, a qualified lawyer, but the culture in which she grew up is much closer to the biblical mindset—and indeed the paradigm of most people who have ever lived—than our own secular materialism.

I'm not suggesting that we should kiss our brains goodbye and ignore the empirical evidence of science, but rather that we should, as people of faith, also be open to other, less materialistic, more mysterious ways of processing reality.

When the Philistine king Abimelek took Abraham's beautiful wife Sarah as his own (not realizing who she was), God warned him in a dream to repent. And the fascinating thing about this is how seriously he took that dream. He didn't question it for a second, but immediately sent for Abraham and returned Sarah to her husband (Gen. 20).

God's Language in the Bible

In the Bible, dreams and visions are—for the most part—viewed interchangeably: visions being "waking dreams" and dreams being "visions of the night." As the book of Job observes:

> God may speak in one way, or in another,
> Yet man does not perceive it.
> In a dream, in a vision of the night,
> When deep sleep falls upon men,
> While slumbering on their beds,
> Then He opens the ears of men. (Job 33:14–16 NKJV)

Since dreams and visions are so similar, and the principles by which they may be interpreted are, for the most part, transferrable, I'm going to focus principally on hearing God through dreams in this chapter, having addressed other types of vision elsewhere in this book (for example, in chapter 4).[2]

The fact is that almost every major character in the Bible received highly significant dreams or visions from God. Some were symbolic, others were warnings, and many were a means of specific guidance. And this was not just an occasional phenomenon for the mystically inclined but one of the *main* ways God chose to speak to his people. Prophets in the Old Testament were often called "seers" for this very reason because, as the Lord says, "I . . . reveal myself to them in visions, I speak to them in dreams" (Num. 12:6). Conversely, the absence of dreams and visions in the land was considered a sign of divine judgment (see 1 Sam. 3:1; 28:6; Lam. 2:9; Mic. 3:6–7).

The patriarch Jacob famously received his calling one night when he dreamed of angels ascending and descending a stairway to heaven in a place he named Bethel (Gen. 28:12). Later he received instructions in another dream to return home to his father-in-law Laban, who was himself advised in a dream how to respond to Jacob's return (Gen. 31:10, 24).

In the next generation, Jacob's son Joseph received a series of prophetic dreams as a boy, which he handled badly (Gen. 37). As an adult, having learned from his mistakes, Joseph became a skilled interpreter of dreams in Pharaoh's courts, even shaping national strategy through the revelations he received through dream interpretation (Gen. 40–41).

Gideon's unlikely victory over the Midianites was foreshadowed by a dream (Judg. 7). King Solomon encountered God in a dream and asked for wisdom (1 Kings 3). Isaiah was given his calling by God in a dramatic visionary experience (Isa. 6). The prophet Daniel received and interpreted dreams throughout his long and spectacularly influential life in Babylon (2:28; 4:5–27; 7:1–28; 10, for example). The prophet Joel predicted that the primary mark of the outpouring of the Holy Spirit in the last days would be a release of dreams and visions among young and old alike (Joel 2:28–29). This was, of course, the passage picked up and quoted by the apostle Peter on the day of Pentecost (Acts 2).

The primary mark of the outpouring of the Spirit on all flesh in these last days, according to Joel, cited by Peter, is not speaking in tongues, shaking, or falling to the ground. It is an increase in dreams and visions. If you are filled with the Spirit, you should therefore expect God to speak to you in this way.

And so, of course, when we step into the New Testament, dreams continue, and even increase. Read carefully and you'll see that the familiar narrative of Jesus' birth, which we celebrate at Christmas, is in fact the story of a remarkable series of dreams. It was in a dream that Joseph received reassurance to marry Mary and instruction to name the baby Jesus (Matt. 1:20–21). It was in a dream that the wise men from the east were warned to avoid King Herod on their journey home (Matt. 2:12). It was in a dream that Joseph was urged to flee with his fledgling family to Egypt (Matt. 2:13) and in another dream that he was told when to return (Matt. 2:19).

And then, at the other end of Jesus' life on earth, at the time of his trial, Pilate's wife was so distressed by a dream that she warned her husband to have nothing to do with Jesus (Matt. 27:19). This is particularly interesting because, if we accept that it was God's plan for Jesus to die, her dream could not have been a divine directive.

Instead, Pilate's wife must have been sensing in her dreams something of the profound atmospheric turmoil surrounding Christ's suffering (more on this later).

After Jesus' resurrection, a series of carefully choreographed dreams and visions contribute to many of the gospel's greatest advances. In Acts 9, Saul is converted through a vision that blinds him, and Ananias is sent by a vision to heal and commission him (vv. 10–11). In the following chapter, Acts 10, an angel appears in a dream to the Roman centurion Cornelius, directing him to send for the apostle Peter (even supplying his address). It is a vision that commissions Peter to reciprocate, resulting in the gospel leaping beyond Judaism into the gentile world. In Acts 16, the apostle Paul (as Saul is renamed) receives a dream of a man, who may have been an angel, redirecting his apostolic mission into Macedonia (v. 9), and then in Acts 18 he receives another dream in which God encourages him to continue preaching in Corinth (vv. 9–11).

Angels: God's Messengers

> *Believers, look up—take courage.*
> *The angels are nearer than you think!*
> —Billy Graham

A fascinating feature in this list of biblical dreams is the frequency with which angels appear and speak. The word *angel* literally means "emissary" or "messenger," and they have certainly been an important way in which God has spoken to humanity for thousands of years, from the angel who told Hagar she would become pregnant in Genesis 16, to the angel who told Mary she would become pregnant in Luke 1. In fact, there are fifty-one references to angels in the Gospels alone, and they play a vital role in Jesus' birth (Matt. 1:20, 24), death (Luke 22:43), and resurrection (Matt. 28:2, 5). Respected author Dallas Willard observes, "It is certainly appropriate to describe the Bible itself as a book full of angels, from Genesis 16:7 onward."[3]

I believe that angels are still active today, serving as messengers of God, bringing his word to ordinary people. Some 70 percent of Americans today believe in angels, and many even claim to have been helped personally in some way by one.[4] In the early days of the 24-7 Prayer movement, we experienced at least two angelic visitations in the first prayer room. These encounters, described in my book *Red Moon Rising*, undoubtedly fueled faith (along with some healthy fear) at a critical time when we were launching out in prayer and giving birth to a worldwide movement.[5]

We shouldn't be surprised by this kind of thing. Jesus taught that angels would continue to have a prominent role at the end of the age (Matt. 13:39–43; 24:31; 25:31). So did the apostle Paul (2 Thess. 1:7). And the very last book in the Bible mentions angels no fewer than eighty times! As those seeking to hear from God, we should certainly keep our homes, our hearts, and our eyes open for angelic visitors, for "some people have shown hospitality to angels without knowing it" (Heb. 13:2).

Some Kind of Miracle

Ben Carson, the pioneering African American neurosurgeon and former presidential candidate, grew up as a "ghetto kid" in a broken family in a series of poor, crime-ridden neighborhoods, but his dream was to become a psychiatrist or a doctor. By sheer determination he made it to pre-med school at the prestigious Yale University, but, finding himself surrounded by the brightest and the best, he was riddled with insecurity and found himself struggling academically, especially with chemistry. As the end of his first semester approached, Carson knew that he was very likely to fail this class, and that would effectively end his dream of pursuing medicine.

The day before the exam, in sheer desperation and terror, he tried praying. "My mind reached toward God—a desperate yearning, begging, clinging to Him. 'Either help me understand what kind of work I ought to do, or else perform some kind of miracle and help me to pass this exam.'"[6]

Having prayed, Carson returned to his revision, furiously scribbling formulas on scraps of paper and trying to memorize information he still didn't understand. Finally, at midnight, "I flopped into my bed and whispered in the darkness, 'God, I'm sorry. Please forgive me for failing You and for failing myself.' Then I slept."[7]

And then came the dream that changed his life:

> While I slept I had a strange dream, and, when I awakened in the morning, it remained as vivid as if it had actually happened. In the dream I was sitting in the chemistry lecture hall, the only person there. The door opened, and a nebulous figure walked into the room, stopped at the board, and started working out chemistry problems. I took notes of everything he wrote.[8]

Remembering his dream the following morning, Carson concluded that his mind must have been so busy with chemistry at bedtime that he'd simply continued working out problems in his sleep. But (and this is important), he took it seriously enough to write down as much of the dream as he could remember, including the problems he'd seen on the board. A little while later he set off nervously to join six hundred other students in the exam hall for their all-important chemistry paper.

> Heart pounding, I opened the booklet and read the first problem. In that instant, I could almost hear the discordant melody that played on TV with *The Twilight Zone*. In fact, I felt I had entered that never-never land. Hurriedly, I skimmed through the booklet, laughing silently, confirming what I suddenly knew. The exam problems were identical to those written by the shadowy dream figure in my sleep.[9]

Ben Carson found that he was able to answer most of the questions by transcribing from memory the writing he'd seen on the board in his dream the night before. It was an extraordinary experience. Eventually he got up and left the hall in a daze, trying to process what had just happened and whether the things he'd written down had made any sense at all.

The answer came through soon enough. Ben Carson had passed his pre-med chemistry exam with a score of ninety-seven. It was to be a turning point in his life, not just academically but also psychologically. From that moment onward he had a new sense of destiny. His insecurity was gone. There was no longer any doubt in his mind that God "had special things for me to do."[10]

By the age of thirty-three, Ben Carson was the youngest chief of pediatric neurosurgery in the United States. At the age of fifty he was named by *Time* magazine as one of America's twenty foremost physicians and scientists. In 2008 he was bestowed the Presidential Medal of Freedom, the highest civilian award in the United States. In 2016 he ran for president, ceding eventually to Donald Trump. And the key moment in this meteoric rise was a dream so baffling that it can really only be explained in one of two ways: either we must conclude that Ben Carson made the whole thing up—that one of the most distinguished and respected men in America has in fact been lying for years, consistently and unnecessarily, regarding a very minor detail from his freshman exams. Or we must conclude that God did indeed step in to answer his prayers at the critical moment in his life, setting him on course for an extraordinary career of exemplary public service.

"I'd never had a dream like that before," reflects Carson in his memoir:

> Neither had anyone I'd ever known. And that experience contradicted everything I'd read about dreams in my psychological studies.
>
> The only explanation just blew me away. The one answer was humbling in its simplicity. For whatever reason, the God of the universe, the God who holds galaxies in His hands, had seen

a reason to reach down to a campus room on Planet Earth and send a dream to a discouraged ghetto kid who wanted to become a doctor.[11]

Practical Keys for Dreamers

I hope that the dream stories I've shared so far—from Ben Carson in America, Sean the tiler in England, Asrin in Iran (chapter 1), and many of the most respected characters in the Bible—are provoking you to take dreams far more seriously as a way of hearing God. But if, like me, you rarely remember your dreams, and when you do they generally seem to be meaningless (or, at least, thinly veiled manifestations of anxiety, fear, or lust), you may well be wondering how on earth it's possible to grow in such a subjective realm of divine revelation.

Let me propose three useful practices for anyone wanting to hear from God in dreams: *asking for* dreams, *honoring* dreams, and *interpreting* dreams.

Asking for Dreams

The first and most obvious thing to say is that dreaming is not a gift you can conjure up or force. You should certainly ask for it, but because it's a gift, you have no automatic right to insist on God speaking to you in this way. Some of my friends are prolific dreamers, but many are not. Personally, I'm far more familiar with visions by day than dreams by night, and that's okay. I suspect it's just the way I'm wired. I'm comforted by the observation that there's no biblical record of King David, or indeed of Jesus, hearing from God in a dream. So please don't feel pressured to dream! Hearing God in this way should always be considered an exciting possibility rather than an onerous necessity—a *could*, not a *should*.

However, I would certainly encourage you to ask the Lord to speak to you through dreams before you go to sleep at night, especially when you are in particular need of his guidance. Researchers note that when people go to sleep carrying an urgent question or concern in their minds, they are more likely to dream about it during the night as their brains process the events of the previous day. What's more, studies of cognitive function during sleep have shown that dream recall increases during times of personal crisis, so there may well be seasons of life—perhaps during times of transition—when it can be particularly important and effective to ask for dreams. It's noticeable in the stories I've shared so far that Asrin in Iran, Sean the tiler, and Ben Carson all received their remarkable dreams at moments of personal crisis. This isn't their normal daily experience!

When I turn out my bedside light at night, as my head sinks into the pillow, I often whisper a simple prayer: "Thank you, Father, for this day. Fill my dreams and speak as I sleep." When I wake the next morning, I may or may not be able to recall my dreams, but I certainly don't worry if I can't. I trust that God answered my prayer in whatever way he saw fit, and I know that my posture toward him has remained open through the night, even in my sleep.

Pause & Pray

The apostle Paul gives the church in Ephesus a glimpse into his private prayers for them. First, he asks God to give them "the Spirit of wisdom and revelation," and second, "that the eyes of [their] heart may be enlightened" (Eph. 1:17–18). More than anything else, this is what we need today. Not just eyes in our heads to see the material realm but also eyes in our hearts to see the spiritual realities all around. I pause now to ask the Holy Spirit to enlighten the eyes of my heart, that I may become far more aware of the spiritual realm all around.

Honoring Dreams

Daniel . . . wrote down the substance of his dream.
—Daniel 7:1

Scientific tests using electroencephalographic readings of brain activity indicate that most people dream vividly for at least ninety minutes in every eight hours of sleep. If a subject is awoken during rapid eye movement (REM) sleep, they can almost always recall a dream that they were having at that time. (This is not the case in other states of sleep.) What this shows is that everyone dreams—even those of us who can't generally remember our dreams. Your unconscious mind remains active while your body sleeps. That's why you will often wake up with a particular song on your mind or with unexpected feelings such as annoyance or joy in your heart. The Bible says that it's even possible to carry on a conversation with God in your sleep, as did Solomon (1 Kings 3) and Daniel (Dan. 7).

One of the ways you can "honor your dreams," if you've been asking the Lord to speak to you in this way, is simply to keep a notepad or some other means of recording your dreams by your bed. If you wake in the night from a dream, take it seriously. If it seems significant in any way, write it down. If you don't, you are highly unlikely to remember it the next morning. And if you ask God to speak in this way but consistently forget everything he tells you, don't be surprised if he stops giving you dreams!

Occasionally you will be quite surprised by what you find on your phone or on the notepad by your bed the next morning! During the hours of deep sleep, when your normal filters are removed and your usual busyness stops, God often speaks in quite remarkable ways, as we have seen. The mother of the church father Augustine prayed many years for the salvation of her wayward son with the passion only a parent can know. One night she received a dream in which she saw him worshiping by her side in heaven. This was all the assurance she needed to keep believing and praying until eventually he surrendered his life to Christ.

The dreams we recorded in the night may well provide insights into the spiritual realm that call us to persevere in prayer. But at other times, dreams that felt utterly profound in the darkness will seem ridiculous by the light of day. Beware of dismissing such things too quickly, however. I'm sure that Pharaoh could easily have dismissed his bizarre dream about skinny cows eating fat ones, but by taking it seriously, he discovered the very word of God for his nation.

Interpreting Dreams

> *I, Daniel, was watching the vision and trying to understand it.*
> —Daniel 8:15

The art of dream interpretation often involves making sense of the imagery with which the unconscious mind expresses itself. In his book *Dreams: God's Forgotten Language*, John Sanford says, "Dreams speak in a symbolic language; and in order to understand them one must understand their symbolism."[12] This is what Joseph did when he interpreted the meaning of the seven cows in Pharaoh's dream as harbingers of boom and bust.

Some people develop entire lexicons of dream interpretation, allocating particular meanings to long lists of symbols and numbers. One of the many problems with this approach is that it treats dream imagery as if it is a fixed universal language, when it is perhaps much more akin to improvised jazz. Joseph's interpretation of Pharaoh's dream does not mean that any cow in any dream at any time and in any place must henceforth inevitably mean the same thing!

Another problem with the lexicon approach is that it bypasses the important process of spiritual discernment in which we listen to the Holy Spirit and talk with other people. Both Joseph and Daniel were careful to say that the interpretation of dreams was not a skill they had learned but a gift they had received from God (Gen. 40:8; 41:16–39; Dan. 1:17; 2:28; 4:18). We will never understand dreams and visions until we ask God to give us insight. The lexicon approach fails to accommodate both the individuality of the dreamer and the subjectivity of each context. In the story of Joseph, the baker dreams of bread, the cupbearer dreams of wine, and Pharaoh dreams of cattle and corn. God speaks figuratively using distinct imagery appropriate and familiar to each one. As the rabbi Abraham Heschel points out regarding prophecy, "The prophet is a person, not a microphone.... The prophet's task is to convey a divine point of view, yet as a person he *is* a point of view. He speaks from the perspective of God, and perceives from the perspective of his own situation."[13]

Numerologists will point out, quite correctly, that the number seven can represent perfection in the Bible. This is fascinating stuff, and worth bearing in mind, but remember that it can also represent judgment (Gen. 7:10; Rev. 21:9), jubilee (Deut. 15:1), or forgiveness (Matt. 18:22). That's quite a selection! And it might equally represent something not mentioned in the Bible, such as a No. 7 bus, or a seventh birthday party, or a house number in a street. Equally, it might not mean anything at all. The point here is that we need contextual discernment, not rigid, religious formulas!

John Sanford goes on to say something refreshingly straightforward: "One way to uncover the symbolism of a dream is for the dreamer to talk about it. It is, after all, the *dreamer's* dream and has occurred in his or her psychic world, so it is reasonable to assume that the dreamer might hold the clues to the dream's meaning."[14] Here we have another reason why it's important to process significant dreams with those we respect and trust. And, of course, this was a common practice in Bible times when some people, such as Joseph and Daniel, were particularly respected for their gifting in the field of dream interpretation.

On one occasion, King Nebuchadnezzar asked for Daniel's help in remembering the details of a troubling dream, whereupon Daniel replied, "There is a God in heaven who reveals secrets, and He has made known to King Nebuchadnezzar what will take place... that you may understand *the thoughts of your mind*" (Dan. 2:28, 30 NASB, italics mine). One translation says, "that you would know your innermost thoughts,"[15] This is a striking summary of the essentials of modern dream theory. Millennia before Freud and Jung and psychoanalytic theory, the Bible regarded dreams as a window to the secret motivations and hidden thoughts of the "innermost mind" (or the "unconscious," as Freud would later describe it).

However, the Bible is equally clear that while some dreams are created by our innermost minds, others are emphatically given by God. This distinction really matters: "'For my thoughts are not your thoughts, neither are your ways my ways,' declares the LORD" (Isa. 55:8). One of the disturbing symptoms of religious psychosis is a conflation of one's own thoughts with those of God.

Most of our dreams are caused by our unconscious minds ordering and making sense of complex data. Maybe this is what Pilate's wife was experiencing in her disturbing dream about Jesus: deep misgivings she'd been ignoring or repressing during the day that surfaced powerfully in her dreams at night. I have often experienced similar things on a lesser scale. For instance, I will sometimes wake in the night troubled by something I've said or done the previous day, or "noticing" for the first time how someone spoke or reacted in a recent encounter. Occasionally I will become aware in my half-waking state of my own deeper motivation in a particular situation. This is because my innermost mind is processing the day, making sense of its events and giving me perspective. And, of course, the Holy Spirit can speak into such processes, challenging me to put something right the next day.

One of the most basic questions to ask when seeking to make sense of a dream is, "Is this just me or is it God?" Is this coming from the natural workings of my own mind or from the supernatural revelation of God's mind? Sometimes it will be a mixture of both, as Ben Carson's dream shows. On one hand, his mind was busy processing a particularly intensive bout of chemistry revision alongside anxiety about his impending exam, and all of this manifested in his dream. But on the other hand, there was clearly a supernatural component to his dream far beyond anything that could be generated simply by "the thoughts of [his innermost] mind."

If a man comes to me saying that he's received a clear dream about marrying his girlfriend and wondering whether it might be a word from God, my immediate response is likely to be, "Not necessarily!" His dream is just as likely to be coming from his own natural desire as from God's supernatural guidance. If he then adds, "But I've been asking God for a sign!" I would still need convincing. Even if he then said that an angel had appeared at the end of his bed, I would want to ask plenty of other questions. (Angels can be deceptive—see 2 Cor. 11:14.)

My first step in such situations is always to check the dream (or other prophetic revelation) against the ABC filter, asking, "Is it affirming, biblical, and Christlike?" (see chapter 4). In the case of this guy wanting to marry his girlfriend, the answer to all three questions would appear to be yes. But because it is potentially such a major, directional word, I would also seek the corroboration of other, less dramatic but equally authoritative sources such as wise counsel, personal conscience, and simple common sense. I might therefore ask him, "Do you think she wants to marry you too?" and, "Are you actually getting along well?" and, "Is she helping you to grow in your faith?" and, "Do your friends think this is a great relationship?" and, "Is this definitely the right timing?"[16]

If he is able to reply positively, without being defensive, to all these questions, I might at last tell him that the dream sounds like a wonderful confirmation from the Lord and that he'd better start saving for a ring!

* * *

Sometimes, even after running all the tests I've outlined in this section, the meaning of a dream you've received will still remain unclear. You'll have established that it's from God and not just a natural process of your own imagination, you'll have passed it through the ABC filter, and you'll even have sought counsel from a trusted source with whom you've processed your own intuitions. You'll have applied all these checks with an undiminished sense that your dream means *something*, but you still won't have the faintest idea what that something might actually be! Whenever this happens, don't fret.

Simply file the dream away for the future so that you can return to it from time to time. It will either become clearer and more relevant with time, or more clearly irrelevant. Personally, I have a number of dreams and other prophecies like this, carefully logged and occasionally visited, which I still don't fully understand.

"No Time to Explain. Attack!"

Before we move on from the realm of the unconscious mind, we must also consider the way in which God whispers to us through the voice of our consciences—our internal sense of right and wrong.

Toy Story 4 is one of the highest-grossing animated films of all time. It even won an Oscar for Best Animated Feature. At the heart of the franchise, as you probably know, is the relationship between Buzz Lightyear, the irrepressible but entirely shallow toy astronaut, and Woody, a much-loved toy cowboy. At one point they are guarding their child's new favorite plaything, a plastic fork named Forky, and Buzz offers to take the next shift. Woody declines, explaining, "That little voice inside me would never leave me alone if I gave up." Buzz is perplexed by this and asks whose voice his friend is hearing. Woody explains that it's his conscience, and Buzz responds with a mixture of derision and envy. "Fascinating," he says. "So your inner voice advises you!"

The joke here, of course, is that Buzz Lightyear has a number of prerecorded slogans that blare out indiscriminately whenever the buttons on his chest are pushed: "No time to explain. Attack!" and "The slingshot maneuver is all we got. Full speed ahead!" Woody doesn't have any such gimmicks—at least none that he can self-activate—but he does have a nuanced inner voice that seems to reflect his truest self. It's almost as if the toy has a soul.

The conscience is to our soul what nerves are to our body—it tells us when we are hurting and endangering ourselves. It is an internal moral compass, given to us by God at birth and subsequently shaped by our environment. Whenever we face ethical choices—whether to switch off the life-support machine, whether to challenge the sexism of a boss, whether to stay awake to keep an eye on Forky—God will guide us in particular through the inner whisper of our conscience.

I say that our conscience is *given to us by God* because our sense of right and wrong is one of the qualities that sets human beings apart from animals. Numerous studies have shown, for example, that even the best-behaved dogs misbehave when their owners are not watching. My dog Crumble, lying beside me now as I write, knows that she is not allowed to help herself to the sandwich on my desk. But if I were to leave her alone for an hour, there is absolutely no doubt about the fate of my sandwich. Crumble obeys rules blindly, like Buzz Lightyear with his buttons, not out of any sense of inner compulsion, comprehension, or conviction but simply out of habit, fear, and the never-ending hope of a permitted treat!

Social anthropologists have conducted extensive research into the universals of human morality. While the particularities of right and wrong are, to a considerable extent, socially prescribed—in one culture it is considered right to file teenagers' teeth into sharp points, and in another it is considered wrong to use electricity—there do seem to be certain universal moral absolutes. Whether you acquaint yourself with the members of a primitive Indonesian tribe or the inhabitants of a gated community on Long Island, you will find a basic consensus against things like murder, theft, and infidelity, and a celebration of such values as courage and honor.[17] It is as though, as the apostle Paul says, "the requirements of the [moral] law are written on their hearts, their consciences also bearing witness, and their thoughts sometimes accusing them and at other times even defending them" (Rom. 2:15).

But although our consciences are given to us by God, they are subsequently shaped by *our environment*. This means that they can be nurtured, refined, and strengthened within godly homes and healthy societies, but they can also be "seared" (1 Tim. 4:2), "corrupted" (Titus 1:15), "weak," and "defiled" (1 Cor. 8:7). We know this is true through personal experience. When we sin for the first time in a particular way, our conscience stabs us with guilt. But if we continue sinning in this way, the objections of our conscience will gradually be dulled and even silenced. Eventually, tragically, we will stop feeling guilt altogether. But the good news is that this damage can be reversed, our consciences can be resensitized, and we can all recover a life of freedom. It's not quick, but it is entirely possible through the simple practices of prayerful self-examination and regular repentance (one of the most helpful tools for doing this being the examen[18]) and through ongoing participation in the righteous relationships at the heart of healthy community.

Because the conscience is influenced to such an extent by its social and moral context, it is not entirely reliable. "My conscience is clear," concedes Paul, "but that does not make me innocent" (1 Cor. 4:4). God certainly speaks *through* our consciences, but our consciences are not the same thing as the voice of God. They are not infallible. Sometimes we may feel guilty about things that simply aren't wrong, especially if we've grown up in a particularly repressive environment. Someone whose background has been extremely frugal, for instance, might feel guilty about spending even a small amount of money on themselves. Occasionally, we may continue to experience a crippling sense of shame regarding past sins, even when we've been fully forgiven. It's important to resist such false feelings of guilt and to stand instead on God's promise that "there is now no condemnation for those who are in Christ Jesus" (Rom. 8:1). And as you keep putting your trust in the facts of God's Word instead of the feelings of condemnation, your conscience will eventually realign itself with truth.

Pause & Pray

Create in me a pure heart, O God,
    and renew a steadfast spirit within me.
Do not cast me from your presence
    or take your Holy Spirit from me.

> Restore to me the joy of your salvation
>   and grant me a willing spirit, to sustain me.
>   (Psalm 51:10–12)

The Vale of Soul-Making

Ostensibly, this chapter has been about hearing God in dreams, but more fundamentally we've been exploring the inner realm of the unconscious as a place in which God dwells and a space in which his Spirit often whispers. While God's word in Scripture may be considered to exist objectively, "out there," the unconscious mind (often described as the heart in Scripture) is the subjective domain of the human soul, so often neglected, rejected, and despised. But the great heroes of our faith are, without exception, those who attended first and foremost to the inner world of their own souls. They viewed the world itself as "the Vale of Soul-making," to use Keats' lovely phrase. These people undoubtedly did extraordinary things—they taught with great wisdom, fought great injustices, built schools, hospitals, and cities—but their priority was always to nurture and adorn that secret place within themselves in which they walked and talked with God.

This imagery of divine hospitality is used by Paul when he writes, "I pray that . . . Christ may dwell in your hearts through faith" (Eph. 3:16–17). In the fourteenth century, Julian of Norwich (featured at the end of this chapter as a "Living Word"), described the human soul as God's "most familiar home and his favourite dwelling."[19] Isn't that lovely? A couple of centuries later, St. John of the Cross described it as "that very tabernacle where He dwells, the secret Chamber of his retreat where he is hidden."[20] Meanwhile, his friend Teresa of Ávila pictured her soul as "a most splendid palace built entirely of gold and precious stones."[21] In all these images there is a sense of the soul as that handsome space within each one of us in which we may most naturally host the One who loves us most.

Orthodox theologian Brad Jersak describes a time of exhaustion in his own life, on the verge of burnout, when he learned to attend to his soul in ways that would surely have resonated with Teresa of Ávila, St. John of the Cross, Julian of Norwich, and the apostle Paul. It began with a strange fantasy—a dark cave with a crackling fire—that Brad started visiting regularly in prayer. Day after day he would simply imagine himself in this space, sitting silently with Jesus, sheltering from a storm outside, not even knowing if this counted as prayer. And then one day he "noticed" a surprising thing: the ark of the covenant had also materialized in the cave.

> This continued for weeks. All verbal prayer had given way to this internal, quiet vision. . . . I began to wonder if this was fruitful, if it was even prayer at all. Perhaps I should have started writing prayer lists again? But I had no heart for that. Even my forays into reading psalms ended with my forehead pasted in the pages of my Bible. All I knew was that my weary dread would surrender to peace whenever I retreated to the cave in my heart where Christ and the Ark would manifest.[22]

Around this time, Brad attended a meeting with other pastors, one of whom was recounting high-octane stories of God moving in supernatural power, but his words left Brad feeling inadequate. "I can't even pray anymore," he reflected. "All I do is lie by the Ark in that stupid cave day after day. I don't even know if it's real anymore."[23] But right then, at that very moment, this zealous firebrand turned to Brad and spoke prophetically into his life:

> "Like Samuel in 1 Samuel 3, you have been willing to remain lying beside the Ark of my Covenant. You've made it your resting place. Therefore, you will witness me restore the voice of the Lord to my people."[24]

With a sense of relief and awe, Brad realized that God was indeed meeting with him in his cave through the power of his own imagination, whispering to his soul in ways he barely understood, telling it slant. "The story of the cave is a personal example of how my prayer life has evolved," he concludes. "It has morphed from a one-way verbal communiqué to the 'God-out-there' into a visual, internal meeting with the indwelling Spirit of Christ."[25]

This is a beautiful journey of increasing intimacy which we may all undertake. It leads from hearing God speak externally through his word in Christ, in Scripture, and in the prophetic (*vox externa*—part 1), to hearing God's whisper within, through our dreams, consciences, and imagination (*vox interna*—part 2). And it is here, in this way, that we slowly make the great discovery:

> There is hardly ever a complete silence in our soul. God is whispering to us well-nigh incessantly. Whenever the sounds of the world die out in the soul, or sink low, then we hear these whisperings of God.
>
> —Frederick William Faber

Living Word: Julian of Norwich (1342–c. 1416)—Hearing and Seeing God in Dreams and Visions

Would'st thou know the Lord's meaning? Know it well. Love was his meaning.
> —Julian of Norwich

On May 8, 1373, Julian of Norwich received her last rites. Just thirty years old, she was gravely ill and expected to die. But instead, she received a series of sixteen visions, primarily of Christ on the cross, and she was also completely healed. For the next twenty years she meditated on the extraordinary visions she had received, recording her reflections in a book,

Revelations of Divine Love. In so doing, Julian became the first known woman to write a book in English and a living example of God's voice through dreams and visions.

Julian's experiences drew her deeply into a life of prayer, and she chose to live in almost complete solitude in a small cell built on to the side of St. Julian's Church (from which she took her name) in the bustling English city of Norwich. Her cell had two windows: one that looked into the church sanctuary so that she could participate in public worship and receive Communion; the other window looked out on to the street so that people could come to her to receive prayer and counsel.

Julian's writing is mystical and marked profoundly by a message of God's all-encompassing love. "Would'st thou know the Lord's meaning?" she asks at one point. "Know it well. Love was his meaning." The quote for which Julian is best known (because it features in a poem by T. S. Eliot) also captures her absolute certainty in the love of Christ: "All shall be well and all shall be well and all manner of thing shall be well."[26]

Julian's writing is profound, occasionally disturbing, and even surprising. In one of her visions, she saw Christ at a party:

> My mind was lifted up to heaven and I saw our Lord as a lord in his own house where he had called his much-loved friends and servants to a banquet. I saw that the Lord did not sit in one place but ranged throughout the house, filling it with joy and gladness. He himself, courteously and companionably, greeted and delighted his dear friends with love shining from his face like a marvellous melody that has no end. It is this look of love shining from God's face that fills the heavens full of joy and gladness.[27]

Jesus Christ is almost always depicted in the arts looking earnest, bored, or mildly angry. But here, in the earliest English book by a female writer, we have a completely different vision of Jesus, and it's really rather wonderful. He is hosting a party, moving from person to person with love shining from his face, filling the house with joy.

Pause & Pray

Lord, let not our souls be busy inns that have no room for thee or thine,

But quiet homes of prayer and praise, where thou mayest find fit company,

Where the needful cares of life are wisely ordered and put away,

And wide, sweet spaces kept for thee; where holy thoughts pass up and down

And fervent longings watch and wait thy coming.

Listening Exercise:
Practicing the Examen

As far as we can discern, the sole purpose of human existence is to kindle a light in the darkness of mere being. It may even be assumed that just as the unconscious affects us, so the increase in our consciousness affects the unconscious.
—Carl Jung

In this chapter we have focused on some of the most important ways in which God whispers to and through our subconscious minds, particularly in our dreams and our consciences. The listening exercises for the last chapter ("Hearing God's Whisper through Silence, Solitude, and Sabbath") will also be useful here in attuning yourself to your own intuitions. Another tool for connecting regularly with your own inner world in order to attune yourself with God's whisper is the prayer of examen.

Practicing the Examen

The examen (or "examination of consciousness") is a simple, four-step prayer model, popularized by the Jesuits in the sixteenth century (see Living Word: Ignatius of Loyola, chapter 3), as a tool for self-examination and spiritual transformation. Francis Xavier, the pioneering Jesuit missionary, urged his disciples, "Twice a day or at least once, make your particular examens. Be careful never to omit them. So live as to make more account of your own good conscience than you do of those of others."[28]

The examen has been practiced in different ways for many years, but essentially always involves four elements: prayerful reflection on the details of one's recent life, discernment of God's presence, acknowledgment of personal sin, and a resolution to change and grow. The Lectio 365 devotional (Night Prayers) breaks it down like this:

- **Reflect** on the details of the day that's gone, replaying it like a film in your head, particularly noticing the moments that provoked strong emotions or unexpected behaviors.
- **Rejoice** in the evidence of God's presence, not just in the day's obvious blessings but also savoring its subtler signs of his kindness: a good meal, a meaningful conversation, etc.

- **Repent** of the ways in which you've sinned in thought, word, and deed, paying particular heed to the subtler, more insidious attitudes you might otherwise brush under the carpet.
- **Res(e)t** Having identified the good, the bad, and the ugly in your day, rejoicing and repenting accordingly, ask the Lord to grant you rest (inspiring your dreams!) and giving you a reset for a fresh start tomorrow.

Questions for Self-Examination

- How reliable is my conscience? Is it oversensitive or undersensitive in any particular area?
- In what ways is God at work in my life, however subtly or slowly?
- When and why did something or someone last provoke a strong emotional reaction within me?

For Further Reflection

Dallas Willard, *Hearing God: Developing a Conversational Relationship with God* (Downers Grove, IL: IVP, 2012).

Lectio 365 (Night Prayers) app from 24-7 Prayer.

Mark and Patti Virkler, *Dialogue with God: Opening the Door to Two-Way Prayer* (Newberry, FL: Bridge-Logos, 1986).

The Emmaus road story is inescapably an account of God speaking through the actualities of community, creation, and culture. When Jesus was born, God's people already had his word in the Bible (the Hebrew books at least), but it clearly wasn't enough. They also had his word through prophets and prophecies, but this wasn't enough either. They knew God's whisper in the still, small voice of Elijah and in their consciences, dreams, and visions. In fact, they had almost every expression of God's word we've studied so far in this book, but none of it was enough. Eventually, God's word had to become flesh—not in a book but in a body, not just mystically in heaven but materially "among us" (John 1:14). There is no aspect of God's creation through which he cannot and does not speak. This chapter is, therefore, about discerning the voice of God in the whole of life, not just in religious contexts but also in the actualities of community, creation, and culture.

7

Hearing God's Whisper in Community, Creation, and Culture

When he was at the table with them . . . their eyes were opened.
—Luke 24:30–31

———————————

The whole earth is a living icon of the face of God.
—John of Damascus (675–749)

The Emmaus road story is inescapably an account of God speaking through the actualities of community, creation, and culture. It begins with a leisurely conversation on a dusty road about current affairs sometime before sunset and culminates with an ordinary meal in a suburban home sometime after dark. Along the way, Jesus is so utterly unremarkable in his appearance, so resolutely not weird in the language he uses, the customs he observes, and the food he eats that for several hours no one on Planet Earth realizes that this is, in fact, the resurrected Son of God.

* * *

"Fancy a pint?"

Our guest speaker, Paul Cowley, had delivered a brilliant talk at church, and people were coming forward requesting prayer. Many were also, no doubt, hoping to chat with Paul himself, but a glance at his face told me everything I needed to know. He was understandably exhausted after preaching all day at four of our services, and the ensuing conversations weren't going to be quick.

Like naughty schoolboys, we snuck out of the ancient church building while the guy I'd left in charge began deploying the prayer team and the band kept playing softly. Surreptitiously we ducked into the pub next door, with Paul's old army mate Eric Martin now in tow, hoping we hadn't been spotted.

By the time I reached the bar, my cover had been blown. I recognized the man nursing a Guinness beside me from the service, and his sheepish grin confirmed that he recognized me too. Laughing, I invited him to join our table, figuring that anyone who makes it halfway to the bottom of a pint glass before the final hymn has the kind of story that needs to be heard almost as much as it needs to be told.

There's some kind of secret code used by ex-servicemen. Somehow they can always identify fellow soldiers. And, sure enough, within a couple of minutes, Paul and Eric were quizzing our new companion about his days in the army and regaling him in return with their own hilarious exploits. Somehow it seemed the most natural thing in the world when Eric began to describe how he'd come to faith in Jesus, how he'd eventually led Paul to Jesus too, and how he now spent his time sharing the gospel with military personnel around the world with Alpha for Forces.[1] Both men's stories were clearly having an impact on our guest, and the fact that they both outranked him seemed to help too!

Before long he was sharing freely about his tough life, and I was drawing a diagram in beer on the table to explain the gospel. And then, just at that moment, a lady came bursting into the pub looking flustered, spotted our new friend, and demanded, "So what do you think you're doing here?"

Then she just sort of froze, staring around the circle as if she couldn't quite believe her eyes. When at last she had regained her composure, she explained that she was actually a new member of the church and that our companion was her wayward brother, who'd agreed to come that night to hear a fellow ex-soldier talk about Jesus. She'd been hoping he might sign up for an Alpha course, but instead he'd walked out before the end of Paul's talk.

She hadn't been surprised to find him drinking in the nearest pub, but never in a month of Sundays had she expected that he'd be huddled around a table discussing faith with the preacher, the pastor, and the guy from Alpha for Forces. The Good Shepherd who leaves the ninety-nine sheep to go after the one had, it seemed to her, left the church service that night in pursuit of her brother in the pub next door. And so her prayers were answered: he agreed to attend Alpha and duly discovered the Lord for himself.

In this little encounter we see God working and speaking through ordinary people in an ordinary pub, and even through a rather unspiritual decision to skip prayer ministry to go instead for a drink. Yes, of course God had spoken through Paul Cowley's sermon, and no doubt he had also moved powerfully in the prayer ministry, and through the whole church service, but he'd also spoken powerfully in the pub next door.

This is just a tiny expression of that massive truth we call the incarnation, when "the Word became flesh and made his dwelling among us" (John 1:14). Two thousand years ago the Word of God left the courts of heaven to be born in a dirty barn beside (or beneath) some kind of hostelry or home. The Creator became part of his own creation in order to speak to us in ways we would be able to perceive and receive more easily. Pierre Teilhard de Chardin, who combined being a Jesuit priest with being a scientist, paleontologist, and philosopher, put it like this: "By means of all created things, without exception, the divine assails us, penetrates us and moulds us."[2] (You may just want to pause and let the fullness of that statement sink in: God speaks through *all created things without exception*.")

Pause & Pray

Where in the so-called secular world can I see God at work right now?

Is there a non-Christian voice through which he might be speaking to me?

Any paradigm that systematically divides sacred from secular, locking God in the church and the world in the pub, is a violation of the incarnation and fundamentally sub-Christian. I don't drive a Christian car, but I do try to drive as a Christian. In Christ, nothing in all creation remains secular but sin, for "the earth is the Lord's, and everything in it" (1 Cor. 10:26). We see this illustrated clearly in the couple from Emmaus who participate in the world's first Sunday Communion service, with Jesus himself officiating. But it doesn't take place in any kind of religious context. Instead, they are simply gathered in an ordinary home, around a meal table, with the sounds and smells of domestic life all around.

*　*　*

On the day that the Word became flesh in Bethlehem, God's people already had God's word in the Bible (the Hebrew books at least), but it clearly wasn't enough. They also had his word through prophets and prophecies, but this wasn't enough either. They knew God's whisper in the still, small voice of Elijah, and in their consciences, and in dreams and visions too. In fact, they had almost every expression of God's word we've studied so far in this book, but none of it was enough. Eventually, God's Word had to become flesh—not in a book but in a body, not just mystically in heaven but materially "among us."

And so we conclude this book as we began it: with God's final word in Jesus. At the start I said that he is the preeminent way in which God speaks and that we must therefore get to know him for ourselves if we are ever to become familiar with his voice. And then, in the intervening chapters, I've set out some of the principal ways in which we may expect him to speak (the Bible, prophecy, dreams, and so on) and some of the practical tools with which we may learn to listen (hermeneutics, *lectio divina*, the ABC filter, and so on).

But now we must step back from these principles and practices to focus once more on the big picture—the heart and soul of this book—which is encountering Christ Jesus for ourselves. Not just in sacred environments like church and Bible study but also in supposedly secular ones like that pub next door. And not just in supernatural ways like dreams and visions but in natural ways too, like that quiet conversation with a stranger. This chapter is, in other words, about learning to discern the voice of God in the whole of life—not just in religious contexts and through spiritual exercises but in the actualities of community, creation, and culture.

Welcome to the Funny Farm

> *One of the immediate changes that the gospel*
> *makes is grammatical: we instead of I,*
> *our instead of my, us instead of me.*
> —Eugene Peterson

Sammy and I went to visit a rescue center for monkeys and owls on the Isle of Wight. It was all quite lovely but also rather peculiar. For starters, we couldn't work out what monkeys and owls had in common. Do they share similar habitats? Do they get on particularly well? Why not include other exotic pets like pythons, alpacas, and those Vietnamese potbellied pigs that presumably, sadly, also need rescuing? Perhaps an owl specialist met a monkey specialist at a zookeepers' convention and they fell in love and started a sanctuary together? (Sammy says I have a tendency to overthink these things, and, reading this back now, I can see that she may have a point.)

Anyway, for whatever reason, this particular animal sanctuary specializes in both monkeys and owls, and, in spite of everything, it's fabulous. The animals are all rescues, which makes wandering around particularly fun. There's a cross-eyed gibbon whose legs are apparently too short, a one-eyed owl called Nelson, a rhesus macaque with an awkward habit of happy-slapping its keepers, and a punk-haired mangabey called Djimmy who had been found forlornly loping along a busy German highway.

This is a place where all the weird-looking misfits, the bullied runts, and the hopeless rejects from other zoos get together and fit together precisely because of their strangeness. Hollywood it ain't. The plaques on almost every cage tell touching tales of abandonment, eccentricity, tragedy, and joy. As I say, it's all really rather lovely.

As we wandered around, from one sad story and one cute face to the next, something started to feel strangely familiar. And gradually it dawned on me that this is a lot like the church! We are, let's face it, a community of oddities, a menagerie of tragic rescues, an eccentric collection of broken backgrounds that barely belong together were it not for Christ who "chose the foolish things . . . the weak things . . . the lowly things . . . the despised things—and the things that are not—to nullify the things that are, so that no one may boast before him" (1 Cor. 1:27–29).

Jesus consistently showed particular kindness to those who found themselves on the margins, those who were broken, those without airs and graces. And nothing much has changed. He continues to gather the strangest assortment of folk into his family (take a good look around next Sunday and you'll see).[3] We really are a peculiar assortment of people, and yet we are also those chosen by Jesus to know and speak his word.

This was a lesson that had to be learned the hard way by one particularly famous Oxford don when he first became a Christian: "I thought that I could do it on my own," confessed C. S. Lewis, "by retiring to my rooms and reading theology."[4] Eventually, reluctantly, he began attending church and made an important discovery:

> I came up against different people of quite different outlooks and different education, and then gradually my conceit just began peeling off. I realized that the hymns (which were just sixth-rate music) were, nevertheless, being sung with devotion and benefit by an old saint in elastic-side boots in the opposite pew, and then you realize that you aren't fit to clean those boots. It gets you out of your solitary conceit.[5]

Increasing numbers of people today share C. S. Lewis' initial sentiment. They would much prefer to hear God on their own personal terms, by "retiring to their rooms to read theology," or by streaming world-class teaching in a favorite café, or by listening to progressive Southern gospel during Zumba classes, or by walking in the forest in the rain. And there's nothing wrong with such things (thank the Lord that C. S. Lewis enjoyed reading theology). It's just that somewhere out there there's "an old saint in elastic-side boots" who may very well have the word of God for your life.

Perhaps you remember that Bible story about Naaman, the great military general who went to see the prophet Elisha because he needed healing from a skin disease. After Naaman had traveled some seven hundred miles all the way from Damascus to Elisha's house, the prophet didn't even bother coming to the door. Instead, he sent a message telling the great man to go and bathe seven times in the murky River Jordan. Naaman was furious. He pointed out that there were bigger, cleaner rivers back home. But eventually he was persuaded to obey, and, when he did so, his condition was completely healed (2 Kings 5).

Naaman got the word he *needed*, not the one he *wanted*. Sometimes you have to choose. What if the thing you *want* God to say is not the thing you *need* God to say? Will you still hear and obey? Naaman found this hard. He was offended *culturally* because he wasn't treated as he felt he deserved. He was offended *intellectually* because generals are strategists, and Elisha's orders were such patent nonsense. He was offended *personally* because he'd traveled for many days and the prophet had been unwilling even to walk to the door.

Most people insist on hearing the voice of God on their own terms. The thought that he might ask us to immerse ourselves again and again in something as uncool as an uncool church—where the music is sixth rate, and the pastor doesn't exactly roll out the red carpet, and his teaching is frankly ridiculous, and its members all look like they voted the wrong way—may very well be as offensive to us culturally, intellectually, and personally as bathing in the Jordan would have been for Naaman.

What might the River Jordan represent for you? Perhaps God wants to speak to you through a Christian tradition you've previously disparaged. Or through a person who annoys you as much as Elisha annoyed Naaman. Or through a very junior employee like Naaman's servant girl who set the whole thing up. We must learn to listen more carefully to those people the culture ignores, because God speaks most consistently from the margins—through children, through the poor, through those who suffer.

It was not until Naaman humbled himself in this way before a rude and eccentric prophet that he finally found the miracle he needed. It was when C. S. Lewis began to sing sixth-rate hymns with "different people of quite different outlooks and different education" that his heart was primed to hear. And it was when the couple on the road to Emmaus allowed a stranger to gate-crash their private conversation that God's Word broke into their lives. All these people had to leave their "solitary conceit" in order to hear God speak through someone else.

There's a story from the lives of the desert fathers about an old man who fasted for seventy weeks, allowing himself to eat only once a week, because he was zealously seeking a word from God. Eventually, he said to himself, "See how much labour I have undertaken and it has been of no profit to me. I will go, therefore, to my brother and ask him about it."[6]

He went outside, and an angel of the Lord was sent to him, to say, "The seventy weeks you fasted did not make you any closer to God. Now because you have been humbled and are going off to your brother, I have been sent to explain the passage to you."[7]

Like many people today, that old man considered the words of a brother secondary to a supernatural revelation. Meanwhile, God, who had clearly been unimpressed by his seventy-week fast, viewed his newfound willingness to take counsel from a brother as a mark of humility and surrender. Sometimes, no matter how much we might pray and even fast for a supernatural word from God, or a dramatic discovery in Scripture, the Lord refuses to oblige. Instead, he waits for us to humble ourselves like Naaman, C. S. Lewis, and that old desert father, to seek his voice "merely" through another person.

Pause & Pray

Given the choice, would I prefer God to speak to me dramatically and supernaturally, rather than through an ordinary conversation with another person? If so, why? Who might be carrying God's word for my life at this time? Is there any initiative I need to take? Anyone from whom I should seek advice?

Hearing God through Others

God has willed that we should seek and find his living
Word in the testimony of other Christians, in the
mouths of human beings. Therefore, Christians need
other Christians who speak God's word to them.
—Dietrich Bonhoeffer

I'm sure you've experienced God speaking into your life through other people. Perhaps it was a moment of great clarity as a sage gave you counsel, or powerful preaching that set your heart on fire, or a prophetic word that somehow spoke directly into your life, or simply an ordinary conversation that Jesus seemed to join (as he did that day on the Emmaus road). As it says in Malachi 3:16, "Those who feared the LORD talked with each other, and the LORD listened and heard." Isn't that reassuring? Sometimes God listens in on our conversations and receives them as prayers.

There was a time in the life of Francis of Assisi when he needed a word from God. He knew that his calling was to serve the poor, but he wasn't sure how best to do it. Was he supposed to go into the world to serve the poor practically or to retreat from the world in order to pray for their needs? It was an important decision with enormous implications, not just for his own life but also for the movement he was leading, and so he decided to ask a small group of trusted friends to seek God's counsel for him.

Weeks later, he gathered this group, washed their feet, prepared them a meal, and gave them fresh clothes. Only when they were sufficiently refreshed did he kneel before them to ask them the simple, straightforward question that would determine the rest of his life: "What does my Lord Jesus command from me?" Francis had complete trust—no shadow of doubt—that these people had received God's word for his future.

Solemnly the friends replied, "He commands that you should go to the poor."

Without another word, Francis obeyed, and the world changed immeasurably as a result.[8]

I love the pragmatism with which Francis engaged in this important process of discernment. First, he didn't try to hear God on his own, but neither did he broadcast his dilemma indiscriminately to anyone who might possibly have an opinion. He was meaningfully accountable. Second, he didn't demand a fireworks show from the Lord—no angelic visitations, supernatural dreams, or prophetic confirmations were required. (Quite an antidote to those people today who will barely start a Bible study without three major forms of guidance!) Francis was happy simply to receive the counsel of trusted friends as the very word of God for his life. In fact, you get the sense that he *preferred* to hear from God unsensationally in this relational way. Third, Francis was deliberate in giving away authority without abdicating responsibility. He received his friends as the very messengers of God, caring for their needs before asking them that extraordinary question: "What does my Lord *command* from me?" (Not, "What do you guys think?") And then he obeyed their answer without hesitation. It was a scary level of trust.

Anam Cara

We all need friends like those of Francis, who can bring God's word to us whether it comes in the guise of wise counsel, encouragement, or loving rebuke. This may sound obvious, but I'm often shocked by the levels of loneliness and relational dysfunction within the church, especially among men, and most acutely and concerningly among Christian leaders who have hundreds of acquaintances but no real friends.[9]

The ancient Celts considered spiritual friendship so important that they had a particular term to describe it: *anam cara*, which literally means "soul friend." It was unthinkable that any follower of Jesus would "go it alone," without someone else alongside them to bring God's word and wisdom. In his bestselling book on the subject, John O'Donohue traces the term back to early Irish monasticism,[10] in which every monk's *anam cara* was his personal tutor, companion, confessor and spiritual guide:

> With the *anam cara*, you can share your innermost self, your mind and your heart. This friendship was an act of recognition

and belonging. When you had an *anam cara*, your friendship cut across all convention, morality and category. You were joined in an ancient and eternal way with the friend of your soul.[11]

This kind of relationship can take many forms—a prayer partnership, spiritual direction, or (best of all) simply the kind of deep Christian friendship in which "iron sharpens iron" (Prov. 27:17), "speaking the truth in love" (Eph. 4:15), where you "spur one another on toward love and good deeds" (Heb. 10:24).

The three most important things to consider in establishing such relationships are:

1. *It should be a friendship*—not duty but delight—(and this is where *anam cara* may differ from the more formal relationship you might establish with a mentor or spiritual director). You need to enjoy one another's company and be relaxed together.

2. *It should be safe.* Your *anam cara* requires radical honesty of you. In fact, the value of your relationship will be set by the price you are prepared to pay in personal vulnerability. This also means that they must be trustworthy and discreet.

3. *It should be framed.* Be clear about expectations (five minutes of framing can save five years of reframing). Roughly how regularly are you going to connect? Is this a peer-to-peer dynamic or a more parental one? How long will you relate in this way before pausing to review? It's far better to say, "Let's do this for a year, review and renew," than to get trapped in a stale relationship, and it's also far less scary!

In my own life I am blessed to have several people who support me in this way, some as peers and a couple with the authority of spiritual fathers. First and foremost, we enjoy each other's company, but it's more than just hanging out. There is also an intentionality to our relationship. We speak truthfully to one another, pray for one another, and seek to be diligent and constant in encouragement too. We connect regularly, and I continually give these people permission to ask me awkward questions, to challenge and encourage me, and ultimately to bring the Word of the Lord into my life.

When I lived in Kansas City, I was mentored by a man called Floyd McClung. Floyd was brilliant at asking questions and completely comfortable with the kind of long silences that leave the rest of us sweating.[12] For this reason he had been nicknamed "Sigmund" (as in, "Sigmund Floyd").

We were having coffee one day when he turned to me and said, "Hey, Pete, everywhere I go in the world right now I'm meeting people who think you're one of their very best friends." He smiled broadly and fell silent, allowing me to bask quietly in the glow of his apparent compliment. But then he continued, "What I want to know is, how can that be genuine? How can so many relationships in so many contexts be in any way meaningful or sustainable?"

Ouch! Floyd had opened my soul in less than three minutes (two of which were total silence). With a single question he had skillfully provoked a painful but beautiful conversation regarding relational fidelity, the insecurity behind projections of popularity, and a load of other stuff. It was the kind of conversation that shapes you, the kind we all long to have, and the kind of three minutes you remember fifteen years later when social media has taken the pathology of fake friendship to a whole new level.

Of course, Floyd was being a good friend to me that night—speaking truth in love—but he was also teaching me how to be a better friend to others. He was speaking God's word to me personally and practically in a way that the ancient texts of Scripture, and even remarkable prophetic utterances, very rarely can. We all need people like that who speak God's truth into our lives. And we can also all be friends like that for others.

It's possible to have more than one *anam cara*, but as Floyd showed me that night, you can also have too many! True soul friendship is a rare gift—a treasure of great worth. It doesn't just land in your lap. It may take years of trial and error to find and refine relationships like these, especially if you're living in a culture like the one in which I grew up, where there is very little understanding of discipleship and the requirements of deep Christian friendship. If this sounds familiar, quit waiting for your *anam cara* to emerge out of the mists. You're going to have to lead on this by instigating soul-level friendships. But in doing so, try not to be too intense. Resist the zealous urge to propose lifelong pacts of mutual accountability! (You probably shouldn't even mention the word *anam cara* at first.) Instead, you might just bring a little more intentionality and vulnerability into an existing friendship in order to see how the other person copes. You could suggest praying together, if that is not currently a feature of your friendship. You might ask this person for specific advice, like Francis with his friends. Or you could take a calculated risk and open up about an area of shame or pain.

Such simple steps can subtly stretch an existing friendship to new depths (#1 on p. 204), long before you introduce any formal framework (#2 and #3). Sadly, some Christians are simply too broken to move beyond a fairly superficial level of friendship. You'll hit a concrete floor on their capacity for honesty and depth and will need to lower your expectations a bit. But others may well surprise you with unexpected oceans of grace. As you begin to pray more, share more, and trust more with these people, your relationship will steadily deepen into a true soul friendship.

You'll find that the best *anam cara* are rarely Christian leaders (beware the man or woman who spends a lot of their time holding a mic!). The best soul friends are ordinary lovers of Jesus with enough time in their schedules, enough equity in their hearts, and enough miles on the road to encourage, comfort, and challenge you consistently in the most important friendship of your life.

Hearing God in the Culture

There are no unsacred places;
there are only sacred places and desecrated places.
—Wendell Berry

Since we know that God speaks in all things and about all things (in the pub as well as the church, and through friends as well as the Bible), we should certainly expect to hear his voice in the culture far beyond the walls of the church. And in many ways, this is the greatest discovery of them all, the culmination and conflagration of everything else we have explored in this book: that the Maker of all things has not abandoned his Great Project. The Creator is still creating the cosmos and the cultures in which we live. He is still actively at work within his world, speaking brilliant new things into existence (babies and films, galaxies and songs). Our universe is still expanding! People are still falling in love! Scientists have not yet run out of things to discover. Novelists are somehow still stumbling upon ideas worth exploring. Priests continue to greet coffins with the great defiant cry, "I am the resurrection and the life" (John 11:25).

There is no aspect of God's creation through which he cannot and does not speak. We wake up each day to discover that "His tender compassions never fail. They are new every morning" (Lam. 3:22–3 AMP). We open our Bibles and, lo, he speaks! We still ourselves for a few moments, and there he is again! We open our newspapers and find him still speaking if our ears remain open to hear. We arrive at work and he deliberately, playfully whispers a little word to our souls through that colleague who doesn't yet know he exists. Our eyes linger a little too long on the shape of a stranger and the Lord speaks sharply through our conscience. We watch a film and it moves us to pray. We switch on the radio and he speaks through a song. Looking up at the sky as the stars come out, we strongly sense an ancient truth:

> The heavens declare the glory of God;
>> the skies proclaim the work of his hands.
> Day after day they pour forth speech. (Ps. 19:1–2)

Few people in history have understood and communicated this truth better than the apostle Paul on the day that he addressed the people of Athens at the Areopagus:

> The God who made the world and everything in it is the Lord of heaven and earth and does not live in temples built by human hands. . . . Rather, he himself gives everyone life and breath and everything else . . . so that they would seek him and perhaps reach out for him and find him, though he is not far from any one of us. "For in him we live and move and have our being." (Acts 17:24–25, 27–28)

Paul goes on to quote not from the Bible but from one of the most famous poems of the ancient world, "As some of your own poets have said, 'We are his offspring'" (v. 28).

This is a line from "Phaenomena" by the ancient Greek poet Aratus (315–240 BC). It was well known in the ancient world, and, since its author had once lived in Athens, we may assume that it held a particular place in the heart of that great city. Paul is not just exploiting the culture here in order to communicate and connect, as Christians often do. Rather he is celebrating the culture and thereby demonstrating the very point he has just made—that "the God who made the world and everything in it" inhabits his creation; he is "not far from any one of us," and our very existence comes from him and continues to be outworked in him.

"Phaenomena" begins with an invocation to Zeus, the Greek god of thunder who was thought to rule over all the other gods in Mount Olympus. It's a poem, in other words, invoking the name of the top pagan deity. Because Paul was a strict former

Pharisee, profoundly and utterly opposed to any form of idolatry, and actually now as a Christian still radically committed to the Ten Commandments, we would expect him to rail against such blasphemy, or at the very least to avoid its texts. We know for sure that he was "greatly distressed to see that the city was full of idols" (Acts 17:16).

It's worth pausing to register Paul's distress because some of us probably feel very differently. We are so comfortable within our context that we are in danger of assimilation. We no longer find any aspect of its idolatry "greatly"—or even mildly—distressing. Our problem is not with hearing God's voice in the culture, but rather with completely confusing the spirit of the age with the Spirit of God. We switch off the gift of "discernment of spirits" when we go to the movies, or when we attend a lecture, or when we shop at the mall. We would never consider abandoning a box set because of its darkness or depravity, or withdrawing from an acquaintance whose influence was consistently detrimental to our holiness. Our consciences are rarely troubled by the culture.

But Paul clearly was not like this at all, which makes his words at the Areopagus even more remarkable. Although he is "greatly distressed" by their idolatry, he takes an Athenian poem dedicated by a stoic poet to "the king of gods" and identifies a single phrase that points beyond itself toward the one, true God.

His years studying the Scriptures and learning to hear the voice of God have brought him to this extraordinary place in which he can trace the whisper of God in a pagan text amid a culture littered with idolatrous shrines. And in many ways, this is the aim of this whole book: that we become so familiar with the word of God in its most obvious forms—in Scripture, in prophecy, in dreams, and in soul friendships—that we are enabled to hear God speak in all the earth through people and things that are not in any way consciously Christian. By learning to hear God in the sermon on Sunday, we begin to hear his voice in the news on Monday. By learning to see

Christ in Christians, we begin to meet him in strangers and notice that "the Word of God is not only being uttered in the sacred scriptures, but more primordially in creation, more existentially in history, more imaginatively in works of art, more immediately and personally in human experience."[13]

So how do we train ourselves to hear all the wonderful things God is saying in the culture, without confusing the many words of the world with the word of God? There is a simple process, almost like three dance steps, that I find helpful: first to *turn* toward the culture, then to *discern* what it is saying, and finally to *return* consistently to Christ.

Learn to Turn toward the Culture

> *The first responsibility of culture makers is not to make something new but to become fluent in the cultural tradition to which we are responsible. Before we can be culture makers, we must be culture keepers.*
> —Andy Crouch

There's a fascinating sentence, easily missed, in the famous story of Moses and the burning bush. We are told, "When the LORD saw that he had gone over to look, God called to him from within the bush" (Ex. 3:4). It's as though God was not necessarily going to speak to Moses, but because he was inquisitive—because he made the effort to go over to see that flaming bush—Moses heard the voice of the Lord.

There is something important here about being attentive to the ordinary events and circumstances of life. At the Areopagus, Paul had clearly memorized a part of Aratus' great poem. He had also been studying the architecture and artifacts of the city (Acts 17:23). It's also fair to assume that he was well schooled in the classics as well as the Scriptures. Paul could hold his own in business too, working as a craftsman, plying his trade making tents.

Some of us fail to pay attention to the wider culture because we live in a parallel religious universe, having been taught that the outside world is inherently dangerous. (Did you see that film *The Village*? Probably not.) We only attend Christian concerts, we only read Christian books, and so on. It's as though Jesus came to earth solely to save us for the sake of an all-consuming hobby. In the rhyme sometimes attributed to nineteenth-century cardinal John Henry Newman, "I sought to hear the voice of God And climbed the topmost steeple, But God declared: Go down again—I dwell among the people."

Many more of us fail to pay attention to the things God is saying in the culture because we are simply too busy. Leadership expert Ruth Haley Barton observes:

> We are blind to the bush that is burning in our own backyard and the wisdom that is contained within it.... We long for a word from the Lord, but somehow we have been suckered into believing that the pace we keep is what leadership requires. We slide inexorably into a way of life that offers little or no opportunity for paying attention and then wonder why we are not hearing from God when we need God most.[14]

If we are serious about hearing God, we will make time and commit energy to become students of the world in which he has placed us by nurturing a relentless fascination with the passions and assumptions of those he has given us as neighbors; we will turn aside regularly to wonder why ordinary things burn so brightly. In the famous words of Elizabeth Barrett Browning:

> Earth's crammed with heaven,
> And every common bush afire with God,
> But only he who sees takes off his shoes;
> The rest sit round it and pluck blackberries.[15]

Learn to Discern the Culture

Having turned toward the culture, we must recognize the fact that it is a very mixed bag indeed. The Bible warns us clearly and consistently that there is a viciously deceptive enemy at work in the world disguised as an angel of light (2 Cor. 11:14). He is variously described as a liar, an accuser, a thief, and a prowling lion. We desperately need the gift of "distinguishing between spirits" (1 Cor. 12:10) so that we can separate God's word in the culture from the devil's lies. We should ask for this gift regularly and then seek to exercise it diligently each day. Reflective prayer disciplines, such as journaling, seeing your *anam cara*, and praying the examen will help us to differentiate between the good, the bad, and the ugly in our lives.

The spirit we are looking for is, of course, the Spirit of Christ. So we are continually scanning the horizon for things in the culture that sound like, look like, or point toward Jesus (which is clearly what Paul did with the "Phaenomena" poem). This is nuanced, of course, so we will have to listen carefully to his whisper within our own consciences, because some aspects of the culture that point some people toward Christ (certain ideas, pleasures, and artistic forms) may constitute an offense to others.

The apostle Paul gives clear teaching about this exact principle in 1 Corinthians 10, with regard to one of the great controversial issues of his time—eating food sacrificed to idols. First, he advises his readers to relax: "Eat anything sold in the meat market without raising questions of conscience, for, 'The earth is the Lord's, and everything in it'" (vv. 25–26). This is very much the line I have been taking so far. But then Paul continues, "If someone says to you, 'This has been offered in sacrifice,' then do not eat it . . . for the sake of . . . the other person's conscience' (vv. 28–29). The key question we must ask ourselves, he concludes, is whether this is something we can receive as a gift from God for his glory (v. 30).

In seeking to navigate the infinite complexities of the culture in which we live, we must listen continually to the whisper of our own conscience (see chapter 6) but also be sensitive to the consciences of other people, ultimately asking ourselves, "Is this God's gift to me, and can I receive it for his glory?"

Sammy and I became deeply embroiled in a particular Netflix series a while ago. As the plot unfolded and the characters developed, we became more and more drawn into their world. But gradually, by the end of its third series (at which point we had watched no fewer than eighteen episodes), my conscience began to trouble me. I don't think I'm a prude—I had been comfortable with the story to this point, even though it had included some sexual content, quite a bit of violence, and a lot of swearing. In fact, I had been able to receive the series as a blessing from God, even sensing him speaking to me at times through some of its themes and characters. But as the third series wore on, the violence and sex scenes seemed to me to have become continuous, gratuitous, and hollow. My spirit was disturbed. Images were being planted in my mind that I didn't want to entertain. I could no longer put my hand on my heart and say that this content reflected Paul's priorities in Philippians 4:8: "Whatever is true, whatever is noble, whatever is right, whatever is pure, whatever is lovely, whatever is admirable—if anything is excellent or praiseworthy—think about such things." And so I bailed out on series four even though I was desperate to find out what happened next and felt heavily invested with the characters.

The interesting thing is that Sammy's conscience was not troubled in the same way. She kept watching the series quite happily and eventually tipped me off that things got much lighter and healthier in the fifth series. I was delighted to rejoin her for the series conclusion.

Learn to Return to Scripture

As we continue to apply appropriate discernment to the culture in which we dwell, we will return continually to the bedrock of

God's word in Scripture, in fellowship with other Christians, and ultimately in our personal encounter with Christ. This is how we remain sharp in our discernment of the culture so that "the world around you [doesn't] squeeze you into its own mould" (Rom. 12:2 JBP) and also how we remain open to the Holy Spirit in the way that we interpret and apply the Word of God. As the great theologian Karl Barth famously reminded us, we need to carry the Bible in one hand and the newspaper in the other. Yes, we interpret the culture in the light of the Bible, but we also allow God's voice in the culture to inform us, perhaps opening our eyes to an ancient truth that we have previously missed in God's Word. Thank God that Martin Luther did this, and William Wilberforce, and Martin Luther King Jr. too.

* * *

Throughout this book we've been walking the Emmaus road, discovering first how to discern *God's word* in the Scriptures, in prophecy, and ultimately in Christ, and second how to discern *God's whisper* in the realms of dreams and conscience, friendships, and culture. It's deliberately only been a taster menu, a simple guide to a vast and important field of spiritual formation. I'd encourage you, therefore, to explore more and go deeper in the particular areas that interest you, using the listening exercises associated with each chapter and the resources recommended in the further reading sections, including the Lectio 365 devotional and the *Lectio Divina* Course, which is designed to accompany this book.

But there is one final, beautiful aspect of the Emmaus story to consider as we conclude, which draws together all the other threads and themes in this book so far.

> When he was at the table with them, [Jesus] took bread, gave thanks, broke it and began to give it to them. Then their eyes were opened and they recognized him. (Luke 24:30–1)

The moment of recognition comes as Jesus reenacts the Last Supper. It is, if you like, a moment of Communion. Perhaps Cleopas and Mary even glimpsed the scars on his wrists as he lifted the bread. We have no reason to suppose that they had been present the previous Thursday in that upper room, but every reason to believe that they would have heard about it, if this is indeed Mary who had been at the foot of the cross and if they had therefore spent the Sabbath with members of that close-knit community that had formed around Christ.

There is some evidence that a church grew up in Emmaus, presumably in that very house (where else would you want to meet?). You can certainly imagine them gathering around that same table, retelling the story of that day again and again, reenacting that first Communion on that first Christian Sunday for years to come.

It is in the sacrament of Communion that we encounter the resurrected Christ. He raises the bread, and we are reminded that this is more than bread. It is a powerful symbol representing "every word that comes from the mouth of God" (Matt. 4:4). It speaks to us even as it feeds us, as both *logos* and *rhēma*, the Bible and the prophetic. And yet, metaphors aside, it is indeed bread: the fruit of the land, the work of someone's hand. Our daily bread is material as well as spiritual, coming to us through the hands of ordinary people speaking to us through human conversation even more than more mystical forms of revelation.

And then, when Jesus breaks the bread, we are reminded of his body so cruelly broken for us on the cross. We take his broken body into our own broken bodies, and somehow in this moment we become the body of Christ, born again and again and again: the community through which he still speaks, the walking, talking embodiment—literally—of his Word in the world.

Every time we share Communion, the word of God is spoken out again in Jesus (through his life, death, and resurrection, through the Scriptures, through his Spirit, through the church), and we receive that word into our lives.

It's fascinating to speculate on the suddenness of Christ's departure at the end of this story. It is actually while he was still in the process of giving them the bread—as he "began to give it to them" and before he had finished doing so[16]—that "he disappeared from their sight."

It's almost as though Jesus wants to let the bread do the talking. He's given them all they need in the Bible study on the road and now the crumbs they are chewing. He didn't want Mary Magdalene to hold on to him in the garden earlier in the morning, and apparently he doesn't want Mary and Cleopas to do so either. It's time for them to take what he has given them already and to work the rest out for themselves. And this they do, hurrying out immediately into the night, walking the two hours back to Jerusalem in the darkness, talking all the way, no doubt, about the things Jesus has said. And then, when they arrive, they announced the thrilling news to their fellow disciples: "It is true!"

Jesus revealed himself to them in an astounding personal encounter, and now they would be witnesses to his resurrection for generations to come. He opened the Scriptures to them in a way that left their "hearts burning within," perhaps for the rest of their lives. They have broken bread with the resurrected Son of God, and nothing could ever be the same again.

Having *heard* God's word in the Scriptures, having *experienced* his word with burning hearts, and having personally *encountered* God's Word in Christ, let us too become carriers of that word to the world.

> Who is the third who walks always beside you?
> When I count, there are only you and I together
> But when I look ahead up the white road
> There is always another one walking beside you.[17]
>
> —T. S. Eliot

Living Word: George Washington Carver (1864–1943)—Hearing God's Whisper in Culture and Creation

All my life, I have risen regularly at four in the morning to go into the woods and talk with God. That's where He reveals His secrets to me. When everybody else is asleep, I hear God best and learn my plan.

—George Washington Carver

The achievements of the eminent scientist George Washington Carver would be exceptional in any age, but the cultural context in which he achieved them makes his contribution to humanity particularly remarkable. Born into slavery in Newton County, Missouri, during the American Civil War, he was kidnapped as a baby and returned to his owner for the price of a three-hundred-dollar horse, his mother having died in the process. As "the orphaned child of a despised race," he was excluded from school, and his health was so poor that he wasn't expected to live past the age of twenty-one. As a young man, his natural brilliance gained him a place at a university in Kansas, but when they discovered his color, he was unceremoniously turned away.

And yet George Washington Carver went on to become one of the most prominent scientists of the early twentieth century: a leading agriculturalist, inventor, teacher, painter, environmentalist, champion of the poor, pioneer of sustainable farming, and adviser to three presidents. One of them, Franklin Roosevelt, established a national monument in Carver's honor—the first such monument to any African American and the first to a nonpresident.

The defining moment in this extraordinary life was the day that George Washington Carver became a follower of Jesus:

> I was just a mere boy when converted, hardly ten years old. There isn't much of a story to it. God just came into my heart one afternoon while I was alone in the "loft" of our big barn while I was shelling corn to carry to the mill to be ground into meal. A dear little white boy, one of our neighbors, about my age came by one Saturday morning, and in talking and playing he told me he was going to Sunday school tomorrow morning. I was eager to know what a Sunday school was. He said they sang hymns and prayed. I asked him what prayer was and what they said. I do not remember what he said; only remember that as soon as he left I climbed up into the "loft," knelt down by the barrel of corn and prayed as best I could. I do not remember what I said. I only recall that I felt so good that I prayed several times before I quit. My brother and myself were the only colored children in that neighborhood and of course, we could not go to church or Sunday school, or school of any kind. That was my simple conversion, and I have tried to keep the faith.[18]

Carver didn't just "keep the faith," he also furthered its cause in countless ways, teaching a Bible class for more than thirty years, praying each morning out in nature where God would speak to him about his many scientific projects, and applying the concrete truths of the gospel to many of the gravest challenges of his day.

At a time when many people viewed faith and science as warring worldviews, George Washington Carver saw them as entirely integrated, even naming his laboratory "God's little workshop," He was frequently ridiculed by the scientific community for claiming divine revelation and pointing to his faith in Jesus as the mechanism by which he could effectively pursue and perform science.[19] He often described a prayer time in which the Lord commissioned him to make the humble peanut his life's work, explaining that other things would be too big for his intellect! In doing so, he changed the lives of countless poor farmers by discovering more than three hundred uses for peanuts—from shampoo to milk and glue.

Carver's faith also propelled him on to the front lines of environmentalism as he developed important models for more sustainable farming of cash crops, including soya beans, sweet potatoes, cotton, and, of course, peanuts. As someone who heard God clearly in creation, he spent much of his life seeking to steward it better for God's glory. "I love to think of nature as unlimited broadcasting stations," he wrote, "through which God speaks to us every day, every hour and every moment of our lives, if we will only tune in."[20]

Carver also viewed faith in Jesus as the key to defeating racism and improving the plight of the poor. No doubt remembering his own past, he made it his goal in life to "help the man farthest down" the ladder.[21] Turning down professorships at eminent universities, he remained at the humble Tuskegee Institute for forty-seven years, teaching successive generations of black students farming techniques for self-sufficiency. Through his teaching and his research, George Washington Carver undoubtedly helped to lift the American South out of poverty after the Civil War.

As a scientist, environmentalist, and activist for the poor, George Washington Carver is a testament to the fact that God speaks in all things and about all things: from the causes of poverty to the humble peanut. In many ways he was therefore a prophetic figure, speaking into so many of today's most urgent issues, from racial injustice to the environmental crisis, and doing so entirely from a Christian perspective. The words inscribed on the Roosevelt Medal awarded to George Washington Carver in 1939 remain an eloquent summary of a very remarkable life:

> To a scientist humbly seeking the guidance of God,
> and a liberator to men of the white race as well as the black.

Listening Exercise:
Hearing God's Whisper in His World

What is honored in a country will be cultivated there.
—Plato

In this chapter we've focused on hearing God in the whole of life, not just in religious contexts but rather in the actualities of community, creation, and culture, through the ordinary people, places, and pastimes that fill our days.

Creative Discernment Exercises
Prayer Walk (Individual Exercise)

The heavens declare the glory of God;
the skies proclaim the work of his hands.
Day after day they pour forth speech. (Ps. 19:1–2)

Take a prayer walk in creation, simply asking the Lord to speak to you through what you see. This works just as well in an urban context as it does in the countryside—evidence of God's creation is visible everywhere. Be sensitive to his promptings as you walk: study the details, marvel at the beauty, consider the infinite complexity of it all, and ask, "What does this say to me about God's character?" and, "What might he be saying to me through this particular moment, this place, this thing he has made?"

Culture Vulture Exercise (Group Exercise)

This exercise can be used in any context of cultural engagement: watching a film, listening to mainstream music, reading the newspapers, or discussing a work of fiction in a book club. It's designed to develop discernment skills in Christians as they seek to relate their faith to the wider culture.

Introduce the theme by reminding the group how God speaks through all of creation, not just the overtly Christian bits (perhaps referring to my comments about the apostle Paul at the Areopagus earlier in this chapter). Ask members of the group to share a time when God spoke to them or met with them through a person who's not a Christian, or in a surprising context (from the supermarket to the cinema), or in some other unexpected way. Their responses should give you a neat platform from which to explain the basic principle of Christian engagement with the world:

1. *First, we remove our shoes* to recognize that we are walking on holy ground. God is one step ahead of us, speaking and acting even in environments that deny his existence, because he is the Creator and Sustainer of all things:

"The earth is the LORD's, and everything in it, the world, and all who live in it" (Ps. 24:1). We have no right to rebuke what is bad in the culture until we have recognized where God is already at work in and through it. So the first thing we do is to search for God's presence and celebrate it.

2. *Second, we learn the language*, recognizing that for the most part a different culture is neither particularly good nor bad but just different. Its clothes and customs, its music and language are for the most part not wrong but just morally neutral, and our job is not to replace these things but rather to respect them. This is a fundamental principle of cross-cultural mission, which we must increasingly apply at home. So the second thing we do, having recognized God's presence in the culture, is to respect all that is good—or just different—within it.

3. *Third, we pick a fight*, recognizing that there are things within every culture that are sinful, fallen, and broken. We don't just accept the culture wholesale but approach it with discernment, *recognizing* God within it and *respecting* its different cultural norms but also *rejecting* its sinfulness. We have no right to pick a fight with a culture until we have learned its language and found God within its gates.

Explain to the group that you are now going to apply these three filters to a particular expression of the culture. You could watch a film together, or agree to read and discuss a popular novel, or you could simply distribute magazines and newspapers. Encourage the group to ask, "Where can I see or hear God in this cultural context?" and also, "Where can I see brokenness and darkness at work here?" When you reconvene, you will be primed for an exciting conversation about how God is speaking in some surprising contexts. Too often we only train our people how to hear God in religious contexts, so it's thrilling to be discipling one another to encounter the resurrected Christ, who comes to us in the real world, disguised within the culture, just as he did that day on the Emmaus road.

Questions for Personal Reflection and Group Discussion
- Which people consistently seem to speak God's language to me, bringing his word to my heart and mind?
- In what ways can I hear God speaking and see him working in my school, workplace, or city? What is he saying?
- (Scanning today's news) What might God be saying to me personally through today's world events?
- Picking either a favorite film or song, I take time to journal, exploring why I love it so much (pretty easy) and in what ways God speaks to me through it (less easy).

For Further Reflection
Andy Crouch, *Culture Making: Recovering our Creative Calling* (Downers Grove, IL: IVP, 2008).
The *Lectio Divina* Course from www.prayercourse.org.

It took perhaps three hours for the couple from Emmaus to realize that they were hosting the living Word of God. But the moment their eyes and ears were opened, their overwhelming attitude was, "Yes!" Hearing became doing. They hurried out of the house immediately, didn't wait until morning, and walked the seven miles back to Jerusalem, where they found the disciples and "told what had happened" (Luke 24:35). This is the pattern: the more we say yes to Jesus, the more familiar and precious his voice becomes until ultimately, at the end of the road, at the end of the day, at the end of our lives, we look back as the sun sets and whisper in wonder and joy: "Were not our hearts burning within us while he talked?"

8

The Word, the Whisper, and the Way

Then the two told what had happened on the way.

—Luke 24:35

———————————

My sheep listen to my voice; I know them, and they follow me.

—John 10:27

Listening and following. That's it. All the vast libraries of theological thought, millennia of sermons, and the relentless chatter of Christendom can be condensed down into just four surprisingly simple words: *listen and follow Jesus.*

And, of course, this is not a one-off thing. I don't just hear Jesus once and say yes to him once, on the day I first become a Christian. As the weeks and months and years unfold, I try to say yes again and again in great big, terrifying, life-defining ways and also (especially) in tiny, imperceptible ways.

First, and most obviously, this means saying yes to his word in the Bible as we have seen in the first part of this book. He says, "Come follow me," "Repent and be baptized," "Pick up your cross," "Love your enemies," "Go into all the world," and I say, "Okay."

But it also means saying yes to his whisper day by day in more particular and personal ways, as we've seen in the second part of this book. Learning to discern that still, small voice telling me to turn left at the end of the street, listen to my kids, wear the blue T-shirt, put fifty dollars in the offering, sort out my attitude, take a day off, call my mother, strike out in a new direction, share my faith, shut my mouth, pay attention to a certain word in the sermon, pause and pray.

Little by little, as I learn to live in this way, attentively toward God's word in the Bible and to the whisper of his Spirit, I discover the intricate goodness of his guidance, stretching out behind me like shapes traced in the darkness by a sparkler on Fourth of July. Gradually, my neural pathways get realigned by ten thousand tiny yeses, slowly my character is refined by each righteous choice, and ultimately my destiny is defined, not by life's marker moments but by a myriad of apparently inconsequential decisions magnified into beliefs and ossified into behaviors. The ancients said it well: *lex orandi, lex credendi, lex vivendi*—the way of prayer is the way of faith and of life itself. Listen, believe, and obey. Just say yes to Jesus.

*   *   *

Do whatever he tells you.
—John 2:5

It's the wedding at Cana, and they've run out of wine. Mary is trying to push Jesus forward to solve the problem, but he's resisting in the strongest possible terms: "Woman, why do you involve me?" he says to his mom. "My hour has not yet come" (John 2:4). That's a pretty forceful no! But then, moments later, he changes his mind. In direct contradiction to the very thing he's just said, Jesus gets involved in the most significant and dramatic way. It seems that his hour has come after all.

What changes Jesus' mind? It appears to have been Mary's five-word response spoken not to her son but to the nearby servants. I imagine her fixing them with a knowing look as she says, "Do whatever he tells you" (v. 5). Listen and obey. Anything might happen. Just say yes to Jesus.

With these words, Mary single-handedly kick-starts the miracle-working ministry of Jesus. She's been sitting on the angelic prophecies for thirty years, watching her son growing into manhood, knowing him better than anyone else on earth, and now it is Mary (not Jesus) who senses that his time has come. (If you are awaiting the fulfilment of a promise from God, remember to wait actively and watch expectantly like Mary, even if the answer takes years. Keep listening attentively and saying yes consistently to Jesus, and your time will eventually come.)

When the servants at Cana followed Mary's direction, they probably considered it a menial task of little consequence. A bit of heavy lifting for a particularly bossy guest. By filling six stone jars, each with more than twenty gallons of water, they were merely serving those enjoying the party. But, of course, their job was not menial at all. Those on the sidelines of the party were about to write the story line for generations to come. If you feel forgotten or sidelined as an observer on the lives of others, take courage! Stay close to Jesus and do whatever he tells you. A single moment of simple obedience, a simple yes, can echo for all eternity.

In her beautiful memoir, *Even the Sparrow*, Jill Weber describes approaching God with a heart that says, "The answer is yes, but what's the question?"

> Basically: yes. Yes to whatever God thinks I should do because he's obviously smarter, wiser, more creative than I am.... Yes, because he knows the opportunities or peril lurking around the next corner. Yes, before he tells me what I'm saying yes to.... I say yes then I listen with the intent to obey what I hear. Because it's all just a crazy big experiment anyway.[1]

* * *

On the road home to Emmaus, it took Mary and Cleopas perhaps three hours before they realized that they were seeing and hearing the very Word of God. But the moment this happened and their eyes and

ears were opened, their attitude was, "Yes!" They hurried out immediately, walking seven miles in the darkness back to Jerusalem where
they "found the Eleven and those with them, assembled together and
[said], 'It is true! The Lord has risen'" (Luke 24:33–34).

Within five weeks of that epiphany in Emmaus, some three thousand people in Jerusalem were saying the same thing: "It is true! The
Lord has risen!" Within a decade, it's estimated that five thousand
people, in every part of the Roman Empire, were saying it too. By the
end of the third century, there were perhaps five million people in
some sixty-five thousand house churches also declaring: "It is true!
The Lord has risen!" And today there are some two billion people,
on every continent and in most (not all) nations, who call themselves
believers in the resurrected Christ.

If every single Christian today—all two billion of us—were to
spend tomorrow saying an unconditional yes to Jesus, I believe that
we would between us write the headlines of the world the day after
that. Think about it:

- Suddenly, vast amounts of money would inexplicably be given
  to the poor. It could be the greatest redistribution of wealth the
  world has ever seen in a twenty-four-hour period. The markets
  would go crazy!
- Generations of bitterness could begin to be broken as long-
  awaited apologies would finally be offered. There'd be an
  outbreak of reconciliation between warring spouses, neighbors,
  even churches.
- Amazon profits might dive as two billion Christians stopped
  shopping for things they didn't need.
- Worship music might unexpectedly surge to the top of the
  streaming charts, leaving the pundits of pop scratching their
  heads and revising their marketing plans.
- By the law of averages, millions would turn to Christ if two
  billion of us simply obeyed our Lord's command by sharing

the gospel with, say, a couple of people each. And if we were to tell four people about Jesus, theoretically everyone on earth could hear the gospel in a day! The Great Commission would be completed! I say theoretically because, of course, sadly many people do not yet know a Christian and don't even have a Bible in their own mother tongue. But this means that, instead of reaching everyone tomorrow, we would reach many people multiple times. If just one in every hundred of those conversations resulted in a new commitment to Christ, we would welcome eight million men, women, and children into the family of God in a single day. Imagine the rejoicing in heaven!

Of course, this is all mere conjecture, unfortunately. I'm sure your mind is already full of "yes, buts"! Many, many people who call themselves Christians don't really know what it means to have a living, listening relationship with Jesus. And you certainly can't turn institutions around overnight. But what mountains might move if, say, half of us, merely a billion, were to spend the best part of a month saying an unconditional yes to the leadership of Jesus? Or, to put it another way, if we were truly to make Jesus the undisputed Lord of our lives in sufficient numbers? Surely, he might eventually be recognized as the Lord of schools, streets, and even cities?

For this to happen, we don't need non-Christians to become Christians. We need Christians to become Christians. Disciples of Christ who will "do whatever he tells [us]," as Mary said. Sheep of the Good Shepherd who simply "listen to my voice . . . and they follow me" (John 10:27). People like Samuel in the Bible and the other heroes of faith described in this book, who learn to pray, "Speak, LORD, for your servant is listening" (1 Sam. 3:10).

That's what Sojourner Truth did when God spoke to her through a vision, and her wholehearted obedience made her "a sign unto this nation . . . showin' on 'em their sins."

It's what Augustine of Hippo did in response to a child's song.

He was liberated from "a hissing cauldron of lust" by repentance and obedience and set out on an unlikely path to become a father of the church.[2]

It's what Ignatius of Loyola learned to do, having first heard the voice of God while (reluctantly) reading a Christian book. He heard God in a moment that sparked a movement that eventually changed the world.

It's what Heidi Baker did in response to the words of a Navajo preacher on a Native American reservation in Mississippi, and today her joyful obedience impacts hundreds of thousands of the poorest people on earth.

It's what Brother Lawrence did by training himself to hear, see, and celebrate God's presence in the ordinariness of his working life, and it made him a mentor to millions.

It's what Julian of Norwich did, and it made her a pioneering writer and saint.

It's what George Washington Carver did, morning by morning as God spoke to him through nature, and it made him a scientist, environmentalist, and powerful advocate for the poor.

Ultimately, it's what Jesus himself did. He watched and then he copied: "Whatever the Father does the Son also does" (John 5:19). He listened and then he spoke: "I did not speak on my own, but the Father who sent me commanded me to say all that I have spoken" (John 12:49).

I'm aware that these are all pretty intimidating examples. But I'm quite sure that most of these heroes (perhaps with the exception of Ignatius) had no particular desire for fame when they began saying yes to Jesus. In fact, most of them probably thought that following his leadership was a movement away from credibility, influence, and power. Learning to say yes to Jesus may lead you into the limelight, but it's just as likely to lead you out into the twilight of quiet service. It can look like failure or success, fame or anonymity (one of the two travelers on the road to Emmaus remains unknown to this day).

None of this matters. What matters is the middle bit of the verse with which we began, the three words I've not so far mentioned: "My sheep listen to my voice; *I know them*, and they follow me" (John 10:27, italics mine). Jesus Christ knows me! He knows my name, my thoughts, my failures, my fears, and my dreams, and still he loves me. I listen to his voice because he knows me better than I know myself. I follow his example because he cares for me more than anyone ever could or would or should.

Having explored many different ways in which the Lord speaks—through the Bible and prophecy, through dreams, conscience, community, creation, and culture—we must finish where we began: with the ultimate word of God in Jesus Christ. It is Jesus who comes to us covertly, disguised in the ordinary, interrupting our conversations on the Emmaus road. It is his presence that realigns our thinking, his insights that bring the Scriptures to life. He enters our homes before we've had a chance to tidy them, sits down at our meal tables, half uninvited, and breaks our hearts by breaking bread.

Sometimes he speaks dramatically, but mostly quietly with "words . . . full of the Spirit and life" (John 6:63). The more we say yes to the things he says, the more familiar and precious his voice becomes, until, ultimately, at the end of the road, at the end of the day, at the end of our lives, we look back with a mixture of wonder and joy and say:

Were not our hearts burning within us while he talked?

And so we arise, put on our coats, and step out into the night.

Acknowledgments and Thanks

This is my eighth book. You'd think it would get easier, but it's been the hardest of the lot. I couldn't have done it without the people who've prayed for me, egged me on, and generally put up with my grumpiness. I'm particularly grateful to my commissioning editors, Katherine Venn and Ryan Pazdur, for their unstinting encouragement, patience, and counsel and to their fantastically talented teams at Hodder Faith in London, and Zondervan in Grand Rapids, Michigan. Heartfelt thanks are also due to Alex Field at The Bindery Agency and to the magnificent band of readers who quietly upgraded this book beyond all recognition: Brian Heasley, Carla Harding, Chris Westhoff, Gill Greig-Allen, Jo Callender, Phil Togwell, Roger Ellis, and especially Chris Denne (who is one of the most remarkable people I know). I am also indebted to those who held the fort valiantly while I was writing: Mike Andrea at 24-7 Prayer International, Adam Heather at Emmaus Rd., Holly Donaldson, Tandia Hughes, and Rachel Hall at the office. Finally, and most of all, I am grateful to my family—to Sammy, Hudson, and Danny—who have once again put up with me staring at a screen, surrounded by a shanty-town of books and coffee cups, for hours and days and weeks on end, when I'd always much rather have been having fun spending proper time with you!

Recommendations for Further Reading on Hearing God

General

Dallas Willard, *Hearing God: Developing a Conversational Relationship with God* (Downers Grove, IL: IVP, 2012).

Jack Deere, *Surprised by the Voice of God* (Grand Rapids: Zondervan, 1996).

Ken Gire, *Windows of the Soul: Experiencing God in New Ways* (Grand Rapids: Zondervan, 1996).

Lectio Divina

Lectio 365—a free daily devotional app from 24-7 Prayer, written by Pete Greig and friends.

David G. Benner, *Opening to God: Lectio Divina and Life as Prayer* (Downers Grove, IL: IVP, 2010).

Michael Casey, *Sacred Reading: The Ancient Art of Lectio Divina* (London: HarperCollins, 1996).

Personality and Prayer

Chester Michael and Marie Norrisey, *Prayer and Temperament: Different Prayer Forms for Different Personality Types* (Charlottesville: The Open Door Inc., 1991).

Ken Gire, *Windows of the Soul: Experiencing God in New Ways* (Grand Rapids: Zondervan, 1996).

Gary Thomas, *Sacred Pathways: Discover Your Soul's Path to God* (Grand Rapids: Zondervan, 2000).

Mark and Patti Virkler, *Dialogue with God: Opening the Door to Two-Way Prayer* (Newberry, FL: Bridge-Logos, 1986)

Meditation and Listening Prayer

Leanne Payne, *Listening Prayer: Learning to Hear God's Voice and Keep a Prayer Journal* (Grand Rapids: Hamewith Books, 1994).

Bradley Jersak, *Can You Hear Me? Tuning in to the God Who Speaks* (Abbotsford: Fresh Wind Press, 2003, 2012).

Richard Foster, *Sanctuary of the Soul: A Journey into Meditative Prayer* (London: Hodder & Stoughton, 2011).

Bible Study

Gordon Fee and Douglas Stuart, *How to Read the Bible for All Its Worth*, fourth edition (Grand Rapids: Zondervan, 2014).

John Stott, *Understanding the Bible* (Milton Keynes: Scripture Union, 1984).

The Bible Speaks Today series of commentaries from IVP.

Bradley Jersak, *A More Christlike Word: Reading Scripture the Emmaus Way* (New Kensington, PA: Whitaker House, 2021).

Developing Your Prophetic Gifting

Graham Cooke, *Developing Your Prophetic Gifting* (Lancaster: Sovereign World, 1994).

Christine Westhoff, *ReFraming the Prophetic* (online Bible-study), www.reframingtheprophetic.com.

Notes

Chapter 1: Hearing God's Word in Jesus

1. David Lewis (trans.), *Autobiography of Saint Teresa of Ávila* (Scotts Valley, CA: CreateSpace, 2010), 26.
2. London: Hodder & Stoughton, 2019.
3. Mark 12:28–9; Luke 10:25–7.
4. 'All my life, I have risen regularly at four in the morning to go into the woods and talk with God. That's where He reveals His secrets to me. When everybody else is asleep, I hear God best and learn my plan.' Gary R. Kremer, *George Washington Carver: A Biography* (Santa Barbara: Greenwood, 2011), 12.
5. The diary of Florence Nightingale, February 7, 1837, held at the British Library, cited in Heather Kelly, *Florence Nightingale's Autobiographical Notes: A Critical Edition of BL Add. 45844* (Wilfrid Laurier University, 1998), 12. See also Edward Tyas Cook, *The Life of Florence Nightingale vols 1 and 2* (London: MacMillan, 1913): "In an autobiographical fragment written in 1867 Florence mentions as one of the crises of her inner life that 'God called her to His service' on February 7, 1837, at Embley; and there are later notes which still fix that day as the dawn of her true life."
6. For more on Ben Carson's story, see chapter 6.
7. After Hammarskjöld's death, US president John F. Kennedy regretted that he had opposed the UN policy in the Congo and said, "I realise now that in comparison to him, I am a small man. He was the greatest statesman of our century." Sture Linnér and Sverker Åström, *UN Secretary-General Hammarskjöld: Reflections and Personal Experiences (The 2007 Dag Hammarskjöld Lecture)* (PDF, 2008), Uppsala University, 28.
8. Most notably Pascal's "Night of Fire," Monday, November 23, 1654.

9. From a young age Tubman received dreams and visions from God that directed her actions throughout her life.

10. The Pew Research Center's *Religious Landscape Survey* of 35,000 Americans in all fifty US States shows that 77 percent of Americans pray regularly (55 percent daily, 16 percent weekly, 6 percent monthly). Meanwhile, in the less-religious UK, a YouGov poll commissioned by *The Times* and published in December 2018 discovered that atheism had declined from 38 percent of the population in 2016 to 33 percent by 2018, while the proportion of people praying regularly or occasionally had increased significantly over the same period. This complements the findings of research conducted by ComRes for the NGO Tearfund, also published in 2018, showing that 51 percent of the British population pray, as do 20 percent of those who describe themselves as "non-religious."

11. N. T. Wright, *Luke for Everyone* (London: SPCK, 2001), 293.

12. Wright, *Luke for Everyone*, 293.

13. C. S. Lewis, *The Collected Letters of C.S. Lewis, Volume 3: Narnia, Cambridge, and Joy, 1950–1963*, ed. Walter Hooper (San Francisco: HarperOne, 2007), 246.

14. After twenty years of hard work, Elam Ministries completed translation of the New Testament into modern Persian in 2003 and the Old Testament in 2014.

15. See, for example, Exodus 3:4; Numbers 22:28; or Hebrews 13:2.

16. There are numerous versions of this story attributed to various schools, and sometimes it's considered an urban myth. However, extensive research has led back to this one unlikely source in Walgett, New South Wales, where the epigram *audio, video, disco* is still widely used, not least on the school's Facebook page. For understandable reasons the school has also chosen to retain the English rendition of its motto!

17. See, for example, Tanya Luhrmann, *When God Talks Back* (New York: Knopf, 2012), which is an anthropological study of a Vineyard church in the USA, where she based herself for a year in order to study its prayer and worship practices. Also Mark and Patti Virkler, *Dialogue with God: Opening the Door to Two-Way Prayer* (Newberry, FL: Bridge-Logos, 1986).

18. C. S. Lewis, *The Problem of Pain* (London: HarperCollins, 2002), 91.

19. Fredrick William Faber, *Growth in Holiness: The Progress of the Spiritual Life* (Scotts Valley, CA: CreateSpace, 2013), 145, 149.

20. Madeleine L'Engle, *Walking on Water: Reflections on Faith and Art* (New York: Convergent, 2016), 174.

21. Issuing the Lord with ultimatums rarely works and is generally ill advised! Moses says, "Do not put the LORD your God to the test," and Jesus himself repeats this instruction in his battle with Satan in the wilderness (Deut. 6:16; Matt. 4:7). Clearly, there was no way for Asrin to have known this, and the Lord in his grace obliged!

22. Jesus' exhortations to have "ears to hear" occur twelve times in the Gospels and three times in the book of Revelation. The only expression he uses more frequently is "Truly, I say to you." It's a phrase first used by Moses in Deuteronomy 29:4 and then by the prophet Ezekiel (12:2). James D. G. Dunn argues that this expression would also have reverberated from Jesus into the oral teaching of the early church as they retold his words, in *Jesus Remembered: Christianity in the Making, Volume 1* (Grand Rapids: Eerdmans, 2019), 462.

23. This is a wonderful promise for those seeking to grow in their ability to hear the Lord. He says, "Call to me and I will answer you and tell you great and unsearchable things you do not know" (Jer. 33:3).

24. Sojourner Truth and Olive Gilbert, *The Narrative of Sojourner Truth* (Dublin: Historic Publishing, 2017), 58.

25. Truth and Gilbert, *The Narrative of Sojourner Truth*, 128.

26. Truth and Gilbert, *The Narrative of Sojourner Truth*, 128.

27. Truth and Gilbert, *The Narrative of Sojourner Truth*, 128.

28. Truth's "Ain't I a Woman?" speech has passed through numerous iterations. This is from the version published in 1863, twelve years after the event, by Frances Gage, one of the organisers of the original convention. The earliest rendition, published by Rev. Marius Robinson in *The Anti-Slavery Bugle* just a month after the event at which he was present, is equally powerful and it references the Bible considerably more, but it does not use the famous "Ain't I a woman?" phrase.

Chapter 2: Hearing God's Word in the Bible

1. On the day of Pentecost, the apostle Peter did the same thing. When he and his friends, filled with the Spirit, were accused of being drunk, he pointed to the Scriptures, referencing Joel 2:28–32 to contextualize events within the biblical witness, as the fulfilment of ancient prophecy.

2. This is the Amity Printing Company established by the United Bible Societies in China in 1987 and working today with the official bodies of the China Christian Council and the National Committee of the Three-Self Patriotic Movement of the Protestant Churches in China (CCC/TSPM).

3. Some of this data is drawn from Session 6 of the Alpha Course: "Why and How Do I Read the Bible?" Alpha has helped millions of people to process their questions about life and to discover a living faith of their own.

4. The events around these rainstorms coming to Ibiza are described in my book *Red Moon Rising* (Eastbourne: Kingsway, 2004).

5. John Wesley, *Preface to the Sermons*, cited in Henry Craik, ed., *English Prose* (New York: Macmillan, 1916; Bartleby.com, 2010), www.bartleby.com/209/.

6. Brian Tierney, *The Idea of Natural Rights: Studies on Natural Rights, Natural Law, and Church Law 1150–1625* (Emory University Studies in Law and Religion, 1997).

7. Kyle Harper, *From Shame to Sin: The Christian Transformation of Sexual Morality in Late Antiquity* (Cambridge, MA: Harvard University Press, 2013).

8. *The Museum of the Bible* Newsletter, December 2020.

9. Richard B. Dobson, *The Peasants Revolt of 1381* (Bath: Pitman, 1970), 375, quotes from Thomas Walsingham's *Historia Anglicana*.

10. Dobson, *The Peasants Revolt of 1381*, 375.

11. The Form and Order of Service that is to be performed and the Ceremonies that are to be observed in The Coronation of Her Majesty Queen Elizabeth II in the Abbey Church of St. Peter, Westminster, on Tuesday, the second day of June, 1953, accessed September 30, 2021, http://www.oremus.org/liturgy/coronation/cor1953b.html.

12. *State of the Bible Report*, published by American Bible Society and the Barna Group, 2020.

13. *State of the Bible Report*.

14. George H. Gallup Jr. in a speech to the Evangelical Press Association, May 8, 2005.

15. Lawrence Kushner, *Eyes Remade for Wonder* (Woodstock, VT: Jewish Lights, 1998), 50.

16. See, for example, Robert Louis Wilken, *The Spirit of Early Christian Thought* (New Haven: Yale University Press, 2005), chapter 6.

17. Alternatively, some thinkers argue for a rhetorical reading of this passage, suggesting that Paul is citing the opinions of those with whom he disagrees

and subsequently corrects them. Either way, the point here is that exegesis enables us to better understand the original meaning and intent of the writer. For excellent and exhaustive analysis of these verses, see Lucy Peppiatt, *Women and Worship at Corinth: Paul's Rhetorical Arguments in 1 Corinthians* (Eugene, OR: Cascade, 2015) and *Unveiling Paul's Women: Making Sense of 1 Corinthians 11:2–16* (Eugene, OR: Cascade, 2018).

18. See for example Lucy Peppiatt, *Unveiling Paul's Women* and Cynthia Long Westfall, *Paul and Gender: Reclaiming the Apostle's Vision for Men and Women in Christ* (Grand Rapids: Baker Academic, 2016).

19. I particularly recommend *The Bible Speaks Today* series of Bible commentaries, published by IVP.

20. Fourth edition, Grand Rapids: Zondervan, 2014.

21. In the interests of simplicity, I don't wish to get drawn here into the complex and fascinating discussion about the chronological relationship between Paul's epistles and the Gospels—which informed the other? It does seem clear that even the earlier Pauline epistles, which predated the written Gospels, were nonetheless still informed by the oral gospel tradition and that there is therefore a mutuality of relationship at work.

22. The christological hermeneutic undoubtedly reframes our reading of the Old Testament, but legitimate questions still linger regarding the genocide passages in Joshua 6 and 1 Samuel 15. It won't do simply to say, "Oh well, Jesus is not like that," because we risk downgrading the authority of Scripture and falling into the Marcion heresy, which pitted the benevolent God of the New Testament revealed in Jesus against the malevolent Demiurge of the Old. Those who want to explore this issue in greater depth might like to read L. Daniel Hawk's *The Violence of the Biblical God* (Grand Rapids: Eerdmans, 2000). Hawk argues that the rhetoric about mass killing "contains more style than substance," and he appeals to Deuteronomy 7, in which God immediately follows talk of "wiping out" the inhabitants of the land (7:1–2) with a commandment not to intermarry with them (7:3). The command to kill, then, "does not appear to be concerned with eliminating them so much as keeping Israel at a distance from them."

23. As Henri Nouwen says, "For Jesus, there are no countries to be conquered, no ideologies to be imposed, no people to be dominated. There are only children, women and men to be loved." *Peacework: Prayer Resistance Community* (New York: Orbis, 2014), 94.

24. Cited in Raniero Cantalamessa, *Life in Christ* (Minnesota: Liturgical Press, 2002), 7.

25. Cantalamessa, *Life in Christ*, 7.

26. Augustine's *Confessions I–IX (Chapter XII)*, trans. Michael S. Russo (SophiaOmni, 2001), 17.

27. R. S. Pine-Coffin, trans., *The Confessions of St. Augustine* (Baltimore: Penguin, 1961), III.1, 55.

28. T. S. Eliot, "The Fire Sermon" in *The Waste Land*.

29. E. M. Blaiklock, trans., *The Confessions of Saint Augustine* (Nashville: Nelson, 1983), VIII.VII, 196.

30. Rex Warner, trans., *The Confessions of St Augustine* (New York: New American Library: Mentor, 1963), VIII.12, 181.

31. God spoke to Augustine through his "potluck" approach to the Bible, but, as a general rule, this is neither a reliable nor a healthy means of discernment, as I explained earlier.

32. Warner, *Confessions*, VIII.12, 182.

33. *Augustine, Sermons*, 19.2, as cited in Richard Foster, *Streams of Living Water* (London: HarperCollins, 1999), 195.

34. F. J. Sheed, trans., *The Confessions of Saint Augustine* (New York: Sheed & Ward, 1943), 242.

35. Arnold Cole and Pamela Caudill Ovwigho, *Understanding the Bible Engagement Challenge: Scientific Evidence for the Power of 4* (Center for Bible Engagement, December 2009).

36. Francis de Sales, *An Introduction to the Devout Life* (San Francisco: Ignatius Press, 2015), 80.

Chapter 3: Hearing God's Word in Prayer: Lectio Divina

1. David G. Benner, *Opening to God: Lectio Divina and Life as Prayer* (Downers Grove, IL: IVP, 2010), 47.

2. "[Meditation] ceases to be a picture, and becomes a window through which the mystic peers out into the spiritual universe, and apprehends to some extent—though how he does not know—the veritable presence of God." Evelyn Underhill, *Mysticism* (New York: Penguin, 1910), 315.

3. See, for example, Richard Bauckham, *The Climax of Prophecy: Studies on the Book of Revelation* (London: T&T Clark, 1998).

4. As early as the third century AD the church father Origen of Alexandria

used the Greek phrase *thea anagnosis* ("divine reading") to describe a
particular engagement with the Scriptures that sought personal revelation
through the text. This approach, which was itself rooted in Jewish
thought regarding the Torah, inspired the desert fathers and mothers,
who made it a core component in their extraordinary way of life. Since the
monastic movement arose from the precedent set by these desert mothers
and fathers, the *lectio divina* (under another name) served as its mother
tongue from the very start, centuries before Benedict's Rule formalized
its practice.

5. Lectio 365: http://www.24-7prayer.com/dailydevotional (last accessed
   4 August 2021).

6. Babylonian Talmud: Tractate Berakoth, Folio 55b, translated into English
   by Maurice Simon, under the editorship of Rabbi Dr Isidore Epstein
   (available online at halakhah.com).

7. Michael Polanyi, *Personal Knowledge: Towards a Post-Critical Philosophy*
   (Oxford: Routledge, 1998), 58.

8. François Fénelon with Robert J. Edmonson, ed., *The Complete Fenelon*
   (Brewster, MA: Paraclete, 2008), 52.

9. Adapted from Richard Rohr, *Everything Belongs: The Gift of Contemplative
   Prayer* (New York: Crossroad, 2003), 39.

10. Martin Luther, "Preface to the Wittenberg Edition of Luther's German
    Works," in *Luther's Works*, vol. 34, ed. Martin Jaroslav Pelikan, Helmut
    T. Oswald, and H. C. Lehmann (St. Louis: Concordia, 1955), 286, cited
    in Amy Boucher Pye, *Seven Ways to Pray* (Colorado Springs: NavPress,
    2021).

11. Sermon 7 on the Song of Songs, 4.5 in Bernard of Clairvaux, translated
    by G. R. Evans, *Bernard of Clairvaux: Selected Writings* (Mahwah, NJ:
    Paulist Press, 1987), 233–34. Cited in Boucher Pye, *Seven Ways to Pray*.

12. Bernard of Clairvaux, *Sermons on the Song of Songs* (Ohio: Beloved
    Publishing, 2014).

13. If you are struggling to identify such words or phrases in the text, you
    are probably overthinking it. There is nothing particularly strange or
    supernatural about this process. Instead of asking yourself the closed
    question, "Are there any such words?" (to which the answer is clearly either
    yes or, in your case, no), try asking the open question, "Which words or
    phrases are catching my attention?"

14. Mark Twain, *A Connecticut Yankee in King Arthur's Court* (Independently Published, 2021), 401.

15. Richard Foster, *Sanctuary of the Soul: A Journey into Meditative Prayer* (London: Hodder & Stoughton, 2011), 35.

16. A. W. Tozer, *Born after Midnight* (Chicago: Moody, 2015).

17. Alexander Whyte, *Lord Teach Us to Pray* (New York: Harper & Brothers), 251, cited in Foster, *Sanctuary of the Soul*, 41.

18. Mark Batterson, *The Circle Maker: Praying Circles around your Biggest Dreams and Greatest Fears* (Grand Rapids: Zondervan, 2016), 94.

19. James Martin SJ, *The Jesuit Guide to (Almost) Everything: A Spirituality for Real Life* (New York: HarperOne, 2010), 409–10.

20. Martin, *The Jesuit Guide to (Almost) Everything*, 410.

21. Diego Laynez, SJ, cited in Martin, *The Jesuit Guide to (Almost) Everything*, 17.

22. David G. Benner, *Opening to God*, 47.

23. Pierre Teilhard de Chardin, *The Heart of the Matter* (Boston: Houghton Mifflin, 1980), 57.

24. From Malcolm Guite's blog: www.malcolmguite.wordpress.com, December 8, 2012.

25. Ignatius of Loyola, *The Spiritual Exercises: The Second Method of Prayer*.

26. The Lectio 365 devotional is available as an app from all the usual outlets.

27. Martin, *The Jesuit Guide to (Almost) Everything*, 11.

28. Ignatius of Loyola, *Personal Writings* (London: Penguin, 1996), 27.

29. Ignatius, *Personal Writings*, 27.

30. Peter Pearson, *A Brush with God: An Icon Workbook* (Harrisburg: Morehouse, 2005), 17.

31. For a balanced introduction to praying with icons see Richard Foster, *Sanctuary of the Soul*, 38–40.

Chapter 4: Hearing God's Word in Prophecy

1. When the Holy Spirit reveals information that we have no other way of knowing regarding a person, place or situation, it is known as a *word of knowledge* (see 1 Cor. 12:8).

2. This story is told in full in my book *Dirty Glory: Go Where Your Best Prayer Takes You* (London: Hodder & Stoughton, 2016).

3. Similarly, when the apostle Paul describes "the sword of the Spirit, which is

the word of God" (Eph. 6:17), he is not referring to the whole Bible as such, but rather, as Jack Hayford says, "to that portion which the believer wields as a sword in the time of need." (Jack Hayford, "The Word—Part 2," January 23, 2015). In Mary's annunciation she says to the angel Gabriel, "May your *rhēma* to me be fulfilled" (Luke 1:38). In Simeon's *Nunc dimittis* he says, "Lord, now You are letting Your servant depart in peace, According to Your *rhēma*" (Luke 2:29 NKJV). When Jesus tells the disciples to let down their nets for a catch, Peter replies, "Master, we've worked hard all night and haven't caught anything. But because [of your *rhēma*], I will let down the nets" (Luke 5:5). These are all examples of the Lord speaking in distinct ways to particular people in specific contexts at significant moments in time.

4. I am not saying here that prophecy should always be "nice." The purpose of the prophetic, from start to finish, is to call the people of God into alignment with the covenant. At times this involves words of correction, direction, and warning today as it always has. However, when they are starting out in prophecy, I always encourage people to begin with positive messages before venturing into more challenging terrain.

5. Jim Asker, "Bethel Music, Jonathan David Helser & Melissa Helser Top Christian Airplay Chart With 'Raise a Hallelujah,'" *Billboard*, August 22, 2019.

6. "No Longer Slaves," by Jonathan David Helser, Brian Johnson, and Joel Case. Copyright © 2014 Bethel Music Publishing (ASCAP). All rights reserved. Used by permission.

7. Jack Deere, *Surprised by the Voice of God* (Grand Rapids: Zondervan, 1996), 146–47.

8. Seasons of divine silence may also indicate a "dark night of the soul." For a full explanation of this and other important aspects of God's silence, see my book *God on Mute: Engaging the Silence of Unanswered Prayer* (Colorado Springs: David C. Cook, 2007, 2020).

9. The Old Testament mentions schools of prophets in 1 Samuel 19:18–24, in 2 Kings 2 and 4:38–44 (some translations say "company of prophets" or "sons of the prophets"). Also, the prophet Amos possibly mentions a prophetic school in stating his credentials (or lack thereof) to Amaziah the priest in Amos 7:14. The group of prophets in 1 Samuel 19 was comprised of his students who were probably Levites serving in roles related to the tabernacle and ceremonial worship.

10. "God comes to you disguised as your life." The original source of this quote was Paula D'Arcy, who lost her husband and one-year-old child in a car accident when she was twenty-seven. It has been popularized by Richard Rohr, *Falling Upward: A Spirituality for the Two Halves of Life* (San Francisco: Jossey-Bass, 2011), 66.

11. This concept of returning to the last thing God said to you is unpacked in Loren Cunningham's memoir, *Is That Really You, Lord?* (Seattle: YWAM Publishing, 2001). Those wishing to grow in the prophetic may wish to enroll in Christine Westhoff's twelve-module online Bible study, "ReFraming the Prophetic," www.reframingtheprophetic.com.

12. For a fascinating summary of the role of prophecy in the sixteenth-century Scottish Reformation, see chapter 5 of Jack Deere's *Surprised by the Voice of God.*

13. "The Iris Story," https://www.irisglobal.org/about/the-iris-story (last accessed August 5, 2021).

14. Rolland and Heidi Baker, *Always Enough: God's Miraculous Provision Among the Poorest Children on Earth* (Grand Rapids: Chosen Books, 2003), 49.

Chapter 5: Hearing God's Whisper

1. *The Poems of Emily Dickinson: Variorum Edition*, edited by Ralph W. Franklin, Cambridge, Mass.: The Belknap Press of Harvard University Press, Copyright © 1998 by the President and Fellows of Harvard College. Copyright © 1951, 1955 by the President and Fellows of Harvard College. Copyright © renewed 1979, 1983 by the President and Fellows of Harvard College. Copyright © 1914, 1918, 1919, 1924, 1929, 1930, 1932, 1935, 1937, 1942 by Martha Dickinson Bianchi. Copyright © 1952, 1957, 1958, 1963, 1965 by Mary L. Hampson. Used by permission. All rights reserved.

2. Michael Casey, *Sacred Reading: The Ancient Art of Lectio Divina* (London: HarperCollins, 1996), 44.

3. Matthew Bridges and Godfrey Thring, "Crown Him with Many Crowns" (public domain).

4. John Greenleaf Whittier, "Dear Lord and Father of Mankind" (public domain).

5. Inattentional or perceptual blindness are terms coined by psychologists Arien Mack and Irvin Rock in 1992. Numerous studies have been

conducted into this condition, and four causes have been identified: *conspicuity*, *mental workload*, *expectation*, and *capacity*.

6. According to Levine and Witherington, Eusebius "reports that various Church fathers thought that Cleopas was Clopas (Eccl. Hist. 3.32)." Although they add, "The connection between the two names, Cleopas and Clopas, cannot be secured." Amy-Jill Levine and Ben Witherington III, *The Gospel of Luke* (New Cambridge Bible Commentary, 2018), 657–58. Interestingly, Eusebius also writes that Symeon, the son of Clopas and Mary, became the second bishop of Jerusalem, after the martyrdom of James. "He was, so it is said, a cousin of the Saviour, for Hegesippus tells us that Clopas was Joseph's brother." Eusebius, *The History of the Church*, trans. G. A. Williamson (London: Penguin, 1965, 1986), 123–24. More recently, N. T. Wright, in his commentary on Luke, has written, "The couple on the road may well have been husband and wife, Cleopas and Mary (see John 19.25; 'Clopas' there is probably the same person as 'Cleopas' here). Though we cannot be sure of this": Tom Wright, *Luke for Everyone* (London: SPCK, 2001, 2004), 293.

7. T. S. Eliot, "What the Thunder Said," in *The Waste Land*.

8. Brother Lawrence, *The Practice of the Presence of God* (Grand Rapids: Baker, 1999), 15.

9. Brother Lawrence, *The Practice of the Presence of God*, 44.

10. Brother Lawrence, *The Practice of the Presence of God*, 46.

11. Richard Foster, *The Celebration of Discipline* (London: Hodder & Stoughton, 1989), 131.

12. Norman Wirzba, *Living the Sabbath: Discovering the Rhythms of Rest and Delight* (Grand Rapids: Brazos, 2006), 13.

Chapter 6: Hearing God's Whisper in Dreams and the Unconscious

1. John A. Sanford, *Dreams and Healing* (Mahwah, NJ: Paulist Press, 1978), 7, 8.

2. For instance, Gustave Oehler points out, in *Theology of the Old Testament* (Grand Rapids: Zondervan, 2001), 143, that the difference between a dream and a vision is generally blurred in the Bible.

3. Dallas Willard, *Hearing God: Developing a Conversational Relationship with God* (Downers Grove, IL: IVP, 2012), 122.

4. In their book *Paranormal America*, sociologists Christopher Bader, F. Carson Mencken, and Joseph Baker note, "Angels pervade popular culture in books, television shows, and movies" (New York: New York University Press, 2011), 184. A 2007 Baylor Religion Survey found that 57 percent of Catholics, 81 percent of Black Protestants, 66 percent of Evangelical Protestants, and 10 percent of Jews reported having had a personal experience with a guardian angel. And 20 percent of those who identified themselves as having no religion also claimed to have encountered an angel.

5. Pete Grieg, *Red Moon Rising*, (Eastbourne: Kingsway, 2004), 101–4.

6. Ben Carson, *Gifted Hands* (Grand Rapids: Zondervan, 1996), 75.

7. Carson, *Gifted Hands*, 75–76.

8. Carson, *Gifted Hands*, 75–76.

9. Carson, *Gifted Hands*, 74.

10. Carson, *Gifted Hands*, 76.

11. Carson, *Gifted Hands*, 75–76.

12. John A. Sanford, *Dreams: God's Forgotten Language* (New York: HarperOne, 1989), 5.

13. Abraham Heschel, *The Prophets* (New York: Harper Perennial, 2001), xxii.

14. Sanford, *Dreams: God's Forgotten Language*, 6.

15. Daniel 2:30, God's Word Translation.

16. God does sometimes override common sense, but I would always seek significant confirmation—certainly more than a single dream—before advising anyone to act upon a completely counterintuitive impulse.

17. See, for example, C. S. Lewis' thesis regarding universal moral values in *The Abolition of Man* (1943) and particularly in its appendix *Illustrations of the Tao*.

18. To find out more about practicing the examen, see Pete Greig, *How to Pray: A Simple Guide for Normal People* (chapter 10), or begin to use the Lectio 365 "Night Prayers," which are based around this practice.

19. Julian of Norwich, *Revelations of Divine Love*, trans. Elizabeth Spearing (London: Penguin, 1998), 33.

20. St. John of the Cross, *Spiritual Canticle*, trans. E. Allison Peers (Image Books, 1961), stanza i 7,8, cited in Bradley Jersak, *Can You Hear Me? Tuning in to the God Who Speaks* (Abbotsford: Fresh Wind, 2003, 2012), 146.

21. Cited in Jersak, *Can You Hear Me?*, 146.

22. Jersak, *Can You Hear Me?*, 129.

23. Jersak, *Can You Hear Me?*, 130.

24. Jersak, *Can You Hear Me?*, 130.

25. Jersak, *Can You Hear Me?*, 130.

26. T. S. Eliot, "Little Gidding" from *Four Quartets* (London: Faber & Faber, 1963), 59.

27. Robert Llewelyn (ed.), *Enfolded in Love: Daily Readings with Julian of Norwich* (London: Darton, Longman & Todd, 1980), 18.

28. James Martin SJ, *The Jesuit Guide to (Almost) Everything: A Spirituality for Real Life* (New York: HarperOne, 2010), 43.

Chapter 7: Hearing God's Whisper in Community, Creation, and Culture

1. Alpha, which includes Alpha for Forces, is an eleven-week course through which millions of people have come to faith in Jesus.

2. Pierre Teilhard de Chardin, *The Divine Milieu* (New York: Harper Torchbooks, 1960), 36.

3. Churches are the most socially and culturally diverse communities in the UK, according to a 2014 MORI poll of 4,269 people.

4. C. S. Lewis, "Answers to Questions on Christianity," in *God in the Dock* (Grand Rapids: Eerdmans, 1970), 61–62.

5. Lewis, "Answers to Questions on Christianity," in *God in the Dock*, 61–62.

6. Cited in Michael Casey, *Sacred Reading: The Ancient Art of Lectio Divina* (London: HarperCollins, 1996), 44.

7. Cited in Casey, *Sacred Reading*, 44.

8. This story is recounted in various contexts by Gordon MacDonald, editor-at-large for Christianity Today's *Leadership Journal*.

9. For instance, research conducted by the Movember Foundation in 2015 found that about 2.5 million British men and 1.1 million Australian men aged between thirty and sixty-five admitted to having no close friends.

10. Edward Sellner traces the concept of soul friendship back further to the early desert fathers and mothers: "This capacity for friendship and ability to read other people's hearts became the basis of the desert elders' effectiveness as spiritual guides." Edward C. Sellner, "Soul Friendship in Early Celtic Monasticism," *Aisling Magazine* 17, Samhain, 1995. These teachings were popularized by John Cassian, one of the founders of

monasticism in the fourth century, who emphasised that the soul friend could be clerical or lay, male or female.

11. John O'Donohue, *Anam Cara: Spiritual Wisdom from the Celtic World* (London: Bantam, 1999), 35.

12. In his book *Community, the Structure of Belonging*, Peter Block says, "Questions themselves are an art form worthy of a lifetime of study. They are what transformed the hour." 2nd revised edition (Oakland: Berrett-Koehler, 2018), 59.

13. From the introduction to Thomas Merton, *A Book of Hours*, ed. Kathleen Deignan (Notre Dame, IN: Sorin, 2007), 22.

14. Ruth Haley Barton, *Strengthening the Soul of your Leadership: Seeking God in the Crucible of Ministry* (Downers Grove, IL: IVP, 2018), 62.

15. Elizabeth Barrett Browning (1806–61), "Aurora Leigh."

16. The NIV gets this right, translating ἐπεδίδου as "he began to give," which is true to the imperfect indicative tense of the original Greek describing an action that was ongoing for a period of time and where the time of completion of the action is not specified.

17. T. S. Eliot, "What the Thunder Said," in *The Waste Land*.

18. G. W. Carver, Letter to Isabelle Coleman, July 24, 1931.

19. "Man of Science—And of God," in *The New American* (January 2004).

20. William Federer, *George Washington Carver: His Life and Faith in his Own Words* (St. Louis: Amerisearch, 2002), 72.

21. John Perry, *Unshakable Faith: Booker T. Washington & George Washington Carver* (Sisters, OR: Multnomah, 1999), 361.

Chapter 8: The Word, the Whisper, and the Way

1. Jill Weber, *Even the Sparrow: A Pilgrim's Guide to Prayer, Trust, and Following Jesus* (Edinburgh: Muddy Pearl, 2019), 25.

2. Augustine's *Confessions I–IX (Chapter XII)*, translated by Michael S. Russo (SophiaOmni, 2001), 17.

Index

References to images are in *italics*.

Pete Greig is one of the founding champions of the 24-7 Prayer movement, and serves as the Senior Pastor of Emmaus Rd Church in the south of England. He is an Ambassador for the NGO Tearfund and a member of The Order of the Mustard Seed. He co-hosts the Wildfires Festival, The Prayer Course and the Lectio 365 daily devotional.

His books, which are available in a range of languages and formats (including audio), are available from all the usual outlets and include the following titles:

Dirty Glory	**God on Mute**	**How to Pray**
Go Where Your Best Prayers Take You	*Engaging the silence of Unanswered Prayer*	*A Simple Guide for Normal People*
(Red Moon Chronicles #2)		

Stay connected with Pete:

WWW.PETEGREIG.INFO

THE
LECTIO COURSE

Designed to accompany this book, the *Lectio Course* is a free, online introduction to the ancient art of Lectio Divina equipping individuals and small groups to hear God and talk with God in and through the Bible.

Interviews

A series of short videos presented by Pete Greig exploring different ways of hearing God.

Toolshed

An archive of practical and diverse 'Prayer Tools', from how to meditate (on the Bible) and how to interpret dreams.

Cheat Sheets

Downloadable discussion-starters to aid deep conversation and personal application of each topic.

The Sessions

Session 1
Lectio Divina – the ancient art of reading God's Word.

—

Session 2
Meditatio – reading, reflecting & rejoicing in God's Word

—

Session 3
Oratio – asking & praying God's Word

—

Session 4
Contemplatio – surrendering to God's Word

www.**prayercourse**.org

Created by 24-7 Prayer